RESET

RESET

Restoring Australia after the Pandemic Recession

ROSS GARNAUT

LA TROBE
UNIVERSITY PRESS

IN CONJUNCTION WITH BLACK INC.

THE UNIVERSITY OF
MELBOURNE

Published by La Trobe University Press in conjunction
with Black Inc. and the University of Melbourne
Level 1, 221 Drummond Street
Carlton VIC 3053, Australia
enquiries@blackincbooks.com
www.blackincbooks.com
www.latrobeuniversitypress.com.au

La Trobe University plays an integral role in Australia's public intellectual life, and is
recognised globally for its research excellence and commitment to ideas and debate.
La Trobe University Press publishes books of high intellectual quality, aimed at general
readers. Titles range across the humanities and sciences, and are written by distinguished
and innovative scholars. La Trobe University Press books are produced in conjunction with
Black Inc., an independent Australian publishing house. The members of the LTUP
Editorial Board are Vice-Chancellor's Fellows Emeritus Professor Robert Manne and
Dr Elizabeth Finkel, and Morry Schwartz and Chris Feik of Black Inc.

9781760642822 (paperback)
9781743821619 (ebook)

A catalogue record for this
book is available from the
National Library of Australia

Cover image: Robert Cianflone / Staff / Getty
Cover design by Akiko Chan
Text design by Dennis Grauel
Typesetting by Tristan Main

Printed in Australia by McPherson's Printing Group

MIX
Paper from
responsible sources
FSC® C001695

CONTENTS

IN MEMORY OF MEKERE MORAUTA
Born in Kukipi, 12 June 1946; Died in Brisbane, 19 December 2020
Papua New Guinea's first Secretary for Treasury and Finance
Governor of the Bank of Papua New Guinea
Prime Minister 1999–2002

INTRODUCTION

We have just lived through the sharpest decline in global production and trade that the world has seen since the beginnings of modern economic development. The most rapid fall for Australia, and for the world. How long its recessionary consequences last, and how it affects long-term prosperity, political systems and international order, depend on our knowledge and wisdom and how we use them. Our knowledge and wisdom as Australians, and as members of a global community.

As I write, in the last quarter of 2020, the pandemic is under control in Australia and some of our neighbours in the Western Pacific region. It continues to rage and impose increasing costs in North America, the UK, Europe and most of the developing world. For Australia and its more fortunate Western Pacific neighbours, economic activity is expanding rapidly from a low base. But the earlier disruption from disease – and from the shrinkage of economic activity and trading opportunities in the rest of the world – casts a long shadow. The arrival and widespread distribution of a vaccine is necessary for the countries still suffering high rates of infection and death to find relief – and for the whole world to see the return of substantial international movement of people. This may be possible over the next year or so. But there is still a long and hard road to what were once acceptable levels of economic activity in Australia and the world.

Australia's economy performed poorly for most of its citizens in the seven years from the China resources boom to the pandemic. I call these years from 2013 to 2019 the Dog Days. Unemployment and underemployment remained stubbornly high – in the later years, well above the rates in developed countries that suffered greater damage from the 2008–09 Global Financial Crisis. Wages stagnated. Productivity and output per person grew more slowly than in the United States, or Japan, or the developed world as a whole.

This book explains the choice Australians will make over the next couple of years, between a resumption of the Dog Days and a post-pandemic restoration of Australia.

The Dog Days are our destination once more unless we break sharply with the policies and political culture of the early twenty-first century. This would be an unhappy place for Australians – more difficult than the seven years before the pandemic. Living standards would remain lower through the 2020s. Unemployment and underemployment would linger above the high levels before COVID-19 struck. Things would be worse than in the pre-pandemic Dog Days because we would have a legacy of extraordinary public debt. They would be worse because business investment would be lower. They would be harder because there would be less gain from trade – due partly to problems in our relations with China, partly to slower global growth and increased protection in Australia and most other countries. They would be worse because increased unemployment has permanently devalued the skills of many Australians, especially the young; and because many of our most important economic institutions – first of all, the universities – were diminished. They would be weaker because productivity growth, already low before the pandemic, would be lower still. The new Dog Days would be disrupted more than the old by the accumulating effects of climate change and by disputation about how to respond to this. Much lower immigration would hold back total output growth – but might improve the living standards of most Australians.

By contrast, the restoration of Australia would follow from an effective effort to loosen the chains that held us down in the Dog Days. It would reset our fiscal and monetary policy to achieve early full employment, while keeping the growth of public debt within manageable bounds. It would involve substantial reform to increase business investment in trade-exposed industries and lift productivity growth – led by a new approach to taxing business income. It would be built around joining our main trading partners – the developed world and China – in creating a zero-emissions world economy, and realising Australia's opportunity to be the energy superpower of the emerging world. It would build a productive approach to foreign relations in new circumstances created by the rise of China as an assertive great power with values and institutions that are different to our own: the confident assertion of our own sovereign autonomy and national interest while maintaining open trade and investment relations with the whole world to the greatest practicable extent.

Restoration will require acceptance of a high degree of income restraint by Australians, who have already endured the longest period of income stagnation in our history, through the Dog Days and then the COVID-19 recession. This is regrettable, and many Australians will see it as unfair, since the wealthy continued rapidly to increase their wealth and incomes through the Dog Days, and most also did well in the pandemic recession. Experience has demonstrated that such restraint in the public interest is possible in our Australian democracy if most people accept that the benefits are distributed fairly. There will be widespread support for the necessary reforms only if the many people on low incomes and with insecure employment and little wealth – those who were damaged most by the pandemic recession – gain from the

3

change. Fairness is integral to any program to lift productivity, employment and incomes. Fairness has to be achieved by means that do not block the path to higher productivity, employment and incomes. That requires reform in our personal income tax and social security arrangements, built around a guaranteed minimum income: the new Australian Income Security payment.

Full employment with manageable increases in debt is going to require large expansion of trade-exposed industries, to keep the growth of debt within reasonable bounds. It will be difficult to greatly increase productive investment in the trade-exposed industries. We have to lift the international competitiveness of production in Australia. That means running monetary policy with an eye to the effect of the exchange rate on competitiveness. The proposed tax reform will help. It has to be supported by policy that encourages the emergence of industries of the future. Investments now – whether in public infrastructure or private business – will be generating output later in the 2020s and beyond. By the 2030s, Australia and the world will be well on the way to a net-zero-emissions economy – or we will be facing increasing problems from climate change. Investments over the next few years will have to make economic sense in the low-carbon global economy of the future. This rules out a lift in investment and employment in the coal and gas industries that contributed a major part of total growth through the China resources boom and the Dog Days. The good news is that there is immense opportunity for profitable investment to build a prosperous place for Australia in the future zero-emissions economy.

Restoration will require a reset of the Australian political culture, and policy and economic structure, that emerged through the first two decades of the twenty-first century. Why restoration rather than reconstruction? Because the most important changes involve restoring old Australian strengths. Most importantly, restoration of the respect for knowledge and community understanding as the basis of good policy in the public interest. These strengths were present in earlier successful periods of Australian democratic economic reform and development. Here, I am thinking especially but not only of the reform era from 1983 to the end of the twentieth century. This laid the foundations for Australia's productivity boom in the 1990s, and for the longest period of economic expansion unbroken by recession ever in a developed country, which ended in 2020.

Other developed economies performed better than Australia between the GFC and the pandemic recession, but still poorly by the standards set in the second half of the twentieth century. Developing countries as a whole did well in the twenty-first century before the pandemic. The whole world economy has been battered by the pandemic, and recovery is shaped first of all by the trajectory of the disease itself. China has made an early return to strong growth, as it did after the 1997–98 Asian Financial Crisis and the GFC. Other Northeast Asian economies, Australia and New Zealand have been successful in containing the disease. The immediate path ahead is not so clear for other developed countries. Bigger questions hover over the future of many developing economies, as they have been severely disrupted by COVID-19 and lack the resources to get back onto a path of strongly rising incomes in an era of stagnation in global trade.

Joe Biden's victory in the US presidential election of November 2020 changes the global context. The opportunity for change was reinforced by the Democratic victories in the senate election re-runs in Georgia in January 2021. The United States – for a number of years – will give priority to full employment through fiscal and monetary expansion over historically low inflation. Much of the fiscal expansion will be directed towards investment in a low-carbon economy. In this way, the US joins the European Union, the UK, Japan, South Korea and China. That creates a congenial environment for Australian restoration policies. It will isolate us if we opt to stand aside from the new momentum towards decarbonisation of the world economy.

The prize for post-pandemic restoration is large. We would achieve full employment by 2025, after reaching pre-pandemic labour conditions by 2023. Prices and wages would rise in the marketplace once we achieved full employment. From that time, economic growth plus inflation would begin to reduce the weight of the recently accumulated public debt, without lowering the standards of living of ordinary Australians. Businesses would generally do well in an expanding economy. An Australian Income Security payment would provide a guaranteed basic income for all Australians and reduce the anxiety and democratic constraints on reform that would otherwise accompany the income restraint and structural change required for restoration.

The October 2020 budget indicates we are yet to make a choice between the alternative futures. That choice will be made explicitly or implicitly over the year or two ahead.

Dog Days or Restoration?
Following this introduction, the first chapter is called 'The Tree of Knowledge'. It stands for the central role that discovery, dissemination and use of knowledge plays in containing the pandemic and in restoring broadly-based prosperity after the pandemic recession. Chapter 1 draws on a great Australian tradition of extending economic knowledge at times of crisis, engaging political leaders with the new knowledge, explaining it to the community, and acting decisively in its application. Here we use and extend insights from Australian economic ideas that were important in dealing with the massive problems of the Great Depression, postwar reconstruction and a stagnant economy prior to the reforms implemented from 1983 to the end of the twentieth century.

Chapter 2 describes the emergence of COVID-19 in Wuhan in central China in late 2019 and its spread throughout the world, including to Australia. It examines the initial economic impact, as well as the medical one. The second quarter of 2020 experienced the greatest ever decline in economic activity and international trade over such a short period, in the world and in Australia. It pushed unemployment by any realistic measure to the highest since the Great Depression. Chapter 2 notes that economic shocks of this magnitude fundamentally change ideas about how political and economic systems work. They knock political structures and economic development from their established trajectories. The brilliantly successful liberal social-democratic framework established after the Great Depression and World War II lost influence in the large English-speaking countries from the early 1980s. That weakened the United States and the UK, in particular, as they confronted the pandemic and its economic consequences.

One challenge in writing this book so soon in the pandemic has been to tell an evolving story while its major features are still taking shape. The lectures upon which this book was based were presented in May and June 2020. Economic, pandemic and political data have been updated to as close as possible to the date of publication.

In the early months of the pandemic, senior federal government figures talked about the goal of 'snapping back' to economic conditions before COVID-19. Chapter 3 explains why going back to what we had before the pandemic is neither desirable, nor possible.

Chapter 4 looks forward, to the huge challenges Australia faces. The first focus should be on early movement to full employment. Budget deficits should be large enough to fill the immense hole that the pandemic has blown in demand for goods and services – plus some, to allow the removal of Dog Days unemployment. We should seek full employment with an eye on the optimal level of external debt, which requires strong focus on the international competitiveness of the economy. To this end, it is important that monetary policy is no tighter than in the rest of the developed world.

An exacerbation of the underemployment and stagnant incomes of the Dog Days would see gradual corrosion of democratic support for an open, market-oriented dynamic economy capable of delivering rising living standards. It would be associated with endless increases in public debt, until Australia had a genuine debt problem, and limited options for dealing with future shocks to economic stability and growth. It would damage commitment to our liberal democratic political system at a time of intense systemic competition.

Chapter 5 explains that there is full employment when unemployment is so low that wages start to rise in the market and inflationary pressures emerge. We don't know what that level is. We know it is far below the five-point-something that Australian authorities had in mind through the Dog Days. Certainly, it is lower than the 'well below 6 per cent' that Treasurer Josh Frydenberg said would trigger efforts to reduce the budget deficit. It may be 3.5 per cent or lower. We won't know until we have run the economy strongly enough for long enough to see the emergence of market pressure for wage increases. The chapter presents information on the number of jobs that would have to be generated to establish full employment by 2025. It discusses whether this is feasible; and where the jobs could come from.

Chapter 6 discusses how much debt would be too much. It explains why borrowing from the Reserve Bank ('creating money') is appropriate now but may have to be followed by later withdrawal of money from the economy. Creating money to allow government spending to achieve early full employment comes with strings attached. So we should move as quickly as possible to full employment, while keeping debt to the lowest levels consistent with full employment on the earliest possible timetable. That means making sure that a substantial number of the jobs come from expanded investment in the trade-exposed industries through improvement in competitiveness. We should continue to keep an eye on competitiveness after full employment.

Chapter 7 discusses how to increase investment. A reduced corporate tax rate is favoured by big business. This would have a small positive effect on business investment and a negative effect on average Australian living standards. It would increase budget deficits now and in the future. Chapter 7 proposes changing the tax base from corporate income as conventionally defined, to cash flow. This would make it a tax on economic rent. There would be a large increase in incentives to investment without overall loss of public revenue. The tax burden would shift from companies operating in highly competitive environments to those earning economic rents; from those making new investments to those living off earnings from established assets; from those investing in research, development and commercialisation of new technologies and business models to those avoiding risk and innovation; from small and young to large and old businesses; and from Australian businesses paying disproportionate shares of corporate tax to international businesses paying little or no tax at all. Chapter 7 also discusses other measures to increase productivity. Avoiding a high real exchange rate is important to investment. Maintaining open trade is crucial. This means limiting protectionist pressures to exclude foreign items in supply chains. Carefully focused investment in infrastructure has an important role to play.

Chapter 8 discusses how to achieve income security for all citizens. Now is the time to integrate social security and personal income tax around a basic minimum income – the Australian Income Security (AIS). The proposed reform would substantially increase incentives for low-income workers to participate more in the labour force, especially for second earners in households. The AIS would provide a large boost to after-tax incomes of all low-income workers, including for part-time and casual workers who have been severely damaged during the pandemic recession. It would increase income security for people without steady employment. The introduction of the minimum basic income would be expensive, but costs would fall as employment and real wages grew. Its fiscal impact is suited to the requirements of a large budget deficit to increase demand before full employment, and a more balanced budget after that. The AIS could be supported by other measures to raise incomes and productivity, with a focus on investment in education.

My book *Superpower* explained how Australia has great advantages in the emerging low-carbon world economy. Building Australia as the superpower of the new low-carbon economy would provide a high proportion of the business investment in trade-exposed industries required for full employment, and then incomes growth. There is no other comparably large opportunity. The much-discussed 'gas-based recovery' has no economic foundation. Chapter 9 looks at the investments in solar and wind power, electricity storage and transmission that are necessary to decarbonise our power system and then, on a much larger scale, to power new export industries. It introduces some of these promising new industries.

Chapter 10 describes the substantial opportunities from sequestering carbon and growing industrial raw materials in the Australian landscape. The special Australian advantage comes from our huge landmass relative to population. We have far greater areas of woodlands and grasslands per person than other countries; this can be a large and broadly distributed source of employment and incomes, with a large presence in most regions of Australia.

Chapter 11 discusses the international context for Australian restoration. Under the Trump presidency, cooperative relations between countries were weakened. The United States took big steps to weaken the World Trade Organization. The US withdrew from the Trans-Pacific Partnership and the Paris Agreement on climate change. It ceased funding its share of the World Health Organisation (WHO). This chapter discusses ways in which recent degrading of international cooperation might be contained and perhaps reversed. The replacement of President

Trump by President Biden in January 2021 and the strong commitment to zero carbon emissions in all developed countries other than Australia, and also in China, gives us a chance.

Chapter 12 was written in the days after the Australian federal budget on 6 October 2020 and the US elections on the first Tuesday in November. It assesses our choice between post-pandemic Dog Days and post-pandemic restoration of Australia. The decisive and early response to the onset of the COVID-19 pandemic in March 2020 maintained economic activity through and after the initial lockdowns at reasonably high levels. That was a good start, but the October 2020 budget leaves us with the big choices still ahead of us. Do we opt for a return to Dog Days policies, with outcomes considerably less satisfactory than those in 2013 to 2019? Or do we take up the mantle of reform in the Australian public interest, restore the best of the approach to policy that led to the productivity boom, and lay the foundations for full employment and rising living standards? The 2020 budget was a waystation on a longer journey. The rest of the book plots a path to the better destination.

1

THE TREE OF KNOWLEDGE

This book is about knowledge, and how we apply it to the big challenges of our time. Knowledge is the foundation of successful public policy across all political systems. Broadly shared knowledge is the foundation of a successful democracy.

The quality of medical knowledge, and how it is applied, determines how many citizens of each country become sick in the pandemic and die, and how severely the economy is disrupted. The quality of economic knowledge determines whether the economic downturn is brief and shallow, or protracted and profound. The pandemic recession is exacerbating stresses between countries. Knowledge of international relations affects whether this leads to war or peace; to renewed international trade and investment, or to a long global recession. And beyond the urgency of the pandemic, knowledge and our use of it will determine how well we handle the larger and more persistent natural challenges of climate change.

Of course, knowledge alone is not enough. The extent to which knowledge is reflected in the decisions of our leaders and policy-makers depends also on our political systems. I presented the public lectures that shaped this book electronically through the University of Melbourne from the shade of the Tree of Knowledge in the central western Queensland town of Barcaldine. That tree is a fine symbol for the most important message of the book. When tensions between the men who controlled land and finance and those who worked for them in difficult conditions reached great heights in 1891, the shearers and carriers gathered under the stately ghost gum to discuss how they would respond to disappointment. They decided that their starting point was shared knowledge. The sharing of knowledge told them they should use their young democracy to change the law. They were pioneers in making democracy work for citizens. Then, and for several decades after, the Australian and New Zealand colonies had a wider franchise and better-developed democratic institutions than the larger and older English-speaking polities in the northern hemisphere.

Henry Lawson wondered whether the tensions of 1891 would cause blood to stain the wattle. The decisions taken under the Tree of Knowledge kept the crimson off the green and gold.

Paul Keating in an expansive moment once expressed regret that Australia had had no towering political leaders of the stature of Washington, Lincoln and Roosevelt. Those three legends grew from violent struggle. It is a triumph of our history that a Tree of Knowledge, and not the battles of Yorktown and Gettysburg, symbolises a decisive time.

Knowledge and the pandemic recession

Plagues have shaped the growth of human civilisation from the earliest times. The emergence of new viruses that cause epidemics has become more frequent and their spread more rapid in the modern era. This follows from denser populations of humans and domesticated animals, and the intense interaction across national borders that we call globalisation.

During the COVID-19 pandemic, medical knowledge has been used much more effectively in some countries than others. Among developed countries, the differences reflect variations in leaders' regard for scientific knowledge. In developing countries, too, whether leaders respect or reject knowledge has made a big difference – but lacking administrative and financial capacity, some governments that had the will to respond to knowledge lacked the means of doing so.

In the early twenty-first century, most countries with effective governments had established mechanisms to allow a swift and strong response to control the spread of a pandemic. The World Health Organization helped to disseminate knowledge of the risk, and to build capacity to manage it. In the United States, important elements of a strong pandemic response system bequeathed by the George W. Bush and Obama administrations were partially closed as a saving measure in an early Trump budget, and the remnants largely ignored by the US government.

To some extent, COVID-19 presented a new challenge requiring new responses. Each new virus and epidemic has novel characteristics. The search for a vaccine begins soon after a new virus is identified, with uncertainty that an effective vaccine will be found. And while medical knowledge can help to shape initial responses, inevitably governments will be working out elements of the responses as they go along.

In the language used by British economist John Maynard Keynes in *A Treatise on Probability* a century ago, policy-makers are faced with uncertainty rather than risk. With uncertainty, wise leaders know that they do not know many things that will have large effects on the consequences of their decisions. British economists John Kay and Mervyn King (the latter governor of the Bank of England during the GFC) in a recent book describe the condition of 'radical uncertainty', in which one really does not know the probability of success from various actions.[1]

Sometimes, when we don't know whether good outcomes are likely, radical uncertainty requires doing what gives the best chance of success. I used the concept in this way at the National Press Club in Canberra in 2008 when introducing my Climate Change Review. I was asked whether we would succeed in avoiding disruption from climate change. I answered by referring to a memorable test match against Pakistan in Hobart a few years before. Australian wicket-keeper Adam Gilchrist joined opener Justin Langer at the batting crease with Australia in a hopeless position. 'Let's have a go,' Langer said to Gilchrist. 'You never know.' They had a go, and Australia won a famous victory.

Subjective assessments of the chances of success from a big policy choice usually suggest better odds than those presented to the Australian batsmen in Hobart. But radical uncertainty is present in any big public policy decision, because we only ever understand part of the relevant world. Knowledge develops over time, and changes with new observations. Yet knowledge is nevertheless essential to good decisions. Not using knowledge at all makes bad outcomes certain. Using the available knowledge well, taking every chance to increase knowledge as events unfold, and adjusting policy in the light of new knowledge, improves outcomes and may lead to good ones.

Here there is a dilemma for a wise leader. Humans dislike uncertainty. They want to think that their leaders know where the country is headed and the effects of their policies on the destination. Members of a society that are confident their leaders know where they are going and are satisfied this is a desirable destination will accept constraints in the public interest. Without such confidence, they will not cooperate, and it is not always possible for governments to force compliance.

Leadership is first of all the telling of a coherent story about the challenges facing a society, the path ahead, and how the leader proposes to improve the destination. Profound and knowledgeable thinkers seldom succeed as political leaders. The great professors are aware of the reality of radical uncertainty and fail to assure the polity that they know where they are taking the country. The case of a great business leader succeeding in political leadership is even rarer. Great business leaders are accustomed to making decisions in a simple value-maximising framework that need take no account of the complex relationships that are important in defining objectives in a way that holds a society together and creating a widely shared view that personal sacrifice to advance the objectives is in everyone's interest.

Great political leaders absorb knowledge from the experts, including knowledge of what we do not know. They use that knowledge to build policies that give the country the best chance of coming to a position that most people think is good. They explain the reasons for the choices in ways that give confidence that the sacrifices are worth the effort. They acknowledge uncertainty, while projecting confidence that the best path has been chosen. We can see this in the appeals by democratic leaders to their polities at moments of radical uncertainty and consequence. Prime Minister Winston Churchill in June 1940: 'I have myself full confidence that if all do their duty, if nothing is neglected, and if the best arrangements are made, as they are being made, we shall prove ourselves again able to defend our island home, to ride out the storm of war, and to outlive the menace of tyranny, if necessary for years, if necessary alone.' Or Franklin Roosevelt in his inaugural address in 1933: 'This is pre-eminently the time to speak the truth, the whole truth, frankly and boldly. Nor need we shrink from honestly facing conditions in our country today … So, first of all, let me assert my firm belief that the only thing we have to fear is fear itself – nameless, unreasoning, unjustified terror which paralyses needed effort to convert retreat into advance.'

In the democracies, there is an alternative to wise and knowledgeable leaders explaining the choices and acknowledging uncertainty while projecting confidence that the best course has been chosen. The citizens' yearning for certainty can sometimes be met for a while in highly uncertain times by the assertion that there is a simple answer to a complex question. Defence of the simple answer involves rejection of knowledge that is inconsistent with it. The appeal of the assertion is strongest if the answer includes a call to defend a tribe or nation from enemies within or without who are identified as the cause of problems. The alternative includes confident assertion of falsehood. This is the phenomenon that has come to be known as populism. It has become increasingly important in the democracies over the past two decades, especially among right-of-centre parties and groups riding the wave of reaction against globalisation and unhappiness with elites at a time of increasing inequality in incomes and wealth.

The populist leader's confident assertion of an erroneous view comes unstuck when the progress of events reveals the error and the damage that has come from it. The leaders who went furthest in rejecting scientific knowledge about the pandemic at the beginning – President Donald Trump in the United States, President Jair Bolsonaro in Brazil and, for a while, Prime Minister Boris Johnson in the UK – have been damaged politically by the revelation that their failures to heed medical science led to outcomes that were very much worse than they would have been if policy had been built on respect for scientific knowledge. All contracted the disease themselves.

One big geopolitical consequence of the pandemic may be the discrediting of populism – the confident assertion of simple falsehoods by the likes of Trump and Bolsonaro. In November 2020, this was fatal for Trump's presidency. We will gradually learn whether the defeat or degrading of 'populist' leaders in the pandemic was the end of the downgrading of knowledge in public policy in the capitalist democracies, or merely a pause.

A great deal of damage can be done before reality unravels populist leadership. The damage can be greater at times like the present, when there is both strategic conflict with successful authoritarian states and internal disagreement about established economic ideas and political institutions.

The decline in respect for knowledge is present in many democracies in the twenty-first century, but is not evenly spread across them. Its sources include resentment at rapid change and the increased complexity in life, with citizens required to learn new things simply to enjoy continued access to old comforts. The expertise required to navigate the increasing complexities of modern life arouses resentment against 'experts' who are comfortable with these complexities and with imposing them on others. There is also a social and cultural reaction against the loss of established ways of life.

The emergence of the internet as the main provider of information about domestic and international events has had a negative effect on the quality of knowledge available to most people. The low cost of serving small audiences online allows proprietors to 'narrowcast' information: to speak to only part of the national population. The internet absorbs almost all the advertising revenue that once supported the highest-quality news sources. Newspapers and other established media forms now invest less in securing the depth and accuracy of information that they carry. The internet platforms do not generate content of their own, but spread widely the content from other media. The other media have become more strident and less knowledgeable. In an attempt to maintain audiences and revenues, media business models have come to focus on simple exhortations geared to reinforcement of readers' views.

Former prime minister Malcolm Turnbull made this point when speaking at a forum in early December 2020: 'We have seen during this year an acceleration of dark trends in the media landscape ... the rise of social media and the ability of the mainstream media to narrowcast ... we've started to see the dangerous situation where communities no longer share the same facts. A political community, a democracy, depends on a common understanding of what the facts are ... where you have alternative facts and alternative realities you get into a dangerous landscape.'[2]

Stagnant incomes in developed countries – most severe in the United States, where there has been no real income growth on average for ordinary citizens for four decades – raise resentment against people of established wealth, whose income and wealth continue to grow at a considerable rate. In the US and some other developed democracies, the costs of the GFC were not evenly shared, nor the benefits of government intervention – and this increased resentment and the reaction against elites.

From the late twentieth century, economic development everywhere has been supported by increasing international movement of goods, services, people and capital – the phenomenon known as globalisation. This greatly increased the value of global production. The fastest economic growth was in developing countries, at first mainly in China and other Asian countries, and then more broadly. Globalisation was a major force in reducing global inequality, with rapid growth in incomes of most people in China and to a lesser extent in Indonesia, India and other Asian countries. There was acceleration of economic growth even in Africa in the early twenty-first century, where outcomes had been mostly dismal in the later decades of the previous century. All of this held out the promise that in the twenty-first century people all over the world would eventually enjoy the high productivity levels and incomes of those in developed countries.

But one large group of people missed out on the benefits of globalisation through the first two decades of the twenty-first century. These were workers in developed countries, people who relied on wages for their livings, perhaps augmented by transfers from their governments. For some of these people, the same globalisation that lifted the incomes of the business elites of their countries, and of most people in developing countries, reduced their own incomes and access to services. International mobility of capital facilitated tax evasion and became an argument for reducing corporate tax rates. This weakened the fiscal capacity of the state in developed democracies, placing pressure on the provision of services and income transfers that could otherwise ease the fall in living standards. The shift of much of the world's manufacturing industry to developing countries, especially but not only China, led to job losses in developed countries. The effects were concentrated among particular regions and older male workers. Increasing movement of people across national borders also led to downward pressure on some wages in the main countries of immigration, notably Australia, the UK and the US.

Globalisation was only one source of pressure on the incomes of ordinary people in developed countries. But it was a real source. It is a human characteristic to resent more acutely the damage imposed by foreign people. Some powerful elite interests in the developed world saw the advantage in channelling resentments against real and imagined foreign causes.

How did increasing tension over income inequality and blaming foreigners help to undermine respect for knowledge? The well-educated and well-informed on average were better off economically. But I doubt that that was the main cause.

In the United States, resentment about the stagnation and decline of ordinary citizens' living standards, and about the role of foreign trade and immigration in that result, was harvested in support of a more general political program, linking hostility towards the well-educated and the foreign to resentment of the role of government. The general ideological theme was that government intervention was undesirable in many economic and social affairs. It had its origins in the reaction in the US southern states against the successes of the civil rights movement in the late 1950s and early 1960s. Here, the reaction was against the federal government's power under the constitution to impose limits on discrimination against non-white citizens.[3] The 'states' rights' movement found common cause with other interests seeking to limit government action in the economy and society: the National Rifle Association; fossil fuel companies and other businesses seeking to avoid government action on climate change; the tobacco industry's interest in avoiding controls on advertising its products; and more generally the interests of business in reducing taxation and regulation. To form coalitions large enough to win majority support in electoral contests, common cause was found with interests that are not obviously connected to opposition to the government's role in the economy – most importantly, religious groups opposed to women choosing to terminate pregnancies.

The ideological bonds joining these interests are not immediately obvious. I met with advisers to the Congressional Republican Caucus on Climate Change in 2007, on Capitol Hill in Washington, DC, in the course of consultations for my Climate Change Review. Several of my interlocutors wore the distinctive tie of the National Rifle Association, with crossed rifles, US flag and eagle. I wondered at the link between climate change and the freedom to own and carry firearms. The penny dropped as the discussion unfolded: it was opposition to government action of any kind.

The idea that government was the problem and not part of the solution to most challenges became influential in US policy in many spheres. It was most influential on the Republican side of an increasingly divided polity. The idea was inconsistent with conclusions drawn from knowledge about economics, climate, international relations and health, among much else. It could only be sustained by separating public policy discussion from knowledge. The new media and political culture supported that separation.

The election of a president with no respect for objective truth was the culmination of these ideological and political developments. It left the United States vulnerable to the COVID-19 pandemic, and in a weak position to manage its recessionary consequences. It rendered the pandemic more dangerous to international cooperation and order.

And it weakened the international effort to meet the challenges of climate change.

Ideological and political developments in the United States are influential everywhere, but especially in English-speaking countries. US ideological developments were transmitted to the UK and Australia, in particular, through the media organisation News Corp. and the advocacy groups of the right. There have been echoes of President Trump on important issues in both countries, and in the UK at the beginning of the pandemic on the appropriate response to COVID-19. These were influential on policy in the UK, with deadly consequences. They were shouty but not influential on the pandemic in Australia.

Three matters were especially important in determining how quickly and deeply the pandemic spread: first, whether governments took medical knowledge about the virus seriously; second, whether leaders saw governments as having an important role in shaping events; and third, the effectiveness of government in taking action once decisions had been made on what should be done.

The numbers of sick and dead were much lower in countries with governments that accepted and acted on scientific knowledge from the beginning than in those that did not. In the United States, Brazil and the UK, leaders explicitly rejected knowledge that the disease was seriously damaging in its effects. They rejected knowledge that there was value in controlling its spread by reducing contact among people, isolating affected people and areas, using masks when contact with affected people could not be avoided, and intensive testing as a guide to policy on isolation.

Many developing countries stand out for their failure to act effectively once it is accepted that action should be taken because of the weakness of health systems. The United States stands out among developed countries for a chronically inadequate public health system.

Among the democracies, countries that took the medical science seriously and acted promptly and effectively to block the spread of the disease achieved much better health outcomes, and better economic outcomes as well. At their best, democracies have advantages in using knowledge to guide public policy. Open criticism leads to correction of failures to absorb or apply knowledge. Governments that do not use knowledge well can be replaced – as we saw with the Trump administration in January 2021.

The capacity and inclination of the authoritarian Chinese government to restrict criticism and the flow of information contributed to the slow response that led to the spread of the pandemic from Wuhan through China and the rest of the world in early 2020. However, an authoritarian government is not always a barrier to using knowledge effectively in minimising the impact of a disease. Governments that in the end controlled the spread of COVID-19 most effectively included the authoritarian (the People's Republic of China, Vietnam, Ethiopia), the liberal democratic (New Zealand, South Korea, Taiwan, Norway, Australia) and the illiberal democratic (we can argue about definitions, but maybe Singapore and Thailand fall within this category). The superiority of democracy at its best over alternative systems is demonstrated in other spheres.

The Enlightenment and knowledge in Australian history

Democracy and the Australian nation both grew from the Enlightenment. They were built on respect for knowledge. Of course, there has been plenty of ignorance and bombastic assertion along the way; plenty of errors, misunderstandings and lies on important questions. But through most of our history, public policy has been built on a premise that there is truth that can be found through examining evidence and through debate. Proposals for change require arguments that draw on chains of logic and facts. To be associated with ignorance, error, misunderstanding and lies carries a political price. People wanting to influence policy choices seek, or at least once sought, to be knowledgeable. Expert opinions and reports were often sought in contests over public policy.

It is the misfortune of the democratic world that we have to deal with the pandemic and its recession at a time when the Enlightenment respect for knowledge is weaker than it has been since the beginnings of our democracy.

It is our good fortune that this did not stop our political leaders in Canberra and the Australian states and territories and our communities from seeking and heeding expert medical knowledge in dealing with the pandemic. It is important for our future prosperity and democracy that the success earnt by that renewed respect for knowledge is now extended to discussion of the economy, climate change and international relations.

History twists and turns through accidents and surprises. It is surprising, and I hope an accident, that one outcome of the response so far to the pandemic recession has been the destruction of the financial base of Australia's primary Enlightenment institutions: our universities. Governments from both sides of the Australian partisan divide over the past decade have kept universities on a short leash in terms of funding for research and domestic students. Universities maintained their research and teaching strength, and exceptionally high global standing for a country with our population and economic size, by relying heavily on fees from foreign students. They lost a major part of their revenue base when the pandemic blocked the arrival of these students. Surprisingly, universities were denied access to the emergency financial measures made available by the federal Coalition to other large service industries for which restrictions had greatly reduced revenues. Casinos are one comparator.

In an article for *Meanjin*, Glyn Davis recently reminded us of the views of the founder of the Liberal Party, Sir Robert Menzies, on the role of knowledge and universities in our democracy. Menzies saw universities as having a central role in preserving and extending the riches of civilisation and in the success of liberal democratic societies.[4] Maybe the singular treatment of universities in the pandemic recession is an accident. If so, there are good reasons to correct the error quickly. Failure would damage progress towards full employment. Failure would weaken our capacity to raise productivity and incomes. Failure would weaken Australia's standing in our Indo-Pacific region at a critical time for competition between political and economic systems.

The Australian tradition of economic knowledge

Australia has a strong record in developing and applying economic knowledge to public policy at times of economic stress. Between the crises, we do not do so well. We tend to let things drift while they seem to be doing reasonably well. Not many people are interested in the things that are not doing so well, and problems accumulate. Then we work it out and put the economy and country on a better course.

Emeritus professor of economics David Vines at Oxford University is working on a history of Australian use of economic knowledge in policy-making. He notes that the development and application of knowledge of how the economy works contributed to good outcomes at several decisive points in Australian economic history. These include recovery from the Great Depression (when Australia moved faster and further in the 1930s than the US or UK), the postwar reconstruction program that led to the long prosperity from the late 1940s into the 1970s, and the reform era from 1983 that led to the productivity boom of the 1990s and the three decades of economic expansion that have just ended.[5]

Ideas from this Australian tradition of policy-making have been neglected in recent economic discussion. I draw heavily upon them in this book, especially in framing proposals for varying expenditure and competitiveness to achieve full employment with the right amount of debt. The successful initial economic response to the pandemic in early 2020 can evolve into restoration after the pandemic recession, as a fourth case of successful Australian democratic response to a massive economic challenge.

Australian ideas on how competitiveness and expenditure jointly determine the rate of unemployment (or, in the absence of unemployment, inflationary pressure) and the amount of foreign debt played a role in the Premiers' Plan, postwar reconstruction and the reform era. So did a distinctly Australian concern for equitable distribution of the costs of income and expenditure restraint in the public interest. In the first half of 2020, the response to the pandemic recession focused on spending that favoured Australians on low incomes (most importantly, JobSeeker and JobKeeper). The restoration of Australia after the pandemic recession requires two developments of this early response. We need increased competitiveness as well as high levels of expenditure so that full employment can be achieved with a manageable level of debt. And the concern for equity has to be maintained, but expressed in ways that are consistent with rising living standards over the longer term.

2

THE PANDEMIC RECESSION
OF 2020

'Pestilence is so common,' wrote Albert Camus in *The Plague*, in 1942. 'There have been as many plagues in the world as there have been wars, yet plagues and wars always find people equally unprepared. When war breaks out, people say: "It won't last. It's too stupid." And war is certainly too stupid, but that doesn't prevent it from lasting.'

So too with recessions. Too stupid, and so common. So common, and yet they always take people by surprise. And they last. The damage from the Great Crash of 2008 lingers today, even in Australia, which, with South Korea, was alone among developed countries in avoiding two successive quarters of declining output.[1]

There have been manifold points of weakness in the global economy in recent years: the Trump expansion of fiscal deficits through unfunded tax cuts with the economy near full employment when debt and deficits were already at record peace-time highs[2]; the retreats from China's new model of economic growth from 2017[3]; the breakdown in global governance on trade, climate change and security, distended by the US trade wars; the unusually high levels of debt in most economies; and the sustained low investment, productivity and wages growth throughout the developed world. Australia has shared many of the developed countries' points of vulnerability. Some of them have been more acute here than elsewhere. The initial conditions made the world vulnerable and the initial shock was immense. But the initial policy response to blunt its effects was also immense. Some countries face long recession. How many, and whether Australia is among them, depends on the continuing policy response.

The immediate cause of recession can be any of many things. The piercing of unwarranted confidence in the fixed exchange rate in Thailand in 1997, sparking the Asian Financial Crisis. Or the financial deregulation that promoted lending for houses far in excess of their value in America a decade later. For any single country, the trigger can be other countries' recessions and the associated reduced demand for that country's exports, or the associated financial stress.

This time the trigger was the impact of a new virus. Appearing first in the Chinese province of Wuhan, it quickly spread throughout China, East Asia and the world. There was an immediate recessionary effect in China and its neighbours. That in itself was bound to impose great damage on the Australian economy – before the disease and the response to it had disrupted Australia directly. Treasurer Josh Frydenberg said to me in Canberra on 5 March that he was determined to do all he could to prevent recession. I said that was a good objective, because the costs of recessions were large and hard to unwind. Regrettably, what had already happened in China, South Korea, Japan and Southeast Asia, on top of what was already probably a negative March quarter, made it too late to avoid Australian recession. We could, however, ensure the recession was as shallow and short as possible, and that Australians had confidence there was a path ahead to a better future.

The pandemic

Plagues creep up, and then overwhelm us.

A small cluster of cases of an unusual pneumonia emerged in

Wuhan, capital of Hubei province in China, around 20 December 2019. The Chinese health authorities advised the World Health Organization of a 'virus pneumonia of unknown origin in Wuhan' on 31 December.

On 30 December, Li Wenliang, a medical doctor in Wuhan, expressed concern at the seriousness of the virus in a group chat. In response to his early efforts to warn of the spreading of the virus and the importance of early sharing of information, he was accused of rumour-mongering. Dr Li contracted the virus and died on 7 February 2020. That same day, US President Donald Trump praised China's efforts in containing COVID-19 and pledged support. In a radio interview, Trump acknowledged that the virus was deadly and spread through the air.

In January, the WHO made several requests to Chinese authorities for information about the virus as it tried to determine its severity and whether it was being transmitted from one human to another; cases were being reported from a number of countries, including Australia and the United States. Learned bodies within the WHO assessed and shared information, and alerted member states. They provided recommendations and guidelines on preparedness, surveillance and monitoring. On 11 January, Chinese authorities made the genome sequencing available to the international community. On 30 January, the WHO declared that the new virus constituted a Public Health Emergency of International Concern. Around 10,000 cases had been reported in at least twenty-one countries. Several countries had already made their own assessments and swung into action. But most had not. The WHO continued its advice against restrictions on international travel and trade, advice supported by some leaders and experts around the world and criticised by others.

On 5 February, the WHO announced a US$675-million Strategic Preparedness and Response Plan to communicate essential information, limit transmission and protect states with weaker health systems.

A week later, the disease was officially named COVID-19. On 11 March, COVID-19 was declared a global pandemic.

There have been reliable reports of high-level discussions about the virus by the Chinese leadership during the first half of January, including about the seriousness of the virus, its high risk of spread through transmission, and its potential to become a major public health risk. Despite this, Chinese New Year celebrations, including an annual banquet in Wuhan on 18 January, went ahead. On 20 January, China announced that the coronavirus was highly contagious. Three days later, Wuhan was locked down, followed soon after by more cities and then the whole province of Hubei.

Several economies in China's immediate neighbourhood responded quickly and effectively to control the virus. Case and mortality rates have remained low in Thailand, Taiwan, Vietnam, Singapore, Japan and South Korea – as they have in Hong Kong and China – despite some surges in 2020. With strong public health systems and being alert for emergent indications following their experiences of delayed reporting of SARS and MERS, many of these economies had begun responding to a potentially highly infectious threat prior to the Chinese report to WHO on 31 December. A mix of approaches was applied. These included timely, factual information; border and internal restrictions; and home quarantine for travellers from Wuhan or China or persons with signs of the disease.

Sophisticated mobile phone apps, alongside clever use of government databases and CCTV, enabled effective contact tracing. The mobile apps were mandatory in some countries, voluntary in others. Mask wearing and social distancing were used comprehensively. A measure successfully used in one country might have been a failure, unsuitable or unacceptable in another. In Taiwan, practical developments by citizens were encouraged and utilised in the national toolkit.

Thailand began screening all inbound flights on 3 January, On 8 January, it reported its first coronavirus case – the first case recorded outside China. The threat was met with a comprehensive public health strategy. Early border controls, strict lockdowns, restrictions on movement and mask wearing were adopted. On 26 March, Thailand declared a state of emergency after cumulative case numbers rose to over 1000. There was a sharp increase in case numbers during April, which levelled off in early May. Restrictions were then eased. Thailand's cases increased in the following months, but not by much.

Taiwan quickly enacted inspection measures on flights arriving from Wuhan on 31 December and set up a response team on 2 January. Flight inspection measures were intensified by 5 January to include monitoring of all individuals linked with travel to Wuhan in the past fourteen days. On 20 January, the day before its first recorded case, Taiwan mobilised response teams across multiple levels, implemented contact tracing, restricted exports and increased production of medical supplies. Broader international restrictions came into effect around 14 March, and from 19 March foreign nationals were barred from entering. Taiwan was quick to roll out testing and to ration masks. With a population not much less than Australia's, Taiwan had the smallest numbers of cases and deaths among all countries with public health capacity to identify the disease. By early May, Taiwan had had only 439 confirmed cases and six deaths, and local transmission had ceased. Taiwan then lifted some restrictions but kept borders closed to the outside world. Cases and deaths per million people remained the lowest among countries with capacity for sound measurement.

Vietnam, like South Korea, Taiwan, Hong Kong and Japan, is an economy near China that responded to the first news with effective domestic controls and border closures. Remarkably, with its population of 98 million, Vietnam had had only 271 cases by mid-May. On 31 July,

Vietnam recorded its first deaths, two in one day. Case numbers and deaths remained low.

Singapore took early, strong and effective measures. It was screening all inbound travel from Wuhan by 2 January, and from the whole of China by 20 January. By 22 January, screening was intensified to include individuals linked to China within a fourteen-day range. Stay-home restrictions commenced on 17 February for anyone returning from China. Broader international restrictions came into effect on 3 March, and by 24 March Singapore had shut its borders to all foreigners. Early measures in Singapore influenced its Southeast Asian neighbours. Early success led to easing of restrictions in April, which was followed by a rapid increase in confirmed cases, mostly among immigrant workers living in poor conditions. A strict lockdown was imposed. Daily case numbers peaked on 20 April and then fell fairly steadily. Singapore began to lift its strict lockdown mid-June and by the end of August was recording few new cases.

The Japanese government initiated a suite of measures against the 'respiratory disease from Wuhan' from early January. Border controls were not introduced with China or the rest of the world and lockdown measures were largely voluntary. Testing was limited. With good public health capacities and a population accustomed to exercising restraint, Japan at first relied mainly on voluntary self-distancing practices in accordance with avoidance of the three Cs: crowded spaces, confined spaces and close-contact settings. By 1 April, Japan had reported 2500 cases and sixty deaths – many stemming from a single cruise ship. The rate of new cases and deaths then accelerated, most notably in Tokyo. A state of emergency was declared on 7 April, but measures were still mostly voluntary. Cases in Japan peaked on 12 April, after which they declined and remained low until mid-July. A new wave late in 2020 generated far more cases and precipitated stronger mandatory constraints.

South Korea officially introduced limited controls on entry for any foreigners connected to China's Hubei province on 4 February, and on 23 February raised the coronavirus alert to its highest level. South Korea moved promptly with widespread monitoring, testing and quarantining of people with symptoms – but delayed implementing travel restrictions on arrivals from China. By 20 March, it had tested more than 350,000 citizens and confirmed 9237 cases. The low ratio of confirmed cases reflected the uniquely comprehensive nature of the testing.

On 25 January, Hong Kong declared the new coronavirus an emergency and began measures to limit transmission. People in Hong Kong, as in several other East Asian countries, exhibited a strong sense of responsibility to protect themselves and their local communities. By mid-May, Hong Kong had only 1000 confirmed cases and four deaths.

The rest of Southeast Asia did not fare as well.

There was early under-reporting in Indonesia, through a combination of weak public health capacity and reluctance from the top leadership to accept the seriousness of the pandemic. Indonesia confirmed its first case on 2 March and its first death ten days later. Detection and treatment were marred by shortages of testing supplies and ventilators. There were no official controls on movement until a public health emergency was declared on 31 March. This introduced large-scale social distancing measures, with border restrictions in specific areas. On 2 April, international restrictions came into effect. Stronger action commenced on 23 April, with the president announcing a ban on air and sea travel until early June, covering Ramadan. There was concern that movement around the country on the eve of Eid would accelerate rates of infection. Pressure from affected communities led to early announcements of exceptions to the travel rules. By May, Indonesia was a locus of increasing numbers of cases and deaths, and still little prepared to deal with them. By 31 August, Indonesia's casualties were the largest in Southeast Asia, with 174,796 confirmed cases and 7417 deaths. As a proportion of the population, the Philippines (220,781 cases and 3558 deaths) had more casualties than Indonesia.

New Zealand – and Australia after a brief wobble – followed China's immediate neighbours and Singapore in their prompt, strong responses. New Zealand placed entry restrictions on foreign nationals travelling from mainland China on 3 February, requiring fourteen days of self-isolation. Its first reported case was on 28 February and on 19 March it shut its borders. New Zealand's continued attention to public health advice has supported the advantages of geographic isolation in containing the virus.

Australia recorded its first case on 25 January – two days after the Wuhan lockdown. On 5 February, Australia announced a ban for non-citizens arriving from China – the same day Chinese authorities blocked travel out of Wuhan. On 19 March, major airlines suspended international flights. All non-citizens and non-residents were banned from entering the country from 21 March. Citizens and families were required to self-quarantine for fourteen days. Compulsory quarantine (with discretionary exceptions) was introduced on 29 March. At the initiative of the prime minister, a National Cabinet was established on 13 March, comprising federal, state and territory heads of government, to coordinate a rapid tightening of domestic movement and the closure of most activities requiring the gathering of people without opportunities for social distancing. Most states banned interstate movement of people not involved in the supply of essential services. Large-scale mining, manufacturing and construction continued within disciplined social distancing regimes.

Australia had some early difficulties in enforcing border controls, with most early cases deriving from a cruise ship docking in Sydney on 8 March. A second wave of cases, concentrated in metropolitan Melbourne, was largely attributable to failure in the management of hotel quarantine for international arrivals in Victoria. Case numbers and deaths rose sharply in Melbourne. On 17 June, when twenty-one new daily cases were recorded, lockdowns were implemented in some suburbs. When new daily case numbers exceeded 100 on 4 July, the state government cracked down at short notice, with restrictions on movement in some public housing towers. More severe restrictions were reinstated on 8 July across Victoria, with stricter restrictions for metropolitan Melbourne. Impressive early cohesion across Australia unravelled in July, with politicisation of responsibility for failure of hotel quarantine and high deaths in aged care facilities. Other states unilaterally tightened controls on movement across their borders. Victorian restrictions were elevated on 2 August. Victorian coronavirus cases peaked at 723 new cases in a single day on 30 July and then fell steadily as the state government's measures proved effective. By November, community transmission was virtually zero throughout Australia, with Victoria standing out in the world as an example of effective elimination after the disease had established deep roots in the community.

The response in Scandinavian countries bifurcated between Sweden and the rest. Norway, Denmark and Finland each recorded their first cases between 26 and 29 February. By mid-March these countries had recorded deaths and implemented strict lockdown measures and border controls. Sweden's first case was recorded on 31 January and its first death on 11 March. Its response was distinctly different: a light-touch approach, with voluntary social distancing and some loose constraints on gatherings of people. Official reference was made to the advantages of 'herd immunity'. The hope was to keep economic and social activity alive. This came at the cost of substantially more deaths. Denmark began easing restrictions in mid-April, the first EU member to do so. Norway and Finland followed in mid-June. By the end of June, Sweden's death toll was over 5000, dramatically higher than its Nordic neighbours (at this time, Denmark, Finland and Norway had recorded 604, 328 and 249 deaths respectively). The situation in Sweden challenged the pan-Nordic acceptance of passport-free travel. Border restrictions to Sweden remained in place as the other Scandinavian countries started to open up. Sweden's per capita death rate was among the highest in the world.

New Zealand, and China's immediate neighbours – Vietnam, South Korea, Japan, Thailand, Hong Kong and Taiwan – stand out as global success stories in pandemic control. Australia also did well. China was highly effective in controlling the spread of the disease after the initial bad start that allowed the disease to spread beyond Wuhan. These Western Pacific economies had much better health outcomes than high-income countries in the rest of the world, and enjoyed earlier and stronger resumption of economic growth.

In contrast to East Asia and the Western Pacific, reactions to the emerging pandemic were late and slow in Europe and the United States. In the US and the UK in particular, initial responses by heads of government, encouraged by a noisy and influential segment of the media centred on Fox News in the US, downplayed the medical science and the value of a strong public policy response.

The United States had its first confirmed case on 21 January, linked to Wuhan. On 29 January, the White House announced a taskforce led by Vice President Mike Pence to oversee monitoring and containment of the virus. On 30 January, Trump downplayed the WHO's announcement of a Public Health Emergency of International Concern. One day later, he announced the restriction of travel from China – relatively early, but far from comprehensive. During the month of February, Trump tweeted from time to time that the US was handling well its small number of cases, that China was working hard, and that the virus would disappear with warmer weather in April. He reassured the nation with a graph that showed the United States at the top of the range of countries in preparedness to respond to an epidemic. This preparation traced back to the George W. Bush administration, when in 2005 President Bush developed a 'playbook' for pandemic response. The playbook identified face masks, surveillance and a unified media message as critical to an effective response. It was passed to the Obama administration, which developed specific plans for responding to coronaviruses. Elements of the mechanisms were dismantled by the Trump administration. Others were not followed. South Korea and the United States recorded their first cases on the same day. Within a month, South Korea had tested over 350,000 citizens, but the United States – with more than six times the population – had tested not much more than 60,000.

When the outbreak was defined by the WHO as a global pandemic on 11 March, the US imposed restrictions on travel from Europe, for a few days excluding the UK and Ireland. On 13 March, Trump declared a national emergency, but continued to make contradictory statements about the seriousness of the disease and the need for strong domestic controls. The opportunity for early response and coordinated testing was missed, and contact tracing was inadequate. By the end of April, the weather warmed, the virus had not disappeared and the United States had experienced more than 65,000 deaths.

There were hard lockdowns in some states after high incidence of the disease had been established, but not in others with large and increasing numbers of cases. Continued disregard for advice from health experts, an inadequate healthcare system and a serious shortage of personal protective equipment for healthcare workers and the population at large allowed the virus to gain a strong foothold. By mid-July, mask wearing was mandatory in many states, but discouraged in others. Decisions on whether or not to wear masks became tangled in ideological conflict over the balance between personal freedoms and public responsibilities. By 31 August, more than 6.2 million people in the United States had contracted the virus, and over 187,000 had died. The number of cases continued to grow as winter approached, to well above those of the first wave early in the year. After the election in November 2020, the lame-duck administration of Donald Trump seemed to abandon any effort to contain the virus. Hope was placed on early development and distribution of a vaccine. By the end of the year, there had been about 350,000 deaths. It seemed that COVID-19 deaths by the spring would exceed combat deaths in all US foreign wars, including and since the American War of Independence.

As many countries were implementing increasingly strict limitations on the movement of people, in early 2020 the UK thought out loud about a 'herd immunity' strategy. This dalliance was short-lived. The first case in the UK was recorded on 31 January. The imposition of firm controls came much later. It was not until 2 March that the prime minister met with senior ministers and health officials to discuss the virus. Testing was slow, and the medical system was overwhelmed by the disease. By 12 March, there were shortages of testing resources. Strict lockdown measures were not introduced until 23 March. By this time, the disease had established a strong beachhead in the community. In early June, the UK introduced a fourteen-day quarantine for all international arrivals, which later included exemptions for some countries considered to be low-risk. As in North America and continental Europe, a second wave became more severe as winter approached, prompting severe and widespread lockdowns. By the end of the year, a new and more contagious form of the virus contributed to an acceleration in the spread of the disease. Daily case numbers and deaths reached the highest levels recorded from the start of the pandemic. There were fears that the public health system would be overwhelmed.

Continental Europe was the global epicentre of the pandemic from March until it shifted to the Anglo-North Atlantic in April. Germany confirmed its first case on 27 January, followed by Italy and Russia on 31 January, France on 4 February, Italy on 21 February and Spain on

25 February. Italy closed public spaces in some areas on 21 February and moved to lockdowns on 9 March. Spain suspended international flights in early March, then in the middle of the month declared a state of emergency and closed its borders to all non-citizens. The high rate of infection overwhelmed Italian and Spanish public health facilities until a complete lockdown of residents led to declines in rates of new cases and deaths in late April. Germany initially experienced high rates of infection, but a strong public policy response within an effective health system kept rates of infection within the limits of medical capacity. While deaths were lower than elsewhere in Europe, Germany shared in the severe second wave that enveloped Europe as winter approached.

The developing world beyond East Asia became the epicentre of the pandemic from July. Poor testing facilities within weak public health systems mean that we do not know accurately the extent of the problem in many countries.

An early outbreak in Iran was damaging, but by late April it had been brought under control by drastic restrictions on the movement of people. Infection rates remained high throughout the Middle East. Countries in South Asia, like the Philippines and Indonesia in Southeast Asia, were late to recognise the extent of the problem. India recorded its first case on 30 January and its first death on 12 March. One day earlier, on 11 March, the same day the global pandemic was declared, India suspended all tourist visas and all incoming international flights, and banned exports of masks, ventilators and some medications. On 24 March at 8 pm, Prime Minister Narendra Modi declared that from midnight all of India would be under lockdown. The immediate response was chaotic. In mid-May, India faced continued acceleration of the rates of infection and death, extreme disruption of social and economic life and the impossibility of containing the spread of the virus among dense concentrations of poor people. While Indian cases and deaths are staggeringly high, weak public health capacity means that India's figures are grossly underestimated. Lockdowns imposed nationally were eased from early June, but lockdowns continued at the state level.

Latin America also faced extreme disruption. The most populous country, Brazil, confirmed its first case on 25 February. President Jair Bolsonaro responded by insisting that COVID-19 was a minor disease and that broad social distancing measures were not needed to stop it. On 7 March, he travelled to the United States to visit President Trump and upon returning was advised to quarantine after members of his party had tested positive for coronavirus. Instead, he publicly and purposefully defied social distancing measures, greeting fans with hugs and handshakes. On 17 April, Bolsonaro sacked Brazil's minister for health, whose advice aligned with that of global health experts. On 16 May, Brazil lost its second health minister in a month, this time at the minister's own initiative. By 7 May, Brazil's confirmed cases had reached 126,611 with 8500 deaths. Bolsonaro joined Trump's unscientific suggestion that the virus could be treated with chloroquine and hydroxychloroquine. He did not, however, follow Trump in recommending injection of disinfectant. On 8 July, Bolsonaro tested positive for coronavirus but insisted that the people of Brazil were dying for fear of the virus and not from the virus itself. By August, Brazil ranked second to the United States in number of deaths.

The island developing countries in Australia's own region are protected by geographic isolation, but vulnerable from weak and in some cases dysfunctional governance and inadequate public health systems. These countries stretch across Australia's northern sea borders, from Timor Leste through Papua New Guinea and the southwest Pacific. Papua New Guinea recorded its first case on 21 March, a fly-in fly-out mine company employee based in Australia. All FIFO operations were shut down and a state of emergency declared. By early May, only eight cases had been confirmed, but this reflected limited testing capacity more than the extent of infection. On 7 August, the country's second-largest source of exports and public revenue, the Ok Tedi mine, was closed when an employee tested positive for COVID-19. The Morrison government reallocated $22 million of aid to COVID-19 support packages for island countries in the South Pacific. A two-week lockdown of Port Moresby ended on 12 August, with Prime Minister James Marape announcing that residents must learn to live with the virus, as fears for the vulnerable health system were outweighed by fears of economic collapse.

Charts 2.1 and 2.2 illustrate the incidence of officially recorded deaths from the disease across regions and over time. Chart 2.1 covers the early period to mid-March, and Chart 2.2 through to the end of 2020. The specific figures are necessarily underestimates, generally being less reliable in developing countries and where governments were reluctant or late to acknowledge the extent of the disease.

Chart 2.1 Daily deaths by country to mid-March 2020

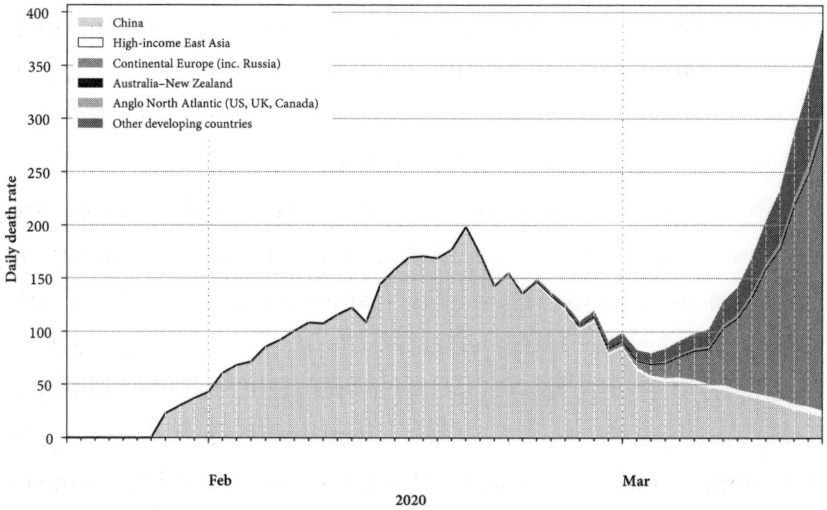

Data source: Center for Systems Science and Engineering, Johns Hopkins University

Chart 2.2 Daily deaths by country to 31 December 2020

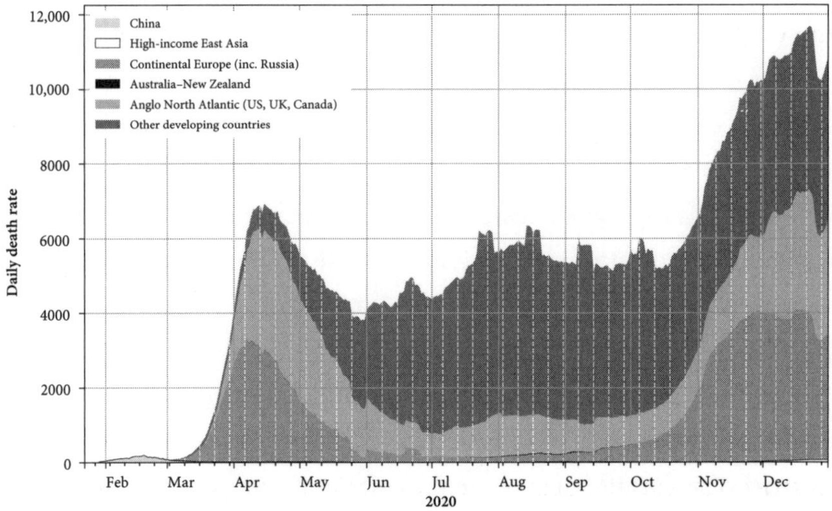

Data source: Center for Systems Science and Engineering, Johns Hopkins University

Chinese deaths – the palest grey in the charts – increased in February, although the number was made to look tiny by subsequent developments elsewhere. Continental Europe (mid-grey in the charts) became the epicentre of the epidemic from the middle of March. Europe reached a peak in early April. Deaths were steadily declining before a new burst of cases in July and August kept expanding until by November they were higher than the April peak. Daily deaths kept increasing for the rest of 2020. The most rapidly growing component of the mid-grey in May was Russia. The whole of Europe contributed to the growth in deaths through the northern winter.

The light grey is the Anglo North Atlantic: the United States, Canada and the United Kingdom, dominated by the United States. Here, a huge peak came not long after the European peak. It eased a bit through the northern summer, but not to anything like the low death rates of Europe. Deaths fell dramatically in New York and the northeast of the United States, where the initial impact of the pandemic had been most severe. They continued to rise elsewhere, with the emergence of new centres of transmission in the south, midwest and west. Cases and deaths remained high and steady in the Anglo North Atlantic, and then lifted again to unprecedented heights as winter approached and kept rising into early January.

The developing world (dark grey in the charts) has experienced an explosion of morbidity and mortality that shows no sign of easing. The twenty-first-century momentum in stronger growth in output and incomes in the developing world has been swept away by the effects of the pandemic at home and the pandemic recession abroad.

By early August 2020, there was impatience everywhere about restrictions on internal and international movements of people. Official constraints were easing in many places, whether or not there was evidence of low levels of community transmission. Case numbers and deaths were rising again in most developed countries – those, like the United States, where it had never been under control; and others, like Germany and Australia, that had been through periods of negligibly low transmission.

By late 2020, community transmission had returned to near zero in Australia, but was out of control in the Anglo-North Atlantic and continental Europe. In the United States, the UK and several continental European countries, daily death tolls were reaching new highs and case numbers threatened to overwhelm hospital capacity in many areas. It seemed that the world would be living with a seriously damaging level of disruption to what once was normal economic interaction until an effective vaccine was in widespread use.

However, in all developed and many developing countries, health specialists had learnt a great deal about care and treatment. Deaths as a proportion of those who contracted the disease were considerably lower than in the early months of 2020.

The search for the holy grail of a successful vaccine was active in many countries. There was hope of early success. Major countries – led by the United States, China, members of the European Union, and Australia for the Southwest Pacific – committed to making vaccines within their control widely available through the developing world. The scientific wisdom said that in the best of circumstances it would be well into 2021 before effective use of a vaccine was widespread in the developed world. It would come later in developing countries. Knowing more about the disease and people's response to it through research and observation over time allowed citizens and governments to define less economically damaging ways of reducing community transmission.

Early in the pandemic there was active debate about whether and to what extent normal economic and social interaction should be curtailed to slow the spread of the virus. Opposition to strong restrictions mainly had ideological origins, with little attempt to base it in knowledge and in analysis of the public interest. In the early discussion, however, some voices conscientiously argued that there was a trade-off between health and economic outcomes: that less restriction may mean more sickness and death, but would lower the damage to economic activity. There was, they argued, a public interest case that the economic costs of restriction outweighed the health benefits. They argued that the combination of widespread, efficient tracing and testing and mask wearing with the isolation and treatment of infected people, and the isolation of people who came into contact with them, was sufficient and that more aggressive measures, such as lockdowns, were unnecessary.

Chart 2.3 plots the early evidence on the relationship between containment of the disease and economic activity. To the extent that there was a relationship at all between health and economic outcomes in the first half of 2020, the fall in economic activity tended to be larger in countries with more severe health impacts.

Chart 2.3 Economic growth versus mortality, in the first half of 2020

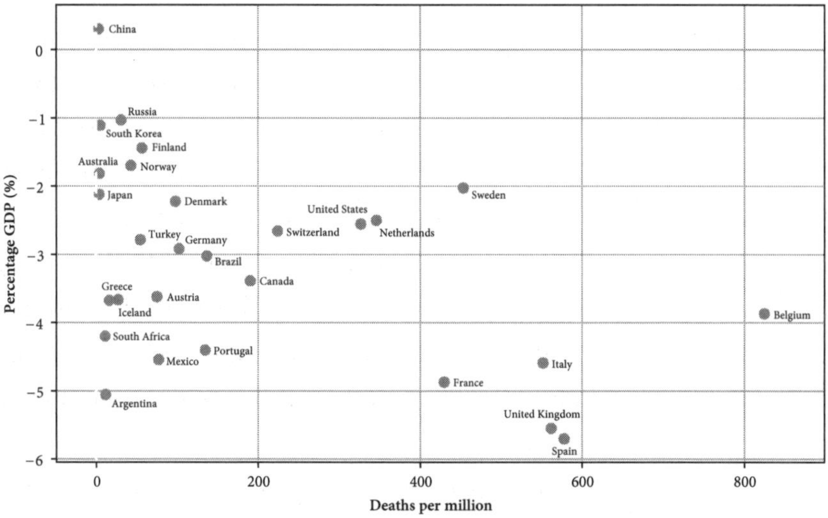

Data source: Johns Hopkins University and International Monetary Fund

The tendency for economic output to hold up better in countries that were more effective in containing the spread of the disease became stronger as the year progressed. The Western Pacific countries with low proportions of cases and daily deaths – led by China and including Australia – were much further along the path to economic recovery in the second half of the year.

The vastly different approaches to pandemic control taken by Sweden on the one hand, and its neighbours Denmark, Norway and Finland on the other, made Scandinavia something of a test case for the competing approaches. Sweden went closest of all developed countries to minimising official restrictions, and arguing that 'herd immunity' would eventually have similarly good health effects to more active intervention, while less restriction would lead to better economic outcomes. Restaurants, shops and schools were kept open. Health authorities actively discouraged the use of masks. Sweden's neighbours in Scandinavia combined private discipline with relatively strong official restriction. Swedish death rates started and remained high. Any 'herd immunity' that may have emerged from high levels of infection in the early months provided no noticeable protection against infection late in the year, as the approach of winter saw a massive new wave break over Europe. By mid-December there had been 7900 deaths in Sweden – on a population-adjusted basis about ten times as high as in Norway and Finland and five times as high as in Denmark. New infections in Sweden were at the highest level ever. The usual intensive-care capacity of Swedish hospitals had been exceeded by COVID-19 cases. Economic output in 2020 was expected to fall by similar proportions across the Scandinavian countries, and was expected to recover more slowly in 2021 in Sweden.

Internal opinion turned against Swedish policy. In a rare statement about government policy, Swedish King Carl XVI Gustaf, said in December 2020 that the people had suffered tremendously in difficult conditions and that 'we have failed'.

The public interest voices against restriction everywhere were diminished by the emerging knowledge that economic as well as health performance was better in countries that took early and strong action against the spread of COVID-19. Experience confirmed that early and strong government action was necessary for good health performance. Dr Anthony Fauci, director of the US National Institute of Allergy and Infectious Diseases from 1984 until now, who has been appointed by President Joe Biden to lead the national anti-COVID effort for the new administration, summed up the evidence in late November:

> It's clear that countries and states that do not embrace restrictions do not blunt the curve as well as those who do. The epitome of that has been the success of Australia.

I know that Victoria is down to almost no cases or even zero cases. In the US, we are in a difficult situation because of the reluctance of substantial proportions of the population to fully implement the mitigation methods.

There is an extraordinary divisiveness in our country. When that spills over into implementation of public health measures – where things like wearing a mask become almost a political statement – it really complicates the issue.

There is a certain something that's beautiful and attractive in the individual human spirit that we have in this country that goes back to our origins. But when you are dealing with a public health crisis that involves the whole country, that individualism sometimes works against you.[4]

The great crash into a global pandemic recession

The sudden onset of the pandemic had an immense, immediate depressive effect on economic activity. There were changes in what governments allowed people to do, and in what people chose to do. I call the former regulatory and the latter behavioural responses to the pandemic. I call the industries immediately affected the restricted industries.

Economic activity in the restricted industries immediately ceased or fell drastically. These were industries requiring long-distance travel or close contacts among large numbers of people. Different levels of regulatory restriction were imposed in different countries. Economic activity crashed in the restricted industries whether or not policy was highly restrictive. International tourism and education were immediately and massively affected everywhere, along with other service industries requiring long-distance travel, and a wide range of domestic service industries, from sport to restaurants, music and theatre. Some industries requiring concentrations of people were declared essential services and did not suffer a decline in output. In Australia, these included abattoirs, supermarkets and other services supplying food to households. Some activities were both essential and organised around scattered workforces – most importantly, agriculture. These were not restricted.

Some countries restricted activity in construction, mining and manufacturing on account of the concentrations of people in operations. Australia did not. The decisions by Treasury and health department officials on where to draw the line made the difference between survival and destruction for many businesses. Officials in Canberra and the states exercised the power and discretion of Gosplan managers at the height of Soviet self-confidence. Some big calls were made. Australia's decision to allow construction, mining and manufacturing to continue was a good big call. It helped to maintain economic activity and these sectors were not a significant source of community infection.

Globally, private behaviour altered even when regulation did not require change. Use of restaurants, theatres and civil aviation declined everywhere. The contrasting pandemic experience in Sweden and other countries in Scandinavia provides insights into the respective effects of regulatory and behavioural restrictions. Activity in industries subject to light restriction in Sweden initially fell almost as much as activity subject to official restriction in Denmark, Norway and Finland.

When regulatory restriction was lifted, people did not move right back to old patterns of behaviour and consumption. Japan and some other East Asian countries were notable for high behavioural restraint despite limited official restriction.

The regulatory and behavioural effects in restricted industries had flow-on consequences elsewhere in the economy. Some of the reduced demand for goods and services fell on imports. This led to lower exports from other countries. Other countries' incomes fell, leading to another round of lower imports, and another reduction of exports in the rest of the world. External demand for goods and services fell in the world as a whole. So did incomes. In addition, reduced opportunities for trade led to falls in specialisation in what countries do best, and so to lower productivity.

The downward spiral of international trade transmitted recession quickly across the world. Some countries were affected more than others by the decline in international trade. Reduced global demand generally causes falls in export prices for commodities and in the terms of trade of countries with large commodity exports – including Australia and most of the developing world. Importers of food and minerals generally experience improved terms of trade. Countries that were closely linked by trade to countries that suffered less than others or recovered quickly were not damaged as badly as others. China's largest trading partners did relatively well. The beneficiaries of early restoration of strong economic growth in China initially included Australia, despite Chinese restrictions on Australian imports of many goods and services, because of the extreme strength of Chinese import demand for iron ore.

All countries sought to counteract the depressive effects of COVID-19 by easing monetary policy, reducing taxation and increasing government spending. The value of expansionary responses had been learnt from the Great Depression and was demonstrated in the Asian and global financial crises. This did not prevent immense falls in output in the first half of 2020 in all countries (see Chart 2.4). These reflected the combined effects of the pandemic shock on restricted industries and the early countervailing impact of expansionary policies. The policy responses had greater effects in the second half of 2020.

Economic output fell at an unprecedented rate in both developed and developing countries in the first half of 2020 (Chart 2.4). Australia, other developed countries and the world as a whole declined more in the first two quarters of 2020 than in the whole of the 1990–91 recession or the GFC. The economic output of developing countries other than China did not fall absolutely in the GFC, but did so in the first half of 2020. Developed countries suffered a much larger decline.

The world's two biggest economies suffered their most rapid contractions ever, and their largest since the cataclysms of the 1930s Great Depression for the United States and the Cultural Revolution (1966–76) for China.

The US Bureau of Labor Statistics counted 14.7 per cent of the workforce as unemployed in mid-April (Chart 2.5) and said that difficulties in collection probably meant the true number was nearly five percentage points higher. Only two years of the Great Depression saw higher unemployment rates.

In the first quarter of 2020, China suffered its first quarterly decline in output since the reform era began in 1978. Massive fiscal and

Chart 2.4 Advanced economy and Australian economic output, first half of 2020

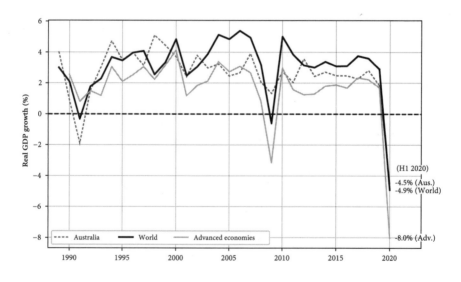

Data source: World Economic Outlook database, International Monetary Fund

monetary expansion and early control of domestic transmission saw a steadying in the second quarter. China alone among significant countries stabilised in the second quarter. China returned to strong growth in the second half of 2020. Output increased in the whole year 2020, but growth was the weakest since the reform era.

In the first half of 2020, Australian GDP experienced the largest fall ever over a comparable period. Investment fell sharply from the low levels of the later Dog Days. Mining held up better than other areas of private investment. Household incomes actually increased, with unprecedented government expenditure on social security. Higher incomes helped to lift consumption, despite a considerable increase in the rate of savings. Unemployment and underemployment rose rapidly (Chart 2.5). Australian unemployment rose less than in the United States to a considerable extent, because of faster and larger policy responses to offset

Chart 2.5 Unemployment and under-employment in Australia, 1992–2020

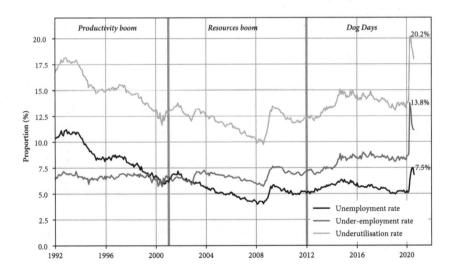

Data source: Australian Bureau of Statistics, cat. 62020.22

recessionary effects. US jobless claims in the second quarter of 2020 increased faster than in any comparable period in the Great Depression (Chart 2.6).

The impact of government responses

As the virus hit restricted industries in the first and second quarters of 2020, governments moved swiftly to combat the decline in output, incomes and employment. Chart 2.4 reflects the net effect of the onset of COVID-19 and the subsequent policy responses in the first half of 2020, superimposed on underlying economic conditions in each country. Chart 2.6 shows the policy response. Australia had one of the strongest early fiscal policy responses (increases in government expenditure and reductions in taxes), but less expansion of government measures to increase funding available to businesses.

Chart 2.6 Summary of fiscal and monetary measures in response to the COVID-19 pandemic, to 12 June 2020 (% GDP)

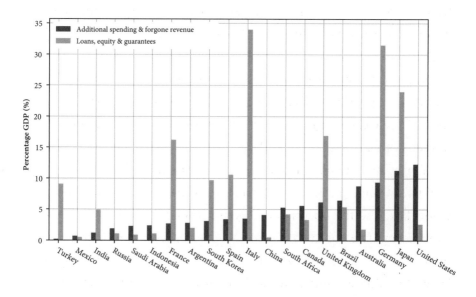

Data source: Fiscal Monitor, International Monetary Fund

Economic activity grew strongly in the second half of 2020, led by countries which had low rates of COVID-19 infection, and deaths and strong fiscal policy responses (China and Australia). There is a view in Australia that since output fell less in 2020 than was anticipated, and later in the year recovery was strong from the depths of the second quarter, the recessionary impact of the pandemic was exaggerated. The truth is that the anticipated contraction was avoided only by the speed and size of the Australian government's fiscal response – one of the strongest budgetary stimulatory responses.

Three general points can be made about the world's policy response to the pandemic recession. First, all developed countries responded quickly, as they did to the GFC in late 2008, but more quickly and more strongly. The responses were different from the GFC in another important way. The weakness of global leadership, with political malaise in the United States and tensions between the two largest economies, caused these responses to be unilateral rather than multilateral. More may have been done and more quickly in a more cooperative global framework. Nevertheless, the success of early stimulus in the GFC a dozen years earlier had entrenched positive attitudes to expansionary policy responses to sudden reductions in economic activity.

Second, the balance was more heavily towards fiscal relative to monetary expansion. This partly reflected the low interest rates at the time of the COVID-19 shock, which left less room than in 2008 for monetary policy to play the leading role.

Third, the balance towards fiscal rather than monetary expansion was stronger in Australia than in any other country. Fiscal policy works faster, so the Australian response was relatively effective in the short term. The combination of easier budgets and tighter money in Australia compared to other countries drove the Australian dollar higher after an initial fall, with its own contractionary effects on import-competing and export industries. Taking January 2020 as the base for comparison, by July the Australian dollar increased in value through 2020 against the euro, the Japanese yen and the US dollar. It had appreciated by large amounts against Australia's main competitors in global commodity markets: Indonesia (coal), Brazil (iron ore) and South Africa (multiple commodities). Appreciation went further in the second half of the year.

The Australian real exchange rate (taking into account differences in inflation as well as currency values) rose strongly between the productivity boom and the resources boom, and held most of those gains in the Dog Days. It strengthened further through 2020. This is an important headwind to restoration.

By late 2020, there was a risk in some countries that the success of early fiscal expansion would give a false impression that the economic damage from the pandemic was not as severe as originally thought, leading to premature withdrawal of stimulus. Australian policy initially provided for relatively early conclusion of stimulatory expenditures, but this was modified as the planned dates for withdrawal approached. The dysfunctional interaction of government and Congress in the US was responsible for larger withdrawal of stimulus late in 2020 than any of the major participants in the policy process preferred. This was a barrier to US recovery. A major stimulus package was passed by Congress immediately before Christmas, and is expected to be followed by more after the inauguration of President Biden.

The collapse of world trade

Chart 2.7 shows the decline in world trade month by month through the three large contractions of the past century: the Great Depression, the GFC and the pandemic recession. As Professor Charles Kindleberger described in his book *The World in Depression*,[5] there was a month-by-month steady decline in world trade for a number of years, until eventually it was less than 40 per cent of what it had been in 1929 (see the dash line). The volume of world trade shrank as much in the first two months of the COVID-19 crisis as in the first fourteen months of the Great Depression (solid line).

The dot line traces the progress of the volume of international trade month by month in the Global Financial Crisis from its beginning in June 2008. It was a steady contraction that continued for twelve months. The volume of world trade in the twelfth month was down about 40 per cent on what it had been back in June 2008. It then steadied, mainly as a result of the huge fiscal and monetary interventions in many countries that began to restore economic activity. In comparison, the solid line shows what happened to the volume of world trade in the early months after the outbreak of COVID-19. M1 is the volume of world trade in December 2019, as the first news of the unusual pneumonia began seeping out from China. There was already a very substantial decline by the second month, M2. By M3, just two months after the outbreak of the disease, there was a contraction of world trade roughly three times as large as in the first two months of the GFC. The low point came in M5. After that, from May, there was substantial recovery in trade volumes. China's return to strong economic growth was influential.

Implications of the Great Crash of 2020

This is a global and Australian shock of historic dimensions. The medical shock remained severe in late 2020 and was getting worse in some large countries. There were prospects of a vaccine being widely available later in 2021, but the pandemic recession will not recede so quickly. Only China among large economies was back on a reasonably strong path of growth by late 2020. Massive fiscal and monetary responses in several developed countries – including Australia, and the United States with its new president and senate – will drive strong

Chart 2.7 Total volume of world trade (Great Depression, GFC and COVID-19)

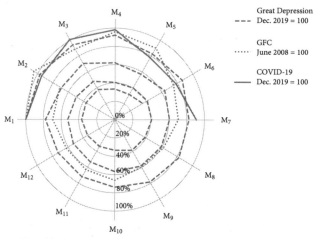

Monthly world trade (total imports), relative to base month (M₁)

Data source: International trade statistics, World Trade Organization

growth in 2021. There is great uncertainty about whether it will be possible to remedy recent damage to the systems of international economic cooperation. And we are headed towards comprehensive failure of financial systems and economic growth through much of the developing world.

Shocks this big change ideas about how societies, economies and polities work. They change what is possible in economic policy.

WRONG WAY; DON'T GO BACK

Not only plagues, wars and recessions but also good times can take people by surprise. So it was with the long continuous period of economic growth in Australia from the end of 1991 until the end of 2019.

Prime Minister John Howard liked a remark that I made at a conference in Melbourne back in 1999 and quoted it many times in and out of parliament.[1] 'There is a good chance,' I said, 'that Australians are about to get the biggest economic shock of the last several decades. The evidence is gathering, and may soon be too strong to be denied, that Australians in 1999 are living through the third period in the century since Federation of sustained economic prosperity.'[2] Prosperity was a shock because the deep recession of 1990–91 was still in our minds. The horrific unemployment had hugely disrupted many lives. And after the recovery began, there was a long grind to bring people back to work.

The sustained prosperity from 1991 went on and on until it became the longest expanse of time unbroken by recession in the history of Australia. Not only of Australia, but in the history of any developed country. It has ended only now, in the pandemic recession of 2020. It took a while, but eventually we became accustomed to good times.

The twenty-eight years of unbroken economic expansion had three parts. For about a decade the prosperity was driven by rapid growth in productivity on the back of the reforms initiated by the Hawke government in 1983. From the recession at the start of the 1990s to the beginning of the twenty-first century, Australia led the developed world in productivity growth. This was remarkable, because the country had spent most of the twentieth century ranking at the bottom of the table of developed countries when it came to productivity growth. I call this first decade of the long expansion the productivity boom.

Australia continued to experience rapid growth in incomes for another decade, until 2013. This second decade was driven by high export prices for metals and energy, joined later by investment in the resources industries. I call this the China resources boom. It drew its strength from the world's most populous country experiencing the strongest, longest and most resource-intensive economic growth ever. During this resources boom, as the world fell into the GFC in 2008–09, timely and bold fiscal and monetary expansion in Australia and China made Australia one of only two developed countries to avoid recession.

During the first two decades of the long boom, from 1992 to 2012, average Australian incomes, measured in international currency, rose from the lower half into the top few of developed countries. By 2013, they were one-quarter higher than in the United States.

Economic growth continued from 2013, but with much slower growth in total output, stagnant output per person, and decline in the typical household's real wages and income per person. I call this third period the Dog Days. In the seven years from 2013 to 2019, the whole developed world experienced slow and grumpy times. Australia drifted to the back of a slow-moving pack. Unemployment has never again fallen to anywhere near the 4 per cent it was on the eve of the GFC. Underemployment has grown and grown. Average household disposable income per person ended the seven lean years where it began. This was a period of income stagnation for ordinary Australians, unprecedented since – and starting to challenge in longevity – the Great Depression of the 1930s. In 2019, average Australian incomes, measured in international currency, were one-quarter below those of the United States.

There have been sixteen mostly six-monthly budget statements by four treasurers since the beginning of 2013. The first fourteen statements projected budget surpluses within a few years. Every projection then suffered a major downgrade. The mid-year economic statement in December 2019 was subject to the most stunningly large downgrade of all – the downgrade coming only eight months later, in the statement delivered in July 2020 in lieu of a May budget. A forecast of a surplus in 2020–21 turned into a forecast deficit of $184.5 billion, by far the largest deficit ever in Australia.

The Reserve Bank of Australia has two main objectives in setting monetary policy. It is required to maintain full employment and to keep inflation within the range of 2 to 3 per cent. Not once in seven years was the economy close to full employment. Not once in seven years did annual inflation reach the midpoint of the target range; mostly, it was below the bottom of the range.

During the Dog Days we appointed four prime ministers and disappointed four. The four disappointed PMs – Gillard, Rudd, Abbott and Turnbull – on average were not bad prime ministers by long Australian historical standards. Dog Days are hard days for prime ministers.

The Dog Days have now disappeared into the pandemic recession. Chapter 2 showed that this recession is already of historic dimensions. Coming out of it well will take policy leadership of historic character. Recessions of this size are times when countries change fundamentally, for good or ill. Change for good, and the pandemic recession of 2020 will be followed by the restoration of Australia. Change for ill, and we will enter the post-pandemic Dog Days.

Why a return to 2019 is not desirable

As restrictions were imposed in March and April 2020, the prime minister and the treasurer spoke of a brief period of reduced activity before the economy snapped back to where we were before. There are compelling reasons why that is neither desirable nor possible.

Let's look first at why snapping back to the Dog Days is unattractive. Chart 3.1 compares growth in Australia's population, per capita production and total output with other developed countries. The productivity boom is on the left, the resources boom in the middle, and the Dog Days on the right. The lowest of the three layers in the chart is output (GDP) growth. The middle is output growth per person. The highest is population growth. The black line is Australia, the dark grey the average for all OECD countries, and the light grey Japan.

Chart 3.1 Population, output and per capita growth

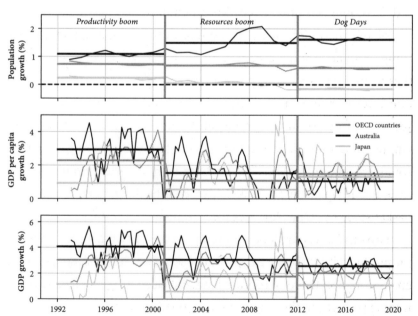

Data source: OECD, quarterly GDP data aand population statistics

In the productivity boom, Australia comfortably led growth in the developed world on all measures. Output per person grew at about 3 per cent per annum – much higher than developed countries as a whole, and three times as high as Japan. In the resources boom, we also led the developed world in growth in all of population, total output and output per person. Japan was a long way behind other developed countries on all measures.

Let's focus on the middle of the three horizontal layers, because output per person is the foundation of living standards over the longer term. GDP growth per capita in Australia was much lower in the Dog Days than in preceding years, and also at the bottom of the developed world, below Japan. The leader of the developed world had become the laggard.

Total GDP growth remained a bit above the United States, Japan and the developed world as a whole. This was due solely to our prodigious immigration and population growth. Population growth increased our capacity to fund national public goods, such as defence. It did not increase household living standards.

Many Australians are accustomed to thinking of Japan as something of an economic basket case. Hence, they are surprised to learn that from 2013 to 2019 we performed below Japan in the most important indicator of economic performance. Japan provides remarkable security of health and incomes and a high standard of living to its whole population, within a rich national culture. On output per person, it has not done as well as most other developed countries. On this measure, if Japan were a basket case, we have been under Japan in the basket since the Dog Days began.

Growth per capita depends on the amount of capital per person and the productivity with which capital and labour are used. Capital per person grew strongly in the resources boom, mainly due to highly capital-intensive mining projects. In the Dog Days, it stopped growing when the overhang from the resources boom had worked its way through the economy.

Throughout the productivity boom, total productivity growth (labour and capital together) was about 2 per cent annually (Chart 3.2). Australia led the league table of developed countries. It fell to less than half a per cent per annum during the resources boom. With high global prices driven by Chinese demand, the mining companies were focused on getting as much material out of the ground as quickly as they could, rather than on producing minerals and energy at the lowest possible cost. Total productivity lifted a little in the Dog Days, while remaining way below the productivity boom.

Large productivity-raising reform stopped at the beginning of the twenty-first century. It became rare for Australian governments to explain the value of policy reform and then to enact it should any well-resourced part of the community feel disadvantaged and campaign against it. Two significant episodes demonstrate how much had changed. The Clean Energy Future package legislated by the Gillard government worked effectively to reduce emissions without damaging

Chart 3.2 Australian total factor productivity growth

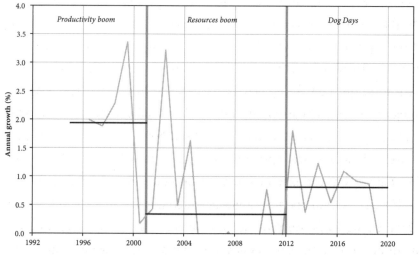

Data source: Australian Bureau of Statistics, cat. no. 5260.0.55.002

economic activity, while avoiding reduction in the living standards of Australians on low and middle incomes. Yet its central element, carbon pricing, was repealed by the Abbott government. The attempt to implement a recommendation from the Henry Tax Review on the taxation of mineral rent precipitated unprecedented investment in the political process by businesses operating in Australia. The largest-ever corporate investment in political influence until those by businessman Clive Palmer in the 2013 and 2019 elections. The transformation of Australian political culture halted further attempts at major productivity-raising reform and entrenched low productivity growth.

Although Australia avoided recession in the Global Financial Crisis of 2008–09, unemployment and underemployment rose, and remained high as we entered the Dog Days in 2013 (see Chart 2.5 on page 53). Low growth in the economy and high growth in population meant no progress was made in reducing underemployment over the next seven years. Compare that with the steady fall in unemployment during the productivity boom and the large but uneven reductions during the resources boom.

Household disposable income per person grew by about half a per cent annually during the productivity boom (Chart 3.3). It grew more rapidly during the resources boom, at about 0.7 per cent per annum, as some of the high export receipts from mining found their way into average incomes. There was virtually no increase in average household disposable income during the Dog Days. Chart 3.3 does not fully reflect how bad things were for average workers during the Dog Days. The mean can be held up by a large increase in incomes for those at the top while the real household income per capita for most people falls. This was the case in the Dog Days, as top executive and business incomes were rising rapidly.

If we are to build better economic outcomes, we need to understand why the Dog Days were so bad. The deep cause was the deterioration of our political culture, with knowledge guiding an independent centre of our polity becoming less influential and vested interests more so in

Chart 3.3 Real household disposable income per capita growth

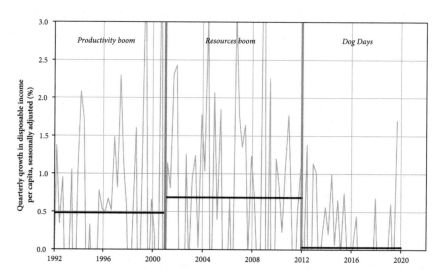

Data source: Australian Bureau of Statistics, cat. no. 5206.0 and 3101.0

policy-making. Immediate causes included two developments that had partially separate origins: the Reserve Bank's running of tighter monetary policy than other developed countries when our economy was running no more strongly; and a historic change in immigration policy.

The Reserve Bank's mistake

The twenty-first century has seen fundamental shifts towards higher private savings and lower private investment in the world economy. This has led capital to become increasingly abundant and generated the lowest interest rates ever in global capital markets.

The changes in savings and investment reflect changes in the structure of economies. These changes do not depend on central bank policies. They will persist for the foreseeable future.

We are starting to understand why global savings are high despite low interest rates. The twenty-first century has seen a falling share of total income going to people on low incomes and without wealth who depend on wages to live; and an increase in the share of the wealthy, who spend a much smaller part of their income. These effects are exacerbated by the increasing proportion of incomes held by the wealthy in international tax havens, accumulating without taxation or drawdowns for consumption. Developing countries that happen to have unusually high savings rates – first of all, China – have increased their shares of global income. More of the world's income growth has been concentrated in developing countries where incomes have been growing rapidly, and it takes time for consumption patterns to adjust upwards to higher incomes. There is less confidence in the United States, UK and some other developed countries in the reliability of the social safety net, inducing higher levels of private precautionary savings. In the developed world and China, ageing populations want to provide for longer retirement.

Among factors reducing investment, the increasing share of services in the economy has reduced the need for investment in plant and equipment. Information technology has allowed more efficient use of capital. A higher proportion of investment is in intangible assets, such as intellectual property. A higher proportion of income takes the form of economic rents, which are sustained without new investment. Lower productivity growth in developed countries in the twenty-first century has reduced the rate of obsolescence of old plant and the need to invest in replacements. Increased economic and political instability and the recurrence of deep recessions has increased perceptions of risk. Finally, a higher and higher percentage of consumption and investment expenditure goes to purchasing IT network services and associated products, in which tangible capital expenditure is tiny in comparison with the value of sales.

Overall, higher savings and lower investment shares have led to huge falls in long-term interest rates for low-risk debt – to around zero in real terms, far lower than ever before. Countries in which businesses, governments and central banks came to understand and respond rationally to the new realities did much better after the GFC than those that did not.

Chart 3.4. Long-term Australian, US and European interest rates

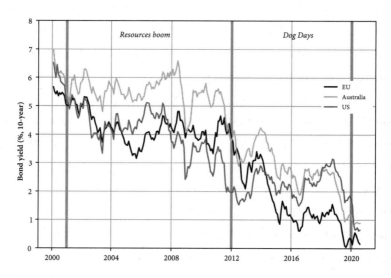

Data source: Federal Reserve economic data, Federal Reserve Bank of St Louis

Chart 3.5 Australian standard and indexed bond rates

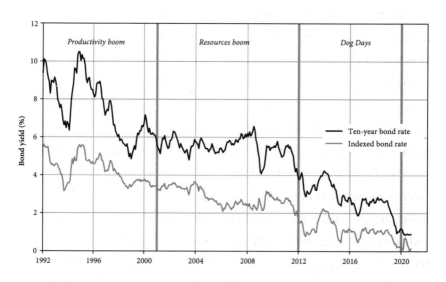

Data source: Reserve Bank of Australia

Chart 3.4 tracks the falls in long bond rates in Australia, the United States and the European Union. These rates are set in markets. Quantitative easing has had some influence in some countries, but at the margins. Australian long-term rates were largely free from direct Reserve Bank influence until the pandemic recession response in 2020.

Interest rates have two components. One reflects the real cost of capital. The other reflects inflation. The interest on a standard bond can be understood as the sum of the real interest rate and the expected rate of inflation.

We can see directly the real cost of capital by looking at interest rates on bonds that are indexed for inflation. The yields on indexed bonds reflect the real cost of capital. The difference between interest rates on ordinary and indexed bonds is the influence of inflation. Chart 3.5 compares interest rates on regular and indexed ten-year Australian Commonwealth bonds. The interest on indexed bonds fell almost to zero in 2020. Inflation expectations were also very low, and yields on ordinary bonds were below 1 per cent.

In this new world of higher savings and lower investment globally, central banks must set low interest rates to maintain high levels of employment and optimal rates of economic growth. In this world, monetary policy in Australia that is easier (lower interest rates) than it has ever been before may nevertheless be too tight for full employment. Other central banks adjusted more swiftly to the new lower cost of capital by lowering the interest rates that they control more than the Reserve Bank lowered Australian policy interest rates. This caused the foreign exchange value of the Australian dollar to be higher than it otherwise would have been. This reduced the competitiveness of Australian industries exposed to international trade – import-competing industries and export industries. This, in turn, reduced investment and growth in output and employment in Australia's industries that compete with overseas production in domestic or export markets.

We refer to import-competing and export industries as trade-exposed. These can be contrasted with domestic industries, which sell their output on the home market without having to compete with imports. Volumes of production in domestic industries depend on the amount of domestic demand. Volumes of production in trade-exposed industries depend on the cost of Australian relative to foreign goods and services – on the competitiveness of Australian production relative to foreign production.

Competitiveness is measured by the cost (for the same quality) in international currency of Australian goods and services compared with foreign ones. Australian competitiveness increases, and with it employment in the trade-exposed industries, if the foreign exchange value of the Australian dollar falls. It also increases if productivity increases more rapidly in Australia than in other countries; or if Australian wages and other costs rise more slowly. If demand at home increases for an Australian trade-exposed product, such as beef, it reduces the volume of exports and does not affect the level of production. By contrast, if we increase home demand for a domestic good or service, domestic supply will increase to meet it, whatever are the Australian relative to foreign costs.

So the total level of employment in Australia is the sum of employment in domestic industries, which is determined by domestic demand; and of employment in trade-exposed industries, which is determined by Australian competitiveness.

We can increase Australian employment either by increasing domestic expenditure, or by improving competitiveness. An increase in domestic expenditure increases production of and employment in domestic industries. An increase in competitiveness increases production of and employment in trade-exposed industries.

One difference between the two routes is that an increase in domestic expenditure and therefore in production and employment in domestic industry increases Australian indebtedness to foreigners. This is because part of the increase in expenditure will be spent on imports, which are financed by an increase in net foreign debt or sale of assets overseas. On the other hand, an increase in production and employment in the trade-exposed industries reduces Australian indebtedness to foreigners. There is an optimal amount of foreign debt that takes into account the cost of repayment by future Australians. Good policy seeks to expand employment coming from domestic and trade-exposed industries in proportions that bring about both the right amount of employment growth and the right amount of debt.

A large amount of employment in domestic and trade-exposed industries comes not from immediate production in those industries but from investment in capacity to produce goods and services in the future. Business investment in domestic industries is determined by expectations of future domestic demand. Businesses invest more if they expect domestic demand to be strong enough in the future for them to be able to sell the extra output profitably. Business investment in trade-exposed industries is determined by expectations of future competitiveness. Businesses invest more if they expect competitiveness to be strong enough in future for them to be able to sell the extra output profitably.

The Reserve Bank's persistent setting of higher interest rates than those in other developed countries – albeit extremely low rates by historical standards – contributed to relatively low growth in domestic demand. More importantly, it contributed to relatively low competitiveness. It therefore contributed to relatively low output, employment and investment in domestic and especially in trade-exposed industries. This was an important reason why in the Dog Days the Reserve Bank was unable to meet either its statutory objective on employment, or the agreed interpretation of its statutory objective on inflation. We managed to have persistently high unemployment and underemployment, persistently low inflation and growing indebtedness, all at the same time.

Australia's failure to reduce unemployment through the seven years leading up to the pandemic contrasts starkly with US success (Chart 3.6). In the United States, unemployment fell steadily and fairly rapidly, from a peak of around 10 per cent after the GFC to about 3.5 per cent on the eve of the pandemic recession. In Australia, unemployment was similar at the end to what it had been at the beginning of the Dog Days.

Charts 3.6 and 3.7 together show that the difference in unemployment tracks the difference in monetary policy. Australia ran much tighter monetary policy than the United States until 2017, by which time US unemployment was much lower.

What is full employment in Australia today? What should we and our Reserve Bank be aiming for? We are at full employment when unemployment is as low as it can get without triggering dangerously strong inflation. Using the ugly acronym that has come into common usage in economics, we are at full employment when the rate of unemployment is at the NAIRU, or non-accelerating inflation rate of unemployment.

The comparison with the United States is instructive. From 1952 to 1974, when both the US and Australian economies were considered to be operating at or close to full employment, Australian unemployment (at 1.5 to 2 per cent) was typically less than half the US rate of 4 to 5 per cent. Neither economy was experiencing inflationary pressures through most of this time.

In the 1960s, the NAIRU was clearly lower in Australia than the United States. Why? Part of the reason was that higher rates of immigration made the Australian labour market more flexible geographically and in deployment of skills. Part was that better and more broadly-based public education and health services left Australia with a smaller proportion of its population with low employability.

Over the past several decades, neither country has experienced rates of unemployment so low that there are strong upward pressures

Chart 3.6 Unemployment in Australia and the United States

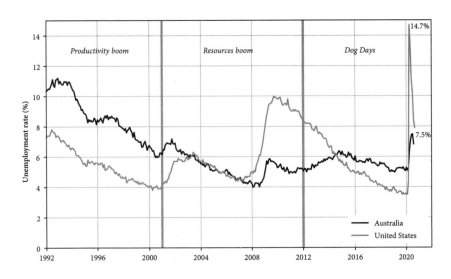

Data source: Australian Bureau of Statistics, US Bureau of Labor Statistics

Chart 3.7 Policy interest rates: Federal funds versus Reserve Bank cash rate

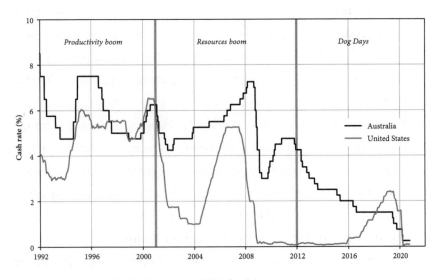

Data source: Reserve Bank of Australia, US Federal Reserve

on wages in the labour market. Neither country has experienced full employment. Trump's massive debt-funded tax cuts tested the boundaries when they took unemployment down to around 3.5 per cent in 2019. At that point there were anxieties about – but no labour market evidence of – high and accelerating inflation. This demonstrates that the US NAIRU in 2019 was no higher than about 3.5 per cent, which was the unemployment rate on the eve of the pandemic. There is no good reason to expect the NAIRU to be higher in the United States than in Australia today. It may be higher, but there is no way of knowing until we have tested how far we can lower unemployment in each country without triggering high and accelerating inflation.

There is no need to guess the NAIRU. We can find out what it is by increasing demand for labour until wages in the labour market are rising at a rate that threatens to take inflation above the Reserve Bank range for an extended period.

The difference between the actual unemployment rate and the NAIRU represents people who are unnecessarily unemployed. The number of unnecessarily unemployed people is actually larger than this, because more people would be encouraged to seek employment if unemployment rates were lower. An average of several hundred thousand fewer people were employed right through the Dog Days than would otherwise have been possible. This is voluntary unemployment – voluntary for the Reserve Bank, because it is unemployment that the Reserve Bank chooses to allow. At current levels of economic activity, having several hundred thousand people unnecessarily unemployed holds annual GDP down about $50 billion below what it could be, and, all other things equal, raises Australian public deficits by nearly $20 billion each year.

The Reserve Bank has started to catch up with the error of its Dog Days ways. In 2019, the assistant governor of the RBA, Luci Ellis, in her Freebairn lecture at the University of Melbourne acknowledged that

Australian unemployment was unnecessarily high. She said that the measured rate of unemployment that could be considered 'full employment' began with the digit 4, not 5. Then, in the first quarter of 2020, in response to the pandemic recession, the RBA lowered the cash rate to 0.25 per cent, the lowest ever. The Reserve Bank said it would keep it at that level until full employment had been reached and inflation had moved into the target range. It also announced that it would buy government bonds in amounts sufficient to hold rates out to three years at 0.25 per cent, until full employment and inflation in the target range had been reached. It remained steadfastly against negative interest rates, which were being applied in Japan and Europe, and against the quantitative easing that had been a feature of monetary policy in Europe, Japan and the United States after the GFC. But then, in November 2020, it reduced cash rates to 0.15 per cent and began a program of quantitative easing – buying large volumes of long-term Commonwealth and state bonds with many durations in the market, beyond what is necessary to hold three-year interest rates at 0.25 per cent.

These are important steps towards bringing Australian monetary policy into line with that of other countries. Taken far enough and continued for long enough, these steps could remove the 'Reserve Bank voluntary' unemployment. But remember, the most powerful influence of monetary policy on employment is through the exchange rate and competitiveness. We only become more competitive if the downward pressure that easy Australian monetary policy places on the Australian currency is greater than the downward pressure that monetary policy in other countries is placing on the foreign exchange values of their own currencies.

The central banks of other countries are not standing still. The US Federal Reserve Bank said in mid-2020 that it would maintain high levels of quantitative easing until inflation had been above its own inflation target by as much and for as long as it had been below in the years preceding the pandemic. That represents a commitment to easier money that goes further than the RBA's new position. Our monetary policy remains considerably firmer than those of other developed countries in November 2020. This is one important reason why in late 2020 our exchange rate has been rising against the currencies of other developed countries and our main competitors in global markets.

The Reserve Bank's monetary policy stance, as articulated in 2020, represents an important departure from Dog Days settings. But the settings remain damaging to competitiveness and to employment and investment in the trade-exposed industries. They remain too tight to allow full employment with optimal levels of foreign debt.

Why did the Reserve Bank make this mistake and persist with it? Some Reserve Bank officers said at the time and say now that although consumer price increases were below the target range, asset prices, especially houses and shares in companies traded on the stock exchange, were increasing more strongly. Lowering interest rates to lower the exchange rate and increase domestic expenditure would have accelerated the increase in asset prices. This would have had unfortunate effects, including exacerbation of inequality in the distribution of wealth. True, there was reason to worry about asset inflation. But this could have been handled by other measures – called macro-prudential policies – that restricted growth in housing prices in particular, despite reductions in interest rates and easier general access to credit.

The fundamental change in immigration policy

The difficulties of achieving full employment with rising incomes for ordinary Australians late in the resources boom and through the Dog Days were compounded by a fundamental change in immigration policy.

The total level of immigration rose substantially, and there was a change in composition away from permanent migration towards temporary migration. The overall effect was to integrate much of the

Australian labour market into a global labour market for the first time. Sustained increases in demand for labour led to more immigration rather than reduced unemployment and higher wages. The shift towards temporary immigrants with lower average value of skills contributed more to this result than the increase in total numbers.

Chart 3.8 sets out the components of population growth through the three decades of economic expansion. Natural increase added between about half and three-quarters of a per cent per annum to the population over this time. Net immigration added an average of about half a per cent per annum during the productivity boom, and about twice as much during the resources boom and the Dog Days.

From 1946, Australian policy had been built on the premise that all immigrants were on a path to becoming Australians. There was an expectation that migrants would become competent in English and participate in all aspects of Australian life. Substantial government support was provided for learning English and more generally for settlement into the economy and society. This changed in the late 1990s and more as time went on in the next two decades. Temporary migration became the main source of growth and reached new heights during the Dog Days. Despite persistent unemployment and rising underemployment, net temporary migration grew steadily.

One instrument of radical change was the new Howard government's introduction in 1996 of the Temporary Business Entry (Long Stay) ('457') visa. 'Business migrants' with rights to stay and work for up to four years were not subject to seriously restrictive tests of whether their skills could be supplied by Australians. Other categories of temporary migration were added and expanded. Increasing the number of temporary migrants stopped wage increases through the strong growth in demand for labour during the resources boom.

Many areas of rural employment came to be dominated by one or other category of temporary migrant. Employment in service industries from restaurants to bars to convenience stores to taxis came to be dominated by temporary migrants, including students from many lands who often hoped to obtain Australian citizenship but didn't have the same rights as Australian citizens in the meantime. Mining companies and suppliers of related services came to employ large numbers of long-stay temporary workers, available at lower pay and conditions than would have been required for Australian workers with comparable skills. Employers lost interest in investing in the skills of young Australians, and soon much of the capacity to impart skills. Many well-off couples came to expect their children to be looked after by au pairs paid at a substantial discount to established Australian wages. In a variation on the theme, family reunion supported the temporary immigration of carers for children and the sick.

Back in 2003, I compared the effects of immigration to Australia and to the United States for immigration minister Philip Ruddock. I concluded that the higher skill content of the Australian program meant that while immigration lowered the pay of low-income workers in the United States, immigration tended to raise the pay of low-income workers in Australia.[3] However, changes in the composition of migration into Australia after 2003 reversed this tendency. Since then, the composition of Australian immigration has moved closer to the American model. Immigration now lowers the incomes and employment prospects of low-income Australians. If the new pattern continues in Australia, it may eventually cause a similar reaction to unskilled immigration as that ridden by presidential candidate Donald Trump in 2016.

Integration into a global labour market held down wages and inflation during the resources boom. It contributed to persistent unemployment, rising underemployment and stagnant real wages during the expansion of total economic activity during the Dog Days. It contributed to a historic shift in the distribution of income from wages to profits.

Increased immigration contributed to total GDP growth, but detracted from the living standards of many Australian working families.

Higher immigration and the explosion of temporary migration had social and cultural as well as economic consequences. One such consequence was cultural and racial diversification, especially in the large cities. This had benefits. Younger Australians of all backgrounds are now more closely familiar with people of Asian backgrounds.

There was also a downside, especially from the interaction of the economic with the social effects of the increase in scale and change in composition of migration. For the first time, large numbers of migrants were not on a path to citizenship. Temporary migrants did not share the commitment to Australia of traditional permanent migrants. They had weaker commitment to becoming part of Australian institutions and closely familiar with Australian language and customs. The temporary immigrants also had less knowledge of their rights in the labour market and were vulnerable to exploitation. Breaches of labour laws on wages and other conditions became common. Reduced public expenditure on settlement assistance, including English-language education, compounded these effects.

We will make earlier and stronger progress towards full employment and rising living standards in the general population if the immigration program is strongly focused on valuable skills. Official statements when 457 visas were introduced asserted that theywould focus on economically valuable skills. This were not borne out in practice. Social as well as economic considerations favour shifting the balance back towards permanent migration. One change could ensure that recipients of the renamed successors to 457 visas would have skills with economic value above the Australian average: require them to be paid at least average weekly earnings.

This is not the place for a detailed assessment of immigration policy, but two general points can be made. First, the humanitarian component of immigration is too small to be of much economic significance. Since World War II, Australia has always had a place for asylum seekers. At pre-pandemic levels, the arrival of asylum seekers adds only about 0.08 per cent per annum to the population. The Commonwealth government reduced the asylum-seeker intake to 0.06 per cent during 2020. Second, there is likely to be electoral resistance to resumption of anything like the immigration levels of the Dog Days. Settling early on an immigration program that is moderate in size and strongly focused on valuable education and skills will help us to avoid contentious and divisive political debate at a time when our society and polity are under great stress. Economic prudence also argues for holding net immigration through the decade ahead to about the level of the productivity boom: around 0.5 per cent of the population per year. This would be about half the level of the Dog Days. The arithmetic in Chapter 5 on the number of jobs required to achieve full employment is built on this level of net immigration.

Why a return to 2019 is not possible

It is not possible for Australia to return to the conditions of 2013–19, even if that were an attractive goal. If economic policy is run just as well as in the Dog Days – no better, no worse – the post-pandemic period will see lower incomes than in the years through which we have recently passed.

Extending recent changes in monetary policy and taking the chance to reset immigration would substantially improve prospects for returning to full employment and rising living standards. These changes are discussed in Chapter 4. We have already made the big change that was required to budget policy; the challenge is to maintain the change for long enough and to supplement it with monetary policy that can generate full employment with a reasonable amount of debt. Other headwinds from the disappointing years will be more difficult to change or turn to advantage. Excellent policy is required for ordinary outcomes over the period ahead. Ordinary policies will lead to bad outcomes.

Our government's October 2020 budget is ordinary. It projects much better economic performance and much higher income growth than in the Dog Days. But it does not propose policy reforms that would make this possible. Some of the headwinds that mean economic outcomes in the 2020s will be less favourable than in the 2010s in the absence of far-reaching reform are:

› the huge legacy of public debt
› a smaller capital stock per person (low levels of business investment in the later Dog Days, taken lower in the pandemic recession)
› major losses in export industries and lower gains from international trade
› reduced productivity
› chronic accumulation of the effects of climate change and an ageing population
› lower population and workforce growth, lowering total output growth (but not output per person).

Public debt

Public debt will inevitably rise over the next few years to an extent and at a rate unknown except in the two major wars of the twentieth century. By 2023, net Commonwealth debt will be more than four times as large relative to the economy as in the aftermath of the GFC.

Servicing and reducing the new debt that Australian governments have accumulated in the pandemic recession may be a drag on future living standards. Chapter 4 discusses the appropriate level of debt and the rate at which it should be reduced. For the moment, it is enough to say that servicing public debt may reduce average living standards by a few tenths of a per cent each year between 2025 and the end of the decade. Possibly, but not necessarily. In Chapter 6, we examine the circumstances in which the drag on living standards would occur.

Lower population growth

The pandemic has brought the twenty-first-century surge in immigration to Australia to a sudden halt. More people left Australia than arrived in 2020. Almost as many people will leave Australia as arrive across our international borders in 2021. The change reflects both behavioural and regulatory responses to the pandemic in Australia and in the countries from which migrants come. Behavioural responses will keep immigration well below preceding levels for at least several years. The sudden halt to immigration is an opportunity to reassess immigration policy; to think through the scale and composition of immigration that will contribute most to broadly shared goals.

Less capital per person

Much capital has been made redundant for the time being by the decline of the restricted industries It is unlikely that patterns of international travel and consumption of domestic services will be unaffected by the pandemic. Some of our capital stock may become obsolete prematurely: some or many of the planes stored in the deserts, some hotel rooms in tourist destinations, and some under-utilised university classrooms and accommodation.

Business investment has slumped. In the best of circumstances, it will remain low for several years. Already in the later Dog Days, it was too low to support rising living standards at full employment. The October 2020 budget anticipates levels of business investment as a share of the economy in the next several years well below the average of the Dog Days – this despite the introduction of costly depreciation allowances to encourage investment.

International business investment in Australia is lower because of diminished expectations for growth in Australian and international demand. It is lower because increased uncertainty about the future path of the economy inhibits investment. It is lower because investment in coal and LNG, which have contributed much investment over the past decade, will be low in future. This will be driven by other countries' climate change policies, and tensions in our relations with China. The decline in fossil energy investment could be balanced and greatly exceeded by a rise in investment in the low-carbon energy sector; that depends on new approaches to climate change and the energy transition. There is greater Australian restriction through the Foreign Investment Review Board – according to the treasurer, to block predatory takeovers of companies weakened by the pandemic recession. China is now a less important source of business investment in Australia – with regulatory restriction much more important, and tensions in Sino–Australian relations.

Fundamental changes are required to achieve necessary increases in business investment. Chapters 7, 9 and 10 discuss the changes.

Reduced gains from international trade

Although productivity growth was very low in the China resources boom, our average incomes grew because we were paid more and more for things we were already making. More and more of us were employed in building the mines and ports for mines – in investment to expand production of export commodities in the future. And more and more of us shifted from doing other things to employment that paid us more. We were receiving larger and larger gains from trade. These particular gains from trade diminished with the fall from 2013 in growth in Chinese demand for minerals and fossil energy commodities. They were partially replaced by increased gains from exports to China and elsewhere of high-value foodstuffs and services, notably services related to international students and tourists – supported in China by the China–Australia Free Trade Agreement concluded in 2015.

International demand has fallen in the restricted industries independently of Australian policy. Australia's third- and fifth-largest export industries immediately before the pandemic, education and tourism, have stopped for the moment and will at best recover slowly. Education exports will be diminished for a long time and perhaps permanently by the financial fracture of the universities during the pandemic and subsequent slide in international standing.

The early and strong return to growth in China was a special advantage for Australia in recovery from the GFC. China now absorbs more value of Australian exports than the next nine export destinations combined (eleven if we include Hong Kong in the China column). China is again experiencing an early and strong return to growth. This time, Australian advantage is to some extent offset by tensions in Sino–Australian relations. These issues are discussed in Chapter 11.

Prices fell during the pandemic in 2020 for nearly all major Australian export commodities. Reduced global demand was exacerbated by other countries' protectionist responses to the pandemic recession. There was a large reduction of crude oil prices, affecting gas prices as well. For coal, a significant decline in 2019 accelerated during the first pandemic year. Chinese policy further reduced demand for Australian coal and gas. Wool prices fell sharply from early 2020; so too other agricultural raw materials. Food demand held up better than most other areas, though some Australian exports, notably wine, were affected by Sino–Australian tensions.

Strong Chinese economic growth in the second half of the year placed a floor under prices, and led to substantial price recovery for many goods late in the year. Iron ore stood out: after falls early in 2020, strong Chinese economic growth in the second half of the year and reduced Brazilian supplies (partly due to COVID-19) led to a tight market and prices approaching those of the later stages of the resources boom. Iron ore is by far Australia's largest export industry. Gold – a safe haven for investors in troubled times – also experienced high prices. Minerals that are inputs into the global energy transition saw high prices and opportunities for investment to expand mining output.

Developing countries (other than China) have been greatly damaged by the pandemic and its recessionary consequences. These together are major Australian trading partners. Australian exports to ASEAN (Association of Southeast Asian Nations) markets are two and a half times that to the United States, and to India. The economic setbacks in Indonesia, India and other developing countries reduce Australian gains from trade.

Reduced productivity

Australian productivity growth was weak through the Dog Days and the resources boom. Without major reforms, productivity will be lower after the pandemic recession. The pandemic and the recession have greatly expanded restrictive government intervention in the allocation of resources. For example, more interventionist management of foreign investment has large negative consequences for productivity. Intervention without clear and generally applicable rules has become more important across energy and utilities more generally.

Inevitably, a period of high unemployment, disproportionately affecting young people, leads to the degradation of labour skills. Disruption of firms and relations among them has reduced productivity.

Chronic effects of climate change and ageing

Climate change is gradually and inexorably increasing infrastructure costs, lowering productivity in agriculture in southern Australia, and requiring heavier spending to counter extreme weather events. My 2008 Climate Change Review suggests likely annual average costs of perhaps a tenth of a per cent of GDP throughout the 2020s. These costs are now unavoidable, and are becoming larger than anticipated twelve years ago. In Australia's case, the costs of climate change itself are compounded by the many costs of uncertainty about climate policy. This could be removed by bipartisan commitment to effective policies. In the absence of such commitment, the costs are probably as large for the time being as those of climate change itself. A steady reduction of about two-tenths of a per cent in output per year from climate change and climate policy uncertainty seems the least burden that we will carry through the 2020s. It may be substantially more. The damage from climate change will continue to increase so long as net carbon emissions remain above zero. Global failure in mitigation policy would see an acceleration of the increase in costs after 2030. Global success, and Australia's full participation in the solution, would see this significant negative turn into a positive for growth.

Many Australians have been aware of the costs of an ageing population since at least the first Treasury Intergenerational Report in 2002. Increasing public health and aged care costs will shave perhaps one-tenth of a percentage point from annual GDP growth through the 2020s. The effects of ageing on labour force participation could remove another two-tenths of a percentage point.

These long-term developments may reduce average output and living standards by around half of a percentage point each year after the pandemic relative to the average for Dog Days. The personal income taxation and social security reforms suggested in Chapter 8 would reduce the drag on living standards to about two- or three-tenths of a percentage point by increasing labour force participation.

Fertility data released late in 2020 suggest a small offset to declining output per person. The lowest fertility rates ever in 2020 suggest that there will be significantly fewer Australians to share output in 2030. None of the missing Australians would have been old enough to work, so their absence will not reduce output. Output per person will be correspondingly higher. Australians living now will hold up their average living standards a little by providing for fewer Australians in the future.

The fateful choice in numbers

Chart 3.9 extends Chart 3.1 to cover two possible futures for Australia: post-pandemic Dog Days and post-pandemic restoration. It adds two periods: 2020–23 and 2023–30. The solid lines represent Australia. The top third of the chart describes population growth; the middle third, growth in GDP per person; and the bottom, total GDP growth. The total is the product of the other two: growth in population and GDP per capita.

The first new column in Chart 3.9 extends the time horizon forward, through the pandemic recession and its immediate aftermath

Chart 3.8 Post-pandemic economic performance: Restoration or Dog Days

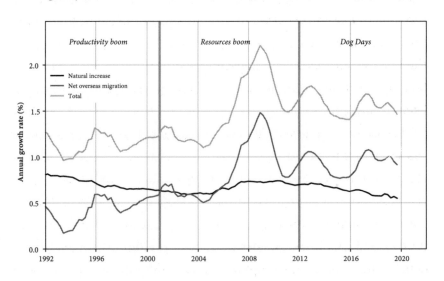

Data source: Australian Bureau of Statistics, cat. no. 3101.0

to 2023. The second row column covers 2023–30. Chart 3.9 describes what I have sketched in this chapter as most likely to happen if we snap back into pre-pandemic policies once we are through the worst of the pandemic recession (the dash grey line). The dash grey line mayb be an optimistic drawing of post-pandemic Dog Days; things might be worse.

Over the next six chapters, I sketch an alternative future: post-pandemic restoration of Australia. The solid grey line describes outcomes if we are able to overcome the institutional weaknesses and pressure from vested interests, and draw upon economic knowledge to make policy in the public interest. This might be a pessimistic view of the restoration possibilities; things could be better.

In the first year of the pandemic, there was a major reset on fiscal policy and a smaller one on monetary policy. That is enough to avoid catastrophic outcomes from the pandemic shock. Extending early policy adjustment into full fiscal and monetary policy reset would strengthen the economic outlook to 2023, but the main differences between the Dog Days and restoration scenarios come after that. This is embodied in the column on the right in Chart 3.9, which covers 2023 to 2030. If we choose post-pandemic Dog Days, there will be a snap back to tighter budget policy and Reserve Bank funding of government before achievement of full employment. A reset for restoration sees full employment in 2025 and lays the foundation for growth in average real output of Australians after that.

On average from 2020 to 2023, Dog Days would see a small decline in per capita GDP, lower but positive population growth, and slight total GDP growth. Growth in all three parameters would be below the low levels of pre-pandemic Dog Days.

The solid grey line describes the outcomes from the application of restoration policies consistently from 2021. Population and per capita output growth would be slightly higher in the pandemic recession.

Chart 3.9 Australian population and GDP growth

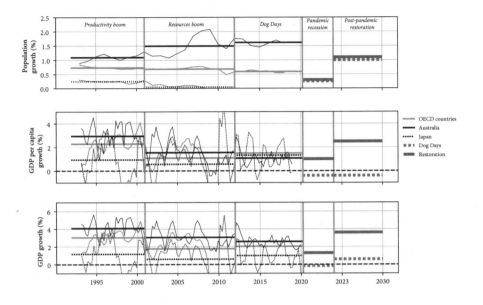

Data sources: OECD quarterly GDP data and population statistics

The larger differences come later. A restoration policy gives us slightly higher immigration and population growth. Tax reform and a basic income would increase participation. Productivity growth would be higher as a result of greater investment, especially in the trade-exposed industries. If the reforms proposed in this book are implemented, we would end up with much higher output growth per person than during the pre-pandemic Dog Days, and very much higher than in the post-pandemic alternative.

Both post-pandemic Dog Days and post-pandemic restoration presume the same 'no big change' in the framework of international cooperation. Both take the current inhibitions in Sino–Australian economic relations as given. In reality, the economic impact of problems in those relations could get better or worse. With Trump in office, continued deterioration in the framework of global economic relations and increasing tensions in Sino–Australian relations were likely. The transfer of power to President Biden is likely to lead to the strengthening of the global framework but not necessarily to eased tensions in Sino–Australian bilateral relations.

Healthy and unhealthy democracies

Australia experienced reasonably strong growth in most citizens' incomes through the productivity boom and the resources boom. There was some increase in inequality in wealth and incomes but, unlike in the United States and UK, not enough to cause stagnation of ordinary people's living standards. Australia did experience widespread wage and income stagnation during the Dog Days.

In the twenty-first century, in the democratic developed countries of the North Atlantic and now in Australia, special business interest groups have got better at capturing the policy-making process. They have invested more heavily in bending policy to favour themselves. This has been accompanied by a weakening of what I call the independent centre of policy discussion – including in the economics profession. This has contributed to the balance between the provision of public goods and the use of private exchange being pushed outside the optimal zone that delivered unprecedented broadly-based prosperity through the second half of the twentieth century. There has been a weakening of the state, and its role in regulating finance and providing public goods and services that are essential to sustained economic growth and general prosperity. Partly due to politics, to ideology and to technological change, there has been an increase in the role of monopoly, and of the rents generated by monopoly.

Globalisation has had powerful effects on the distribution of global income. It has lifted the incomes of billions of ordinary people in the developing world. At the same time, in the absence of social democratic protections, notably in the United States, it has added to the downward pressure on living standards of workers in developed countries. The growth of information technology has also had important negative effects on equity in income distribution.

In the twenty-first century, the modest increase in incomes in most developed countries went almost exclusively to the rich. This was a continuation of a trend that was two decades old in the US by the beginning of the century, but less well established in other developed countries, and much less evident before the Dog Days in Australia. This gradually undermined the legitimacy of established economic and political institutions and leaders – in the United States, undermining alike the influence of the knowledgeable and the ignorant; those promoting the public interest as well as those seeking rents for themselves.

The stagnation of real wages and living standards of ordinary Australians in the Dog Days was too young by the time of the pandemic to have undermined the legitimacy of established institutions and the knowledge they produce. That has turned out to be a crucial difference between Australia and the United States. Australian democracy remains in a healthier state to manage the pandemic than its confrères in the North Atlantic. This fortunate condition would not survive an extended period of post-pandemic Dog Days.

4

FULL EMPLOYMENT WITH THE RIGHT AMOUNT OF DEBT

Tony Abbott's Coalition won government in 2013 on a platform that gave high priority to getting rid of Commonwealth debt and deficits. That was a few years after the Global Financial Crisis, in which Australia avoided recession by expanding public spending. Commonwealth net debt was then about 10 per cent of Australian GDP. The Abbott government outsourced the plan to reduce deficits to a committee and secretariat closely associated with the Business Council of Australia. The resulting budget in May 2014 precipitated a massive negative reaction, and the prime minister's electoral standing never recovered. Measures that would have contributed most of the proposed savings in the 2014–15 budget failed to pass the Senate.

On the eve of the pandemic recession, Commonwealth net debt was about one-fifth of GDP. The percentage had roughly doubled over seven years. As noted in Chapter 3, over that time Australia stood out among developed countries for stagnant output per person and continuing high unemployment and underemployment.

The Morrison government's economic response to the pandemic recession turns Coalition budget policy on its head. The October 2020 budget gave priority to creating jobs above reducing debt. It anticipated net Commonwealth debt more than doubling again as a share of GDP by mid-2024. It will be higher than that unless October 2020 turns out to be the first of sixteen consecutive budget statements since 2013 not to suffer upward revision of medium-term deficits.

The Abbott government erred in focusing on reducing public debt when it was a small share of the economy and unemployment remained high. The prime minister paid for the error with his job. The Turnbull and early Morrison governments continued the error. Since the onset of the pandemic, the Morrison government has corrected it. The government is right to allow debt to rise more, and more rapidly, than at any time in Australian history, in response to an unprecedentedly sharp collapse in economic activity. Whether these actions are enough to set Australia on a path to restoration depends on what happens next: the rate at which the deficit is reduced; the composition of revenue and spending measures; and on whether accompanying monetary and taxation policies significantly increase international competitiveness.

Through the Dog Days, budget policy error was secondary to the Reserve Bank's excessively restrictive monetary policies, discussed in Chapter 3. Reserve Bank policy has undergone a halting partial correction. A full correction to monetary policy no tighter than that of other developed countries which have similarly weak economies would accelerate movement towards full employment while moderating growth in foreign debt.

While the Morrison government has been right to allow unprecedented increases in public debt, the amount of debt still matters. Debt incurred now may reduce the domestic spending that can be sustained after full employment has been achieved. Servicing debt incurred now may require lower living standards later. The extent of this cost depends on circumstances at the time; it may in some cases be zero or low, and in others high. But it needs to be considered. Higher levels of debt also make the economy more vulnerable to future economic shocks.

It would be an error for the government to assign priority to reducing public debt before full employment is in sight and wages are rising. The government's intention to reduce debt would be overwhelmed by low revenue growth and high social security outlays in a weak economy. This happened in the old Dog Days. It would have worse effects now, with much more debt and a weaker economy. The debt ratio would continue to rise, more rapidly than it did between 2013 and 2019. Sooner or later, Australia's international credit standing would come under stress, perhaps in another episode of weakness in the global economy. We would be forced into retrenchment in difficult circumstances.

The focus of this chapter is on broad economic aggregates – macroeconomics, or the economy as a whole. It discusses how we set expenditure and competitiveness policies to achieve full employment at the earliest possible time and with the right amount of debt.

Two paths to increased employment

There are two paths to increasing employment. One is to increase domestic spending. Part of any such increase is spent on domestic goods and services that have no foreign competitors. Think of restaurant meals, haircuts, tickets to the football or a concert, visits to a doctor, the service element of purchases from a supermarket or butcher or bicycle repair shop. That increases the income of people supplying the good or service. It also increases employment – directly, and indirectly when the supplier spends the increased income.

A second path is to lower the cost of goods and services produced in the country, relative to those produced overseas. This makes the economy more internationally competitive. A more competitive economy supplies a higher proportion of domestic demand from local rather than imported sources. It also exports a wider range and more of its own produce. More jobs in such industries allow full employment to be achieved with fewer jobs from increased domestic demand.

The producers in the trade-exposed industries also spend part of their new income, increasing the incomes of people supplying the additional goods and services that they buy.

Various combinations of expenditure and competitiveness allow us to achieve full employment. If an economy is less competitive, a higher level of domestic expenditure is required to attain full employment.

We could achieve full employment for a while by expanding domestic demand whatever the competitiveness of the economy if the amount of debt didn't matter. We would simply increase domestic aggregate demand until enough jobs were created to achieve full employment. The economy would seem to be doing well. The cost would be the increase in government debt. This is the essence of the US expansions after the debt-funded US tax cuts under President Reagan in the early 1980s and President Trump in the late 2010s. In some circumstances, the increase in debt is worth the cost; in others, it is not.

There is an optimal amount of debt that takes into account the distribution of income among Australians, including between those living now and those living in the future, and vulnerability to future external shocks.

The appendix to Chapter 4 sets out in a diagram how competitiveness and expenditure jointly determine how close the economy is to full employment and to the optimal level of debt. The appendix shows that there is a unique combination of expenditure and competitiveness that generates a state of bliss, with full employment and optimal debt.

Government policy is one of many influences on expenditure and competitiveness. Private preferences have large effects, independent of government. Influences include everything affecting private consumption and private expenditure. For example, if residents spend a higher proportion of their incomes, government needs to do less to raise domestic expenditure to the desired levels. If private investors become more optimistic about the future prospects of the economy, they will invest more, and reduce the effort that governments must make to encourage expenditure.

Setting the level of expenditure

How does a government increase expenditure in the economy? It can either increase its own public expenditure or influence the level of private expenditure.

Public expenditure takes two forms. One is through the direct provision of services such as health, education, and domestic and international security. The other is through spending on durable physical assets: roads and railways; electricity lines, gas pipelines and fibre-optic cables; buildings for the use of its own employees (office blocks) or the use of the general public (sports stadiums). It is conventional to call the latter public investment.

The government can affect private expenditure in a number of ways. One is through changes in the amount of purchasing power government transfers to the private sector. The government can change the amount of income it secures from private citizens through taxation or returns in the form of social security transfers, and therefore the amount that is available for private consumption, saving and investment.

Setting the levels of direct public spending and transfers and taxation, and therefore the level of additional public borrowing (the deficit), are together called fiscal policy. In Australia, the broad parameters of fiscal policy are administered by the Treasury, advising the treasurer.

The public sector can also influence the level of expenditure in the economy, by changing the terms on which debt is made available to private consumers or producers. This is monetary policy, today conducted through a central bank – in Australia, the Reserve Bank. The Reserve Bank can vary the interest rates charged by banks, or the amount of money circulating in the private economy, by buying and selling government bonds and other securities. Lower interest rates and larger amounts of money in circulation tend to increase private investment by households (especially on housing) and business. They also tend to increase household consumption. The effect of changes in interest rates is less powerful during times of deep recession.

Lower interest rates and more money in circulation lead domestic and foreign asset owners to increase the amount of money they send to other countries. With a floating currency, this lowers the exchange rate of the Australian dollar. This is a major influence on competitiveness.

By contrast, larger budget deficits and increased domestic demand without any change in the amount of money in circulation increase the amount of money Australians and foreigners together want to hold in Australia, relative to the amount they hold overseas. This tends to raise the exchange rate.

So, fiscal policy and monetary policy both affect expenditure. And the relationship between fiscal and monetary policies has a large influence on competitiveness. (It is now conventional to separate fiscal policy, administered through the Treasury, and monetary policy, administered through the Reserve Bank. Of course, the liabilities of the Reserve Bank are every bit as much public debt as those of the Treasury.)

The effect of a dollar of increased demand for goods and services on employment varies with its composition. For example, reducing taxation on business income in competitive parts of the economy is likely to increase investment more than the same reduction on business income that represents economic rent. (Chapter 7 explains what is meant by economic rent.) Income transfers to low-income people lead to much larger increases in expenditure than tax cuts for people on high incomes.

The balance of public and private expenditure
The boundaries that are drawn between private and public provision of goods and services are affected by economic characteristics

of industries, by ideology, and by the influence of vested interests on policy-making. Where there is opportunity for competition among suppliers, private ownership and exchange through markets generates better outcomes. Where provision of a service is seen to be essential for the effective operation of the community, and where people who do not choose to pay for the service cannot be excluded from its benefits – such as internal and external security, and the supervision of markets and contracts – the service is a public good that is better provided through the public sector.

There are some circumstances in which competition is economically inefficient. For example, overwhelming economies of scale can create natural monopolies, as with electricity transmission lines. In these cases, regulation is required to force the natural monopoly to act in the public interest, or else the state can tax the resulting monopoly rents in the public interest. Where economically efficient regulation or rent taxation are not possible, public ownership has advantages.

Where there are large external costs from operation of a business – for example, through damaging the environment enjoyed by others – regulation or taxation of the externalities may reconcile effective use of competitive markets with good outcomes for the community as a whole.

Ideological support for activities to be undertaken in the public sector independently of the character of the goods and services (socialism), or the private sector (neoliberalism), has been prominent in public discussion of the role of government in the economy. Getting the balance right between use of markets and public provision of goods and services is one of the main determinants of national economic success. Finding the optimality zone between the role of the state and the role of markets in the economy was important to the emergence of modern economic development in Britain a quarter of a millennium ago and its spread through much of the world. The communist governments of the former Soviet Union and Maoist China failed by allowing markets too small a role. China allowed a much larger role for markets with the reforms that commenced in 1978, leading to much stronger economic performance. Getting the balance between the state and markets right was important in the immense success of democratic capitalism in the second half of the twentieth century.

Ideology can shift the balance too far towards private or public provision of goods and services. Adam Smith explained the advantages of private exchange through markets in his book *The Wealth of Nations*, which laid the foundation for modern economics. That was at the dawn of modern economic development. Smith saw domestic and external security as naturally a matter for government. In Australia, ideology saw a shift towards private provision of security services in the late twentieth and early twenty-first centuries. One line of questioning in the judicial inquiry into the failure of COVID-19 quarantine arrangements for people entering Victoria from overseas was whether the provision of security against a pandemic was too important to the public interest to be left to the private sector.

More generally, Australia probably overemphasised state control in the early decades after World War II, and entered the optimality zone only with the reforms of the 1980s and 1990s. It subsequently overcorrected, with too little reliance on public institutions, contributing to problems which emerged in the Dog Days. Another readjustment has been important for managing the pandemic recession. There is a danger that in a prolonged recession, following many disappointments about the performance of private delivery systems, the correction will again go too far.

The division between private and public provision is highly relevant to the challenge of recovery from recession. If people want proportionately more of the services provided efficiently by the public sector and proportionately less of those provided through private markets, then efficient economic development requires a larger public sector. We can illustrate the point with reference to medical services. As the population ages, and medical services become more effective, valuable and expensive, Australians are wanting more money to be spent on them. Since efficient provision of health services has a major public component, this requires a proportionate increase in the public sector.

Freeing ourselves from ideological commitment to a particular size of the public sector is important for the achievement of full employment in the years ahead. Whatever the right size of government overall, investment is needed in the quality of the public sector and in an effective state.

These questions relating to public or private provision also apply to investment in durable assets. Private investment in natural monopolies can only be compatible with the public interest with carefully designed regulation of investment, service quality and price. This oversight is technically challenging, and inevitably complicated by the influence of vested interests. Australia now has private ownership without efficient regulation. We need high levels of investment in electricity transmission to unlock other economic opportunities. We will not get the right amount or composition of transmission investment through decisions by privately owned, transmission companies operating within the current regulatory framework. Institutional innovation is required, or Australia will be denied economically valuable investment that could be helpful to achieving full employment. This is discussed in more detail in Chapter 9.

Being competitive

How does government (including the Reserve Bank) increase the competitiveness of the economy? It can secure a lower exchange rate. It can influence the level of wages and other costs. And it can influence productivity growth, which affects competitiveness over the long term.

All of these determinants of competitiveness require comparisons with other countries. Competitiveness is a relative concept. A more competitive United States or China or Cambodia means a less competitive Australia. That doesn't mean that one country's gains from trade are another country's losses. Increased opportunities for trade and for specialising in what a country does best increase every country's economic welfare. It is just that a country will produce more tradeable goods and services whatever the total opportunities for trade if it is more competitive.

It will not always be economically desirable to be more competitive. If a country has full employment and less than optimal debt, good policy will involve some reduction in competitiveness. This will be associated with an increase in current living standards. This is illustrated in the appendix to this chapter.

The exchange rate of the currency is the most powerful and immediate influence on competitiveness. Easing of monetary policy lowers the exchange rate below what it would otherwise be. Yet Australia can become less competitive even if it is easing monetary policy if other countries are easing monetary policy earlier or more. During the pandemic recession, other developed countries are doing as much as us to loosen monetary constraints on growth, and some much more.

In the era of fixed exchange rates that ended in Australia in December 1983, governments could directly set the exchange rate. The influence of policy on the exchange rate is now indirect. As discussed in more in detail in my book *Dog Days*, a combination of easier monetary policy (expansion of domestic money supply, usually accompanied by lower interest rates) and tighter fiscal policy (a smaller budget deficit) lowers the exchange rate and raises competitiveness.

The depreciation of the currency only increases competitiveness on a continuing basis if its effects on prices for importable and exportable goods and services do not flow into increases in domestic wages and other costs of domestic goods and services. If the currency depreciation is not accompanied by such increases, we say there has been a real depreciation. This is a sustained gain in competitiveness. A reduction of the foreign exchange value of the Australian dollar generally leads to a real depreciation if there is substantial unemployment, but not permanently if there is full employment. The substantial depreciation in the Australian dollar after the end of the China resources boom in 2013 became a permanent increase in competitiveness – a real depreciation. A depreciation in 2021 would have the same effect.

A real depreciation increases the profitability of trade-exposed industries. This leads to an immediate increase in output and employment if there is spare capacity in the import-competing and export industries. Once spare capacity has been taken up, increased business investment is required to take advantage of the opportunity. This leads to much greater demand for goods and services as investment increases productive capacity, and a smaller continuing increase in employment once production from the new capacity begins.

The trade-exposed industries tend to require more physical capital for a given value of output than domestic industries. The distinction is not absolute, but in general higher proportions of goods than services are internationally tradeable. Goods require more physical capital relative to the value of output. Expansion of trade-exposed industries is therefore likely to induce a proportionately larger increase in investment. Higher investment contributes to greater domestic demand.

Investment in trade-exposed industries depends not only on competitiveness today but also on perceptions of competitiveness in the future, because any capital expenditure now increases production in the future. This point can be illustrated by a conversation I had with the CEO of the Japanese car manufacturing company Toyota in late 2013, when he was being pressed by the Australian government to make an immediate decision on whether to continue operations in Australia. He told me that the Toyota manufacturing plant in Melbourne was unprofitable at the exchange rate of the time – over one Australian dollar for one American dollar. However, he said, it would be a profitable plant with an expanding role in the Toyota global manufacturing system at an exchange rate of eighty cents. 'I don't know what the exchange rate will be in future,' he said, 'so I have to be guided mainly by what the exchange rate is today.' He noted that the governor of the Reserve Bank had commented that the Australian dollar may remain high, and businesses had to get used to it. As I write, the Australian dollar is valued at seventy-two US cents, and Australia has no domestic car production. It is a much bigger decision to build a new factory than to continue operating an established one, so Toyota has not reviewed the decision that it took to end Australian production when the foreign exchange value of the Australian dollar was high.

Balancing spending and competitiveness

Chapter 6 discusses the right amount of public debt. For the moment, we simply say that there is an optimal amount of debt, so that good policy requires finding the right balance between domestic expenditure and competitiveness to give us full employment with the right amount of debt.

For a considerable while, we will need high levels of public expenditure funded by borrowing. We will also need more competitiveness. While there is unemployment, we can get both for a while with increased public deficits funded by borrowing from the Reserve Bank, which lowers the foreign exchange value of the Australian dollar.

A lower exchange rate for the Australian dollar only converts into greater competitiveness if it is accompanied by restraint in wages (increasing no more rapidly than in other countries) and reasonable productivity growth (at least as rapid as in other countries). Until the achievement of full employment, low wages growth will happen without effort – as it did in the Dog Days. That will extend the long period of stagnant incomes for most Australians. Over the long term, the living standards of Australians will grow only if competitiveness is secured by productivity growth rather than by wage restraint. That will be achieved by more effective provision of public goods, higher levels of business investment, and structural reform. Beyond full employment, this becomes the objective for the restoration of Australia.

The strong headwinds from the international economy, and the legacy of the Dog Days and the pandemic recession, mean that for the time being the balance has to be struck at a standard of living that is parsimonious compared with contemporary Australian hopes.

The massive fiscal expansion embraced by the Commonwealth government in 2020 provides part of the foundation upon which to build full employment. The increased government debt will need to be used judiciously to raise productivity, living standards and income security for ordinary Australians. It is easy to lose sight of the importance of efficiency in both production and distribution when the focus is on rapid increases in jobs. But lose sight and we condemn Australians to the post-pandemic Dog Days.

APPENDIX TO CHAPTER 4

The broad nature of the choices before us is illustrated in a diagram that is familiar to Australian economics students of my generation. It was developed by ANU economist Professor Trevor Swan, and clarified and made available to the community of economists by our esteemed colleague at the University of Melbourne, Professor Max Corden.

In looking at the big macroeconomic choices, there are two broad levers over policy. One is competitiveness. That is shown on the vertical axis of Chart A4.1. The other is real domestic expenditure. This is shown on on the horizontal axis of Chart A4.1.

Look at the downward-sloping line FE, for full employment. This line shows the various combinations of competitiveness and real domestic expenditure that produce full employment. Increase competitiveness, and we need to spend less to achieve full employment. Increase domestic expenditure and we can achieve full employment with less competitiveness.

The upward-sloping line OB – optimal borrowing – defines the various combinations of expenditure and competitiveness that lead to the right level of debt. Increase competitiveness, and we need to spend more to keep borrowing at an optimal level. Increase domestic expenditure and we need to increase competitiveness to keep borrowing at an optimal level.

Trevor Swan's original presentation of the material in the Swan diagram sought an optimal size of the current account deficit, rather than an optimal stock of debt as the objective.[1] This note and this book identify the stock of debt rather than the flow of current account deficit as the relevant objective. Chapter 6 discusses why I have adopted this approach.

The state of bliss is the point B, at which FE and OB intersect. This defines the combination of competitiveness and expenditure that achieves both full employment and optimal borrowing.

Competitiveness is increased by lowering wages, increasing productivity or depreciating the exchange rate. Increased competitiveness can come from exchange-rate depreciation that does not lead to compensatory increases in wages. Over time, it can come from rates of productivity growth in excess of the rest of the world, or lower wage growth than in the rest of the world.

Competitiveness might also increase as a result of factors over which government has no control, such as successful economic growth leading to increased wages in a major trading partner. The Swan diagram takes such factors as given, and looks at the variables over which the Australian authorities have control.

Real domestic expenditure is increased by the many measures that were described in Chapter 4 – lower interest rates, higher public expenditure, lower taxation.

Real domestic expenditure might also increase as a result of factors over which government has no control – like increased export prices flowing through to higher Australian incomes and demand for Australian goods and services. Again, our diagram takes such factors as given, and looks at the variables over which the Australian authorities have control.

The economy was in the quadrant at DD, with unemployment and suboptimal borrowing before the pandemic (Chart A4.1). Higher expenditure was needed. The pandemic reduced domestic demand further. Much more expenditure is needed.

Increased government revenue from taxes on rent can reconcile full employment with optimal debt with higher levels of domestic expenditure and lower competitiveness (Chart A4.2). Shifting the incidence of corporate income taxation towards rent is one of the reforms suggested in Chapter 7.

In the Dog Days (DD), Australia was consistently running the economy in segment, W, with unemployment and less borrowing than desirable. B1 would have been the state of bliss, with competitiveness at C1 and expenditure at E1. With the economy in the W segment, at DD, full employment and optimal borrowing required increased domestic demand.

Chart A4.1 Achieving full employment with optimal external borrowing

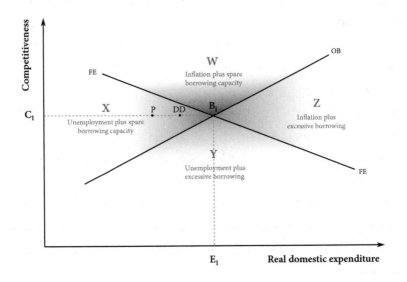

The pandemic (P) shifted us further from the state of bliss by reducing expenditure. That gap has to be reversed if we are to move towards full employment – in the diagram, at B1.

More competitiveness can come through wage restraint, an increase in productivity, or depreciation of the currency. The relationship between depreciation of currency and competitiveness is complex. What matters is change in the real exchange rate, after deducting from the improvement in competitiveness that comes from depreciation, any increase in the domestic wage and cost level induced by the depreciation.

Chart A4.2 looks at a policy change that would affect the combination of real expenditure and competitiveness that would deliver full employment with optimal borrowing: raising more government revenue through a tax on rent. The tax on rent does not affect investment or real economic activity. This shifts the optimal borrowing curve to the

Chart A4.2. Full employment with optimal borrowing after increased tax on rent

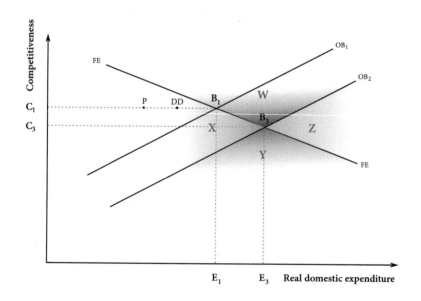

right – from OB1 to OB2. Full employment and optimal borrowing can be achieved by a combination of higher expenditure and lower competitiveness than would otherwise be necessary.

Keep in mind that there was unemployment on the eve of the pandemic. The changes from the pandemic recession require more expenditure and more improvement of competitiveness for full employment with optimal borrowing. Improved competitiveness requires income and wage restraint. The amount of expenditure that can be sustained could be increased, and the amount of downward pressure on wages reduced, if we were to introduce a tax on rent.

5

FULL EMPLOYMENT

We can achieve full employment by mid-2025, while keeping public debt at a manageable level. There are two common definitions of full employment that in practice turn into one. The popular conception of full employment is for all residents to be able to work at the going wage for the number of hours that they would prefer. In modern economics, there is full employment when the rates of unemployment and underemployment are the lowest they can be while inflation remains stable and moderate (the NAIRU, or non-accelerating inflation rate of unemployment, discussed in Chapter 4).

The two definitions point to similar but not identical levels of employment. The lowest unemployment that is consistent with stable moderate inflation would not quite provide employment for all who want it when they want it. The frictions involved in matching the number of people with particular skills and experience in particular places with equivalent jobs mean that it always takes some time for new entrants to the workforce, or people between jobs, to find employment.

The NAIRU is the lowest sustainable rate of unemployment. It is therefore the closest that we can get to the popular conception of full employment.

The Reserve Bank of Australia has a statutory responsibility to achieve full employment. Recently, central banks have been changing their views about what rate of unemployment would correspond to full employment. The chair of the US Federal Reserve, Jerome Powell, noted in a speech to the Jackson Hole conference in August 2020 that in 2012 his fellow members of the Open Market Committee thought the rate of unemployment that amounted to full employment was 5.5 per cent. In 2020, they thought it was 4.1 per cent. The latter seems unrealistically high, being well above the 3.5 per cent achieved without inflation in the year before the pandemic.

In Australia, for many years the Reserve Bank said that full employment would be reached with unemployment of five-point-something per cent. As we have seen, the assistant governor broke new ground in 2019, suggesting that the figure was now about 4.5 per cent. But addressing a parliamentary committee in June 2020, the governor of the RBA, Philip Lowe, said the denudation of labour skills in recession may take the NAIRU back up to 5 per cent. The Commonwealth Treasury's mid-year economic statement released in December 2020 spoke of the NAIRU being 5 per cent.

It may be true that the Australian NAIRU after the recession is higher for a while than before. But there is no reason to think that the number is 5 per cent, anymore than the 3.5 per cent the United States reached just before the pandemic. We simply don't know, and we won't know until unemployment falls to a level at which wages rise at an accelerating rate.

The Reserve Bank could honour its statutory responsibilities for full employment by aiming for an unemployment rate of 3.5 per cent. There would be time to adjust the number up when high and accelerating inflation becomes a matter of concern, or down if we approach 3.5 per cent without inflation accelerating dangerously out of the top of the Reserve Bank's target range.

Factors affecting how many jobs are required for full employment

We can calculate the increase in numbers of jobs required for full employment as the sum of three parts: the reduction of unemployment from mid-2021 levels to full employment; the increase in population in the age group that wishes to be part of the labour force – from the natural increase in population, and immigration; and the number expected to be encouraged into participation in the labour force by full employment and by lower marginal effective tax rates (proposed in Chapter 8).

There is some interaction of employment, population and participation. Population growth falls when there is high unemployment, because both immigration and fertility fall. High unemployment discourages the search for jobs and lowers participation.

Economic growth that comes from a larger population does not significantly change average living standards. In contrast, economic growth that comes from lower unemployment or higher participation increases the income per person that is available for distribution and therefore raises living standards.

More jobs to reduce unemployment and achieve full employment

In its December 2020 economic statement, Treasury indicated it expects the unemployment rate to peak at 7.5 per cent in the March quarter of 2021 and then to fall steadily. I have interpreted that as about 7 per cent in mid-2021. Unemployment fell more rapidly than anticipated in the last two months of 2020, and it is possible that it will be lower than 7 per cent in mid-2021. A lower starting point for unemployment makes the task a bit easier. How many jobs will have to be created to achieve full employment?

If there were no change in population or participation rates or hours worked, we would need about 260,000 additional jobs between mid-2021 and mid-2023 to take unemployment down to the level we saw just before the pandemic – about 5 per cent. This is the rate of unemployment towards which the Treasury and Reserve Bank seem to be aiming.

It is a long time since we were close to full employment – the closest we came in the twenty-first century was on the eve of the GFC, in 2008. Unemployment fell to around 4 per cent then.

We don't know the rate of unemployment at full employment in contemporary circumstances, Pending the testing of boundaries through restoration policies, let's work on 3.5 per cent. Reducing the unemployment rate to that level will require another 200,000 jobs after mid-2023 for full employment by mid-2025.

More jobs for a growing population: Natural increase plus immigration

Population increases through natural increase (births minus deaths) and immigration.

We used to think that fertility (births) was largely independent of policy. Some commentators have credited the 'baby bonus' introduced in 2000 with increasing fertility for a while. Maybe. The early evidence is that the pandemic recession has been influential in the fall of Australian fertility in 2020 to the lowest rate ever. Achievement of full employment may increase it again. But no policy affecting fertility will change the number of Australians wanting employment during the 2020s. Mortality is slowly falling and life expectancy slowly rising, and the pace of change through the 2020s will not be affected significantly by policy. We can expect natural increase to add about half a per cent per annum to the population – converting into a need for about 65,000 new jobs per annum before taking into account changes in the participation rate.

Immigration has important effects on the number of jobs required in the aftermath of the pandemic recession. It also affects the growth of the economy and therefore the rate at which jobs are created. Immigration is greatly influenced by policy, but not only by policy.

Immigration increased population by about 1 per cent per annum during the Dog Days. In the first year of the pandemic recession, it stopped. It is likely to remain low for at least several years, independent of policy choice. Health-related restrictions will greatly limit entry until at least 2022. Electoral pressures to reduce immigration are stronger at times of high unemployment. As a destination, Australia is less attractive when jobs are difficult to find. However, with all the world except China experiencing a fall in average output and incomes in 2020, the latter factor may not be influential this time: jobs are hard to find everywhere, and in some places from which immigrants come, including India and Europe, harder than in Australia. Until there is widespread effective global vaccination – and maybe for longer than that – the success of Australia and New Zealand in controlling the pandemic make these nations more attractive to people from many countries.

I concluded in Chapter 3 that it would be wise to reduce net immigration to the proportions of the 1990s productivity boom – about half a per cent per annum augmentation of the existing population. If this were accepted, the rate of net immigration would be less than half a per cent per annum from 2021 to 2023 and about half a per cent per annum after that. So to provide employment for the increase in population from natural increase and immigration will require about 200,000 new jobs from mid-2021 to mid-2023 and another 260,000 jobs to full employment in mid-2025.

In assessing the number of new jobs that will have to be found to achieve full employment, immigration adds jobs and workers seeking jobs in similar proportions.

Increasing participation

Participation in paid work is affected by many factors: the age structure of the population; social attitudes to the participation of women and younger and older people; the ease of finding employment; wage rates; taxation and social security arrangements; and laws and regulation affecting labour. Taxation and social security have their main effects through the effective marginal taxation rate (EMTR) – how much extra tax is taken plus how much social security payments is withdrawn when more income is earned.

There has been a long-term tendency in Australia for labour force participation to rise – with attitudes shifting about paid employment for women and with the regulations or traditions governing age of retirement changing over time. The participation rate rose to 65.3 per cent when unemployment was low on the eve of the GFC in 2008. It then fell away with higher unemployment. It rose again in the later Dog Days. It reached 66 per cent just before the pandemic – higher than just before the GFC, although unemployment was much higher in the Dog Days. It fell with the collapse of employment during the pandemic but recovered quickly. In November 2020, it was 65.8 per cent – almost back to what it was on the eve of the pandemic.

So far in the twenty-first century there is a tendency for participation rates to rise over time in Australia. It can be expected that this will be augmented by the usual tendency for participation rates to rise with lower unemployment and lower effective marginal tax rates. The augmentation will be stronger in the early years of recovery, with the withdrawal of JobKeeper and JobSeeker and the reopening of restricted industries. There would be additional augmentation of effective participation as reductions in underemployment allowed workers to seek longer hours of work. This is not much more than a guess; but I suggest that a fall in the unemployment rate to 5 per cent by mid-2021 would see the effective participation rate rise by a percentage point. This would expand the labour force by about one and a half per cent, or about 200,000 people. Full employment by mid-2025 with restoration policies and the effects of the Australian Income Security (Chapter 8) would see a lift by another percentage point by mid-2025, creating the need for another 200,000 jobs. After mid-2025, there would be some continuing increase of labour force participation under the influence of the AIS's lower marginal effective tax rates.

How many jobs for full employment?

About 1.2 million additional jobs would be required to take Australia from about 7 per cent unemployment in mid-2021 to full employment in mid-2025. About half of these would be required in the first two years and about half in the second. The first two years would carry a heavier load in reducing unemployment, and the period from 2023 to 2025 a heavier load of catering for a larger flow of immigrants. The two periods would carry similar loads from the increase in labour force participation – the first two years more from the adjustment to lower unemployment, and the later years from the beginnings of adjustment to lower marginal effective tax rates.

To achieve full employment, we would need to expand employment by a touch under 2.5 per cent per annum over the next four years.

Historical experience with required rates of employment expansion

Is this realistic: to move from mid-2021 unemployment to Dog Days rates of unemployment in two years? And then to move from Dog Days unemployment to full employment in another two years? Australian historical experience reveals no obvious reason why this could not be achieved.

A 5 per cent increase in employment over two years is close to the rate of increase in jobs in the two years after the 1982–83 recession, and about the average rate of increase through the productivity boom after the 1991–92 recession. So a return to pre-pandemic labour market conditions by mid-2023 is within historical experience.

After the low point of recession in March 1983, Australian employment increased by 5.3 per cent over the next two years. The rate of growth in jobs increased considerably after that, to an employment peak in May 1990.

Growth from the low point in November 1991–92 was held back by premature tightening of monetary policy. Interest rates were raised by 2.75 percentage points in 1994, when unemployment was still high and without any sign of inflation. To tighten money like that so early in recovery from the pandemic recession would be a Dog Days mistake. That would not happen with restoration policies. Despite that premature tightening of monetary policy, the percentage increase in jobs from 1992 to 1996 was roughly what is required for full employment by 2025.

Australia would achieve full employment by 2025 if annual growth in employment were as strong on average over the next four years as it was on average in the five years from the low points of the last two recessions.

Jobs after mid-2021: The restricted industries

A substantial recovery in the restricted industries is built into the Treasury forecasts of employment in mid-2021, and a complete return to 2019 levels may not occur by the mid-2020s in some industries. The extent of recovery depends on the progress of the pandemic, and on lingering behavioural responses to the memory of the disease. The most likely scenario, with declining incidence of the disease through 2021 and the first half of 2022 with the successful use of a vaccine, would see the continuing partial recovery of restricted industries making a modest positive contribution after mid-2021. The continuing decline in direct and indirect employment in the universities will offset much growth elsewhere. The net increase in employment in the restricted industries in the absence of policy change is likely to be in the tens rather than hundreds of thousands in post-pandemic Dog Days. There would be a large response in these industries, with total employment growth over a hundred thousand, with the policy reform suggested in Chapters 7 and 8.

The universities were rare centres of economic dynamism during the Dog Days. The huge loss of revenue from overseas student fees has been compounded by the sector's exclusion from JobKeeper support. The rationale for exclusion is not obvious. Ministers have explained that the universities are large organisations with substantial reserves. Yet many other large institutions with such reserves received JobKeeper.

Compare the universities with the casinos. Crown Casino employed about 15,000 people before the pandemic; the universities employed about 130,000 in academic and professional and many more in other roles. Both employed many more indirectly, in provision of goods and services including accommodation. Indirect employment was proportionately much larger for the universities. Crown Casino received $115 million in JobKeeper payments in the first four months of the scheme's existence, to August 2020, and more after that. The universities received no JobKeeper support.

The universities have their imperfections, which can usefully be corrected, but few would doubt their superiority over casinos in terms of their national contribution. They contribute to accretion of valuable skills, technological innovation, understanding and suggesting solutions for problems of national importance, our coherence as a society and our standing abroad.

Both universities and casinos experienced catastrophic falls in revenue with the pandemic lockdowns. Universities Australia estimates the immediate loss of 21,000 (full-time equivalent) jobs in the universities themselves, before taking into account the indirect jobs from providing services to foreign students. The decline in employment will continue into 2022. The casinos face headwinds from official responses to breaches in Australian and foreign laws and regulations, so are unlikely to see recovery of employment despite favourable policy treatment.

Restricted domestic services, from music and theatre to hospitality and sport, are responding strongly to control of the disease within Australia. Much of the return to pre-pandemic levels of employment will have occurred by mid-2021. Tourism benefited from JobKeeper and government grants to airlines and some other institutions. The expansion of domestic tourism to some regional areas has substituted for part of lost international demand.

These industries are large employers and would benefit exceptionally from the taxation and social security reforms presented in Chapters 7 and 8.

Other domestic industries

Construction was not a restricted industry. Construction expenditure will fall for at least a year or so, as existing projects are completed and new orders diminished by recession. University construction will fall over a few years from high levels on the eve of the pandemic nearly to zero in 2022. New housing investment fell rapidly in response to reduced immigration and population growth. It is likely to stabilise and resume growth, but lower population growth will hold it below pre-pandemic peaks.

Investment in renewable energy at the peak in 2018 and early 2019 reached about half a per cent of GDP. Policy uncertainty had caused a large fall before the pandemic. The fall accelerated with the recessionary decline in wholesale electricity prices. Certainly in 2021 and probably 2022, these various influences will see renewables construction well below 2019 levels – perhaps by several tenths of a per cent of GDP. Prospects after that depend on whether Australia embraces the opportunity provided by the combination of its own natural advantages and other countries' commitments to decarbonisation.

Trade-exposed industries

Private investment in trade-exposed industries is highly sensitive to expectations of future Australian competitiveness. Continuation of Dog Days policies, with Australian monetary policy remaining more restrictive than in other developed economies with similarly weak economies, would keep the real exchange rate high and competitiveness low. A low exchange rate was a major support for Australian economic activity in the Asian Financial Crisis of the late 1990s, through the US 'tech wreck' at the beginning of the century and the Global Financial Crisis. There was a period of considerable currency weakness as the pandemic struck around March, but this was soon followed by large appreciation against nearly all currencies including those of major international competitors. The high exchange rate is a major drag on competitiveness and investment in the trade-exposed industries.

Weak global demand will be a general source of weakness in the trade-exposed industries. Restrictions on Chinese investment and tensions in Sino–Australian relations will remove what had been an important source of strength through the Dog Days. In the absence of successful measures to increase Australian competitiveness, investment in the trade-exposed industries will be lower in 2023 than in 2021. There is no obvious reason why it would have recovered by 2025 in the absence of new policy support.

There are reasons for low expectations of employment growth in each of the main trade-exposed sectors in the absence of major departures from Dog Days policies.

This is generally a buoyant time for agricultural products in global markets. La Niña climatic conditions have allowed Australian farmers to make good use of opportunities through 2020 into 2021. That has assisted growth in incomes and employment in rural Australia – on a scale that has been noticed in the national economy. The favourable conditions will have run their course and agricultural output will retreat from 2022 or soon after.

Services exports were exceptionally strong through the Dog Days, with education and tourism the main contributors. China was the major growth market. With the easing of restrictions, there will be a return towards pre-pandemic levels for most services, although tensions in Sino–Australian relations will constrain recovery. The financial crisis of the universities will constrain recovery in that important industry.

Trade-exposed Australian manufacturing industry was crushed by the high real exchange rate during the resources boom. Australia was left with a manufacturing sector much smaller as a share of GDP than any other developed country. Much of what remained is vulnerable. The large metals smelting industry is held back by high carbon intensity in an age of decarbonisation, and by the upward shift in Australian gas and electricity prices (see Chapter 9). Decline is much more likely than expansion after 2021 in the absence of shift to the climate change objectives now embraced by all of the other developed countries and by China.

Mining is now by far our largest trade-exposed sector. Within current policies, there are prospects for growth in employment in parts of the sector to exceed modest decline in others. The fossil energy industries, coal and gas, were a source of employment growth through the resources boom and Dog Days. Coal will continue to shed jobs after 2021, with reduced demand in a decarbonising world, and tensions in what had been our largest market: China. Other mining will see some growth, especially in minerals which are inputs into the new low-carbon industry. There is also expansion of gold mining – prices are high through the pandemic recession for this ancient hedge against uncertainty.

State government employment and federal financial relations
In Australia, the Commonwealth public sector has overwhelmingly the main taxation powers, and the capacity to create money through its control of central banking. The states have the main responsibility for labour-intensive public services, including in education, health

and domestic security. The services provided by state governments, including health and domestic security, are in especially high demand following the pandemic. The states have experienced huge falls in revenue. Increased state as well as Commonwealth expenditure is required in response to the pandemic. Maintenance of economically rational levels of services and employment will require major adjustment of federal financial relations.

Some useful adjustment has already occurred. At the depths of the pandemic recession, the federal treasurer and prime minister implored the states to make a larger contribution to economic recovery by spending more – and to run larger budget deficits and lift the level of their debt. The governor of the Reserve Bank also said the states should spend more to increase demand and employment.

The states have responded to the pandemic recession by avoiding contraction of expenditure as revenues have fallen in recession, and by increasing public investment. However, the budget difficulties of all states except Western Australia are likely to lead to reduction of jobs after 2021 in the absence of major reform of federal financial relations.

Employment from JobSeeker and JobKeeper

JobSeeker and JobKeeper played critical roles in holding up aggregate demand, incomes and employment during 2020 into 2021. They were massive programs, injecting over 7 per cent of GDP into the economy through the first year after their introduction. They were much larger in fiscal terms than other measures, and made much larger contributions per million dollars spent to aggregate demand and employment than other anti-recessionary measures. Their early introduction was the main reason for Australia's relatively good performance on output and employment through 2020 and early 2021.

Their progressive withdrawal in itself reduces aggregate demand by a large amount. Many Australian households experienced increases in their incomes as a result of these programs, and were able to increase their savings. Some of these savings will be spent after the winding down of the programs, reducing the reduction in demand from withdrawal. But only for a while. In the absence of major new injections of demand—and none are currently in sight on the required scale – their contributions to demand will need to be replaced by others if we are to avoid unemployment and underemployment sticking at high levels later in 2021 and beyond. The replacement could take the form of new transfer payments to households; or reforms to corporate taxation that cost revenue in the early years while leading to higher levels of business investment; or direct government expenditure on infrastructure or services.

The JobSeeker and JobKeeper programs had highly positive macroeconomic and welfare effects, but made only small contributions to increases in productivity and therefore to future living standards. Better to shift to expenditures that not only contribute to demand and full employment, but also to future productivity and the standard of living. It is important to shift the balance of fiscal stimulus as soon as possible to services (such as health and education) that contribute directly to the standard of living; or to infrastructure that increases productivity or the quality of future lives; or to encouragement of business investment that increases future productivity.

Primary jobs and the employment multiplier

Decisive, strong and early policy responses placed a reasonably high floor under Australian economic activity and employment in the first year after the recognition that COVID-19 was a major threat to Australian living standards. Current policy settings suggest that there will be a levelling out of employment growth from late in 2021, with unemployment and underemployment still well above Dog Days level. Major policy initiatives are required for restoration.

There will be some continued recovery in the restricted industries and some in mining. But new policy will have to drive most of the increase in jobs to take us from around 7 per cent unemployment in mid-2021 to full employment in 2025. Some government measures can increase employment in domestic industries. Others can stimulate investment and output in trade-exposed industries. As we saw in Chapter 4, the policy interventions can only lead to sustainable growth in living standards if they lead to high levels of investment in the trade-exposed industries.

After 2021 there will be some increase in jobs in the restricted industries, some growth in some parts of mining, some growth elsewhere. But most of the 1.2 million new jobs will require new policy.

Some jobs will emerge from the multiplier effect of primary job creation. Once a new job is created, increased incomes from that job will be spent. This increases demand for other goods and services. A substantial part of that demand will be for domestic Australian goods and services. If the increase in demand is expected to continue, sooner or later domestic producers respond by investing to expand capacity. That gives a large boost to increased demand and employment. Estimates of the multiplier effect range around two at a time of high unemployment. Peter Dixon and Maureen Rimmer from Victoria University's Centre for Policy Studies have analysed the United States after the GFC. This work suggests a multiplier a bit below two. Standard estimates used in analysis of impacts of new investment range upwards from about two.[1]

Let's say the multiplier is two. If policy change has to contribute to most of a million new jobs over four years, less than half a million has to come directly from the government policy initiatives. Jobs lost after mid-2021 from any reduction in government expenditure would be deducted from new primary jobs.

Policy for enough jobs

The provision of another 1.2 million jobs in the four years from mid-2021 requires concerted action in many policy areas. It requires the continuation of high levels of public spending, supported by public debt. That means new measures with early impacts on demand equal to the withdrawal of demand associated with the conclusion of the emergency programs, simply to fill a gap, and others to build forward movement. It requires monetary policy that is as supportive of growth as that in other developed countries and the lower exchange rate that would come from that. It would be supported by the reform of corporate taxation and the introduction of a minimum income guarantee, with their large early injections of additional income into the community and economy. And it requires Australia to embrace the powerful global trend towards building the zero-emissions world economy, within which Australia has immense advantages as the energy and landscape carbon superpower.

AN EYE-WATERING AMOUNT OF DEBT

Over the past half century Australia has had such low levels of debt that there are no immediate limits to creating jobs by expanding the budget deficit. The constraint is the risk that circumstances will change and make debt harder to manage in the future.

Achieving full employment with optimal public debt requires the right levels of both competitiveness and domestic expenditure. More competitiveness means that full employment can be achieved with less debt-funded public expenditure. More competitiveness means modestly lower living standards in the short term than would be supported by exclusive reliance on increased expenditure. It can mean much higher living standards in the future.

The right amount of debt is not zero, nor the largest number that can be financed now.

Breaking records

Early in the pandemic recession, Treasurer Josh Frydenberg described as 'eye-watering' the deficits and debts that would appear in the period ahead. The 2019–20 budget deficit was $85 billion. At 4.3 per cent of GDP, it was the largest outside the major wars as a share of the economy. When he took office in March 1983, Prime Minister Bob Hawke was advised by the Treasury that the anti-recessionary (and election-boosting) policy settings he had inherited from the Fraser–Howard government would generate a deficit of 4.6 per cent of GDP. I remember well the eye-watering note from the secretary of the Treasury that described Hawke's inheritance. The deficit in the first Hawke budget ended up being lower than in Treasury's note, and lower than 2019–20, because the government tightened the settings that it inherited. As it turned out, the Hawke–Keating tightening was consistent with faster growth in employment over the next seven years than had ever previously been experienced or has been experienced since then.

The record deficit for 2019–20 is set to be followed in the next innings by one more than twice as high. The great Don Bradman never stood so far above his peers. The deficit for 2020–21 is estimated at nearly 10 per cent of the economy. The December 2020 Treasury mid-year outlook forecasts deficits for another two years that are larger than any in Australian peacetime before 2019–20, and high deficits until 2030. This would raise Commonwealth net debt as a share of GDP to over 45 per cent in 2025 and higher in 2030. The 2023 proportion would be around twice as high as immediately before the pandemic and more than four times as high as at the beginning of the Dog Days in 2013.

Eye-watering numbers, but they are no higher than is required to 2025. Only with restoration policies would the ratio come down at all in the second half of the 2020s. They may not come down in the second half of the 2020s, even with restoration policies. That depends on whether private savings exceed private investment at the time that full employment has been achieved.

Return to Dog Days policies and a weak economy would see continuing increases in debt and deficit until the gales from the next external shock blow the doghouse down.

Low interest rates, optimal government debt and secular stagnation
As shown in Chapter 3, the forces holding global interest rates lower than they have ever been are deeply rooted. Interest rates on long-term debt – say, on debt with terms of ten years or more – are determined by markets with relatively little influence from official policy. The RBA's purchase of securities since early 2020 has had some influence, but real rates would have been near zero even without that intervention.

Mainstream economics presumes that interest rates near zero are impossible, or short-lived if they ever appear. That view has been challenged by twenty-first-century reality.

The idea that substantially positive interest rates are embedded in human preferences was part of the system of economic ideas that developed in the Austro-Hungarian Empire before World War I. Those ideas were brought to the English-speaking world by Ludwig von Mises and Friedrich von Hayek after World War I, and systematised and popularised by Hayek and Milton Friedman after World War II.

The Austro-Hungarian school of economic ideas, with its prioritisation of low public expenditure and taxation, became deeply influential in the US and the UK from the 1970s and remains influential today despite the recurrent failure of economic policies that have been built on it. Martin Wolf at the *Financial Times* has observed that the Austro-Hungarian ideas survived so well because they serve wealthy interests, which gained increasing political influence in the developed capitalist democracies during the late twentieth and early twenty-first centuries.

Von Mises saw humans as having a strong inherent preference for consumption now over consumption in the future. This is called positive time preference. People would not save and make room for investment unless they were rewarded for postponing consumption (that is, for saving) by substantially positive interest rates. If interest rates were low for long, savings would shrink, capital become scarce and interest rates rise.

The most influential US economist of the early decades after World War II, Paul Samuelson, took a similar view about the impossibility of interest rates near zero, following a different tradition of economics. His neoclassical models embodied an assumption of positive time preference, sometimes quantified as about 5 per cent per annum in real terms. His 1937 paper that began this intellectual tradition acknowledged that the assumption was necessary for mathematical convenience, and had no basis in empirical observation.[1] These qualifications were lost in the subsequent use of this class of models.

The leading British public intellectual and economist of the twentieth century, John Maynard Keynes, had a view of interest rates that was more subtle and nuanced and reliably rooted in observation of real economies. In the Keynesian tradition, savings could remain so high and investment so low that interest rates fell to low levels. Low interest rates alone would not induce higher private investment or consumption, or lower savings. In the absence of government stimulus, they could persist forever – alongside high unemployment and stagnation of output. Later economists in the Keynesian tradition pointed to a range of other influences on savings and investment that could keep savings high whatever the interest rate.

Keynes saw the endpoint of successful capitalist development as a state in which capital was abundant and interest rates negligibly low. The essay 'Economic Possibilities for Our Grandchildren', which Keynes prepared for Cambridge undergraduates early in the Great Depression and which was later published in *Essays in Persuasion*, anticipated conditions in which no-one would have a high income simply because they owned capital. Savings would accumulate over time, with diminishing opportunity to deploy them profitably. Real interest rates would fall to negligible levels. High incomes would come only from successful entrepreneurship. We would see the 'euthanasia of the rentier'.[2]

So readers of von Mises and von Hayek, and of part but not the whole of Samuelson, understood that interest rates near zero are impossible.

When zero interest rates emerged in Japan early in the twenty-first century, they concluded they were an aberration derived from the unique characteristics of that incomprehensible people. When low interest rates persisted despite tightening monetary policy in the United States, they were a 'conundrum', as Federal Reserve chair Alan Greenspan said in February 2005. Conundrum or not, long-term expectations of the global balance between savings and investment are overwhelmingly the main determinant of long-term interest rates, and they have determined that interest rates are near zero. When real interest rates near zero became common throughout the developed world after the GFC, negative rates were seen as an aberration derived from hugely expansionary monetary policies. To the RBA, they were anathema, to be avoided at all costs. Everywhere, they were a brief deviation from the norm that sooner rather than later would be corrected by a return to 'normal' higher interest rates.

After the GFC, Federal Reserve Bank chair Ben Bernanke recalled from his student days a lecture by Samuelson in which the great economist provided a different explanation of why interest rates would never be negative. At zero interest rates, there would be an infinite number of profitable investments. It would be profitable to raze part of the Rocky Mountains for the small savings in fuel that it would enable. RBA governor Philip Lowe, in his 2019 lecture in honour of Australian economist Sir Leslie Melville, recalled Sir Leslie's view in the 1930s that zero interest rates would be absurd, as they would allow the satisfaction of every human want. Samuelson and Melville had a point. So long as the institutional arrangements were in place to raze the Rocky Mountains and its equivalents elsewhere, and governments were ready to make rational decisions on investments in socially valuable infrastructure when private investors were reluctant to do so, it would make sense for investment levels to scale great heights in a world of negative interest rates. Interest rates would only be negative for as long as was necessary to get enough shovels moving.

Negative real interest rates may be impossible, but they are all around us in the developed world. They may be transient visitors, but they have now been with us for a long time.

The tendency towards high savings and low investment on a global scale leads to low long-term interest rates. There is no reason to expect a return to 'normal' higher interest rates soon; or, with certainty, ever.

The tendency towards higher private savings and lower investment, generating real interest rates near zero, was discussed in Chapter 3. These same factors can generate what has been called secular stagnation: conditions in which unemployment persists indefinitely in the absence of large government budget deficits. To use the term favoured by Frydenberg in the first half of 2020, 'aggregate demand' can be too low to establish full employment and the highest sustainable rates of economic growth.

Harvard University economist and former US treasury secretary Larry Summers reintroduced the Keynesian idea of secular stagnation at an International Monetary Fund seminar in 2014, in an attempt to explain stubbornly high unemployment in the United States despite expansionary fiscal and monetary policies after the GFC. (Yes, US economists were worried about the slow retreat of unemployment in the decade after the GFC, although there was steady progress during the years when Australian unemployment was stuck at a high level.) Summers, with Jason Furman, returned to this issue in a paper circulated in late 2020.[3]

Persistent low interest rates and secular stagnation share a common cause: the tendency for private savings to exceed private investment at low, zero or negative real interest rates. If these conditions exist – and they did in Australia and throughout the developed world in the 2010s, and do now – full employment is only possible if public expenditure exceeds public revenues: that is, if there is a government budget deficit. There can be full employment, and the economy can grow at the fastest sustainable rate, only if the government is prepared to run persistent and possibly large deficits, possibly even at full employment. In these conditions, public debt continues to rise, possibly even at full employment. Public budgets face no great difficulties so long as these conditions continue – as long as interest rates remain near zero. Problems emerge if interest rates rise. That could leave a government and debtors in the private sector with a large debt service problem.

Adjusting to low real interest rates: Asset prices, inequality
Falling interest rates lead to asset inflation. This increases the wealth of people who have business, housing and other assets. When interest rates fell at a rapid rate in the first two decades of the twentieth century, asset prices rose at a prodigious rate. Owners of assets greatly increased their wealth – more so, if the owners had high levels of debt. The moderately well-off became wealthy, and the wealthy fabulously rich – all through no fault of their own. Occurring at a time of stagnant real wages and high unemployment and underemployment among people with little or no wealth, this became the source of great tensions. In the democracies, it corroded support for the political system. It is part of the background to the rise of Donald Trump in the United States.

Asset price inflation tends to exacerbate intergenerational inequality, as the young own fewer assets than the old. In housing, it locks many young people out of home ownership, which was once seen as an important support for the market economy in a democracy.

High asset prices somewhat increase the consumption of people who own those assets, but not by enough to affect the conditions of secular stagnation.

Some commentators decry the rise in asset prices. The increase can be reduced for some assets through macro-prudential monetary policies – making it more difficult to borrow to purchase particular kinds of assets. Such policies have had substantial effects where they have been applied to housing.

The low interest rates exacerbate inequality in the distribution of wealth. But they are just one of the distributional effects of markets at work. The efficient way to respond to the inequality problem is through the fiscal system. The corporate and personal tax reform proposals discussed in Chapters 7 and 8 would help. More could be done with positive economic effects if there were serious support for reducing inequality.

Business investment responses to low interest rates

With real interest rates near zero, average rates of return on investment fall to very low levels in competitive parts of the economy. Owners of capital cannot get the high returns they once expected and achieved in competitive markets. Businesses owned by people who understand the new realities in global capital markets and adjust their expectations of rates of return continue to invest and expand. Businesses which inflexibly seek the old high rates of return shy away from investment in competitive areas of the economy. They shrink. While they remain important players in the economy, business investment falls – exacerbating the tendency for savings to exceed investment. Or they persuade governments to close more areas of the economy to competition, or to open monopolistic parts of the economy, once the preserve of public investment, to private monopoly ownership. There can be a long period of stagnation in countries with a preponderance of conservative investors, while Darwinian processes weed them out. In countries in which oligopolistic businesses exert high political influence, rents grow and economic output stagnates.

Darwinian processes operate among states and political systems as well as among enterprises in each country. Countries which manage this change by preserving a large realm for competitive market exchange increase their relative economic size and political influence. Countries which manage it poorly shrink and become vulnerable.

Full employment and reasonably strong economic growth in the developed world now require the acceptance of low interest rates and lower expected rates of return. Countries which move fastest and furthest towards acceptance of this reality increase their competitiveness and net exports.

Servicing debt with low interest rates

Commonwealth net debt of a trillion dollars or around 45 per cent of GDP in 2025 is a shocking number from the experience of the last four decades in Australia. However, it is well within the experience of Australia during earlier periods, and of other developed countries. This ratio is much lower than the UK now and at almost any time since the Napoleonic Wars. It is substantially lower than in Australia for several decades after World War II.

In 2020, the ratio of public debt to GDP was 107 per cent in the United States, 110 per cent on average for G7 countries and 177 per cent for Japan. In Australia after the record deficits of 2019–20 and 2020–21, in its December 2020 outlook the Treasury expected net debt to GDP to be 34.5 per cent.

Low rates make the interest costs to the Australian budget small. At current interest rates, a debt of about a trillion dollars – the highest level contemplated so far for Australia in the period – would attract interest of about 0.5 per cent of GDP. That is a small budget story. In Japan, with public debt heading towards twice GDP and with even lower interest rates, the budget cost is currently about zero.

Low interest rates have led to criticism of the traditional ways of measuring the burden of debt. Furnum and Summers argue that the flow of costs (interest) should be compared with the flow of national output (GDP); or the stock of debt with the stock of the present value of future GDP. The current debt burden of the United States is trivially low on either measure.

These are fair points. We would not need to worry at all about the level of public debt if we were certain that the government was always going to be able to borrow without limit at interest rates near zero. The questions of prudent limits to debt are all about the chances of future increases in interest rates.

Might 'normal' real interest rates return?

Might the balance of global savings and investment that is generating historically low interest rates change?

In a world of wise leaders using the best economic knowledge, things would change. Larger public deficits to balance private surpluses would reduce unemployment and raise rates of economic growth.

It would be prudent in the public interest for governments to borrow to build public goods which had continuing value. Many urban transport or electricity transmission projects would have high value at interest rates near zero, and such projects should be built if governments can ensure that they are delivered efficiently.

In addition, developed countries experiencing secular stagnation could export capital to the developing countries, which have large capacity to absorb capital profitably. This would support higher economic activity in the developed countries. Earnings well in excess of the rate of interest would increase the wealth of the communities exporting the capital. The capital outflow would be reflected in a lower real exchange rate, more competitiveness and increased net exports from the developed world. This would be highly favourable for developed and developing countries alike. Such an outcome would not emerge only from private initiative, as it requires a framework of state-to-state and state-to-business agreements to provide confidence in the stability of contractual rights. China is moving determinedly down this path, and some European countries, Japan and South Korea are also active in international development. But the dominant tendency in the United

States, UK and Australia has been to reduce public support for capital flows to developing countries.

It is possible that increased interest rates could come from the sudden immense increase in budget deficits all over the world in the pandemic recession. The Democrats' victories in the Georgia senate reruns in January 2021, which gave them a more certain path to implementation of massive fiscal expansion, led to a small increase in bond yields on global markets. It is not impossible that the sum of the fiscal expansion in developed countries and in developing countries which have access to international capital markets could become so large as to soak up the excess private savings.

The incoming Biden administration is committed to massive early fiscal expansion. It is also committed to higher taxes, which would haul back the deficit over time. How much of the latter – the increase in taxes – survives the political process will influence global as well as US interest rates.

In these circumstances of policy-induced sustained economic expansion, global real interest rates could rise, and nominal rates rise more. Maybe not for long. Unless there were some weakening of the underlying forces keeping private savings high and investment low, at some point governments would come under pressure to reduce the increasing share of public revenue going to pay interest on the public debt. At the same time, heavily indebted firms and households (and there are many, despite private savings exceeding private investment in the economy as a whole) would come under great pressure. Sooner rather than later, this could restore the abundance of savings and low real interest rates. Higher nominal rates from higher inflationery expectations are more likely to persist.

Durable and stable increases in real interest rates would only come from a global reset: policy reform in a large part of the developed world, to restore stronger growth in productivity, greater equity in income distribution, and sustained efforts to support global development. Higher levels of business investment would come with that. The world as a whole has been a long way from that happy place. It is not impossible that Biden's commitment to full employment and large investment in the transition to a zero-emissions economy may provide the opportunity for a global reset. Not impossible; but not likely soon.

The smaller its public debt, the better Australia would do in the happy place created by the global reset. It would be wasteful to have built policy around the certain expectation that the global reset would occur. But we would hedge our bets against rising interest rates by reaching full employment with the largest possible investment in trade-exposed industries. We would be in a better position if our fiscal expansion achieved its full employment goal with the smallest deficit possible – by focusing on those expansionary measures with the largest lift to employment per billion dollars of additional debt. We would be in the best position if expansionary measures increased long-term efficiency and not only immediate employment. We would be better placed if government debt were funded by monetary expansion rather than sale of bonds to the private sector.

On the latter point, Reserve Bank policy until 2020 was resistant to monetisation of public debt. Since March 2020, the Reserve Bank has been indirectly funding much of the increase in the Commonwealth and state debt through its on-market purchase of securities. The Australian dollar investments on the Reserve Bank's balance sheet have increased dramatically. This is a historic change for the RBA: big, necessary and welcome. Our Reserve Bank has been starting to take seriously the effects of tight money on competitiveness. But its balance sheet remains much smaller relative to the size of the economy than those of reserve banks in other developed countries. We were still running a tighter monetary policy than the rest of the developed world in December 2020.

The risk of inflation

High inflation and inflationary expectations raise nominal interest rates even if real interest rates remain near zero. Higher nominal are easier than higher real rates for governments to manage, as the real value of debt falls alongside the inflation-induced increase in interest payments.

We need to consider two types of inflation risk. One would materialise if monetary expansion in the rest of the world were to generate global inflation. The other would arise if global inflation remained low, but excess demand in Australia at some time after the establishment of full employment entrenched high inflation here.

We have noted the possibility that a virulent inflation emerges in the United States after the recovery from the pandemic recession. The near-term inflation risks have disappeared with recession. They will not re-emerge before full employment. The risks are in what might happen beyond full employment.

This is a time of extreme uncertainty in US politics and policy. The risk of a prolonged US recession is much larger than the risk of virulent inflation for the foreseeable future. What might the unforeseeable hold?

Speaking at Jackson Hole in August 2020, the governor of the Federal Reserve reinterpreted the bank's 2 per cent inflation target. He suggested that it should be 2 per cent over long periods of time. Undershooting the target for the decade after the GFC could be balanced by overshooting by a similar amount for a similar period. Taken literally, that amounts to an inflation target of about 3 per cent over the decade ahead. Given the balance of risks, it is a sound approach. But it introduces the possibility that the United States could experience higher inflation over the next decade which, once established, could accelerate. Nominal long-term interest rates in global markets could then be expected to rise with inflationary expectations.

The wise course for the RBA in those circumstances would be to follow the US Federal Reserve. This is not a time for monetary policy heroes in Australia, keeping to the old faith of tight money, a high real exchange rate and low inflation risk through apostasy abroad. The undershooting of the inflation range through the Dog Days would then be balanced with expectations of a period of inflation moderately above the target range of 2 to 3 per cent after the achievement of full employment during the 2020s.

This approach would see a large increase in the Reserve Bank's purchase of securities and expansion of money supply. This would lead to some dollar depreciation. For the time being, the more the better.

Some increase in the price of trade-exposed goods and services would follow the fall in the Australian dollar. The experience with currency depreciation through the long expansion of 1991 to 2019 demonstrates that this is largely absorbed by Australian businesses and households without prompting price increases. This was evident in the aftermath of the currency depreciations during the Asian Financial Crisis (1997–2000), the GFC (2008–09) and the end of the China resources boom (2013–15).

Large monetary expansion in the years of high unemployment leaves a stock of money in the community that could lead to unpredictable increases in expenditure once full employment has been reached. This would then need to be withdrawn if disruptively high expenditure emerged. It could be withdrawn by the Reserve Bank selling back securities that it had purchased during the recession. Alternatively, the government could run a budget surplus, or a smaller budget deficit. With a surplus, it would not need to issue more bonds as old ones expired.

It may be that the tendency for private investment to exceed private savings at full employment is so deep that continued budget deficits are required to sustain full employment. We will learn whether or not that is the case as we approach full employment.

After full employment has been reached, there may be a case for building budget surpluses to bring down the debt ratio faster, rather than tightening money. The five treasurers of the Dog Days can attest that a budget surplus is easier said than done, although none had the benefit of anything like full employment. Treasurers Paul Keating and Peter Costello achieved multiple budget surpluses. Costello had more surpluses, in the more favourable economic circumstances of the China resources boom. In the restoration scenario, an annual surplus of 1 per cent of GDP from mid-2027 would reduce the debt ratio from just over 35 per cent to just over 30 per cent in 2030. That would be worth doing if it were consistent with full employment, mostly for the momentum it would provide for additional reductions over time. The additional reduction in the debt ratio would come at the cost of five months' expected growth in living standards. That takes roughly a fifth of a percentage point per annum off the modest real incomes growth expected between 2025 and 2030.

The arithmetic would be much more daunting in post-pandemic Dog Days. The failure to reach full employment and the slower growth would keep the budget in deficit. At best, deficits would decline slowly. The ratio of debt to GDP would continue to rise. Australia would be highly vulnerable to any new international shock.

Total public debt in the federation

Gross state debt in 2025 is also rising strongly and should be considered to be part of the liabilities of the Australian public sector. As discussed in Chapter 5, growth in state debt is economically efficient in the circumstances of the pandemic recession. Gross state debt is expected to reach around half a billion dollars or nearly a quarter of national GDP by the mid-2020s. This makes Australia less of a low-debt outlier than is suggested by Commonwealth liabilities alone – but leaves the ratios much lower than in other developed countries. The states' expansionary fiscal policy is helpful to restoration in a way that has no parallel in recovery from earlier postwar recessions. Its continuation depends on changes in the character of federal financial relations.

The Reserve Bank is now helping by buying state bonds as part of its quantitative easing program. This is an important and positive innovation in federal financial relations. It is crucial that the bank does not prematurely withdraw that support for state deficits – that it blocks state interest rate rises and other financing problems before full employment has been achieved.

Hauling back demand at full employment

Reset of monetary and fiscal policy does not end with easier money and larger budget deficits to increase demand in domestic and trade-exposed industries.

We have to be ready to haul back demand without destabilising economic growth if strongly rising wages and prices tell us we have reached full employment. We do not know how reality will reveal itself in Australia as we approach full employment. What we do know is that we can avoid some large problems if we prepare for them. If market participants expect the Reserve Bank to sell government securities as we approach full employment, they will also anticipate a stronger Australian dollar. Such expectation would reduce investment now in trade-exposed industries. That would cut across any strategy to reduce the debt required for full employment by increasing competitiveness.

For a decade and a half from the mid-1970s, Australia faced persistent excess demand and high inflation. These were the circumstances in which democratic governments gave independence to the Reserve Bank – de facto under Prime Minister Paul Keating and Reserve Bank governor Bernie Fraser, and by exchange of formal letters under Prime Minister John Howard and RBA governor Ian MacFarlane in 1996. After the costly defeat of a long inflation, the Reserve Bank was given independence to raise interest rates to counter higher inflation whenever it threatened to appear. Like the fabled guns of the British Navy in Singapore, the weapons were pointed in the direction from which attack was expected to come.

But the economic attack came from behind the defensive weapons. The attack came from underemployment and income stagnation, not inflation. Realistic responses to this challenge require more public debt, funded by expanding the balance sheet of the central bank. That is easily done once the Reserve Bank sees the need for it. The politically difficult task requiring independence in the years ahead is not the timely increase in interest rates as inflation accelerates forcefully out of the target range, but the reduction of public fiscal deficits in those same conditions.

Full employment may be marked by wages rising rapidly and at an accelerating pace. At full employment, it may be necessary to reduce growth in demand so as to slow inflation, while avoiding a sharp contraction of economic activity. Monetary and fiscal tightening will both have parts to play. Then we will want to avoid relying mainly on the Reserve Bank's sale of government debt and higher interest rates, with appreciation of the Australian dollar and reduced competitiveness of trade-exposed industries. Reducing budget deficits fast by raising taxation may be necessary to maintain competitiveness if there are strong inflationary pressures after reaching full employment.

If private investors anticipate that control of excess demand in the future will come mainly from tightening money and a higher exchange rate – as it did in the China resources boom – that will deter them from investing now in trade-exposed industries. It is important to put in place mechanisms now that ensure a more balanced easing of demand once full employment has been reached.

Control of demand with a judicious balance between fiscal and monetary policies will serve us best in the battles for economic stability, full employment and income growth that lie ahead.

Put in place mechanisms to achieve that balance, and the defensive guns will face in the direction of likely enemy attack. The Reserve Bank now has de facto independence to raise interest rates and sell government securities when it judges inflation to have risen too far. I say de facto, because the government retains the power to direct the Bank so long as it informs the parliament that it has done so. The history of restraint in the use of the government's power has built a reality of substantial independence. The Reserve Bank's powers lead policy excessively towards monetary and away from fiscal expansion or contraction.

The independent authority that is required now is not a Reserve Bank Board that only has the power to buy and sell government securities and alter interest rates. The circumstances call for an Economic Stability Board, with power to constrain demand by fiscal as well as monetary means – to place a surcharge on major taxes if that serves better than raising interest rates. The board's power to adjust some tax rates would be two-sided, with tax cuts being on the agenda when growth sags below full employment rates and the scope for lower interest rates has been exhausted. If we were designing an independent agency to support economic stability now, we would make it an independent Economic Stability Board and not an independent monetary authority. So let's make this change for the future as part of our reset for restoration.

Now is a good time for funding future growth

The Australian government has taken us into by far the largest fiscal deficits that we have seen in peacetime. It would be unwise to reduce them until the economy is reliably on a path to full employment. Unemployment will stick at high levels if JobKeeper and JobSeeker are closed and not replaced with programs that have a similarly large stimulatory effect. The new programs should be selected to raise the long-term efficiency of the economy, and their capacity to contribute to reduction of the budget deficit as full employment is approached. To have similar stimulatory effect, they would need to inject demand equivalent to several per cent of GDP in the period leading up to full employment.

To ensure that the movement to full employment is accompanied by the largest possible component of investment in trade-exposed industries and the smallest increase in public debt, the fiscal deficits should be mainly funded directly or indirectly by the Reserve Bank, at least until full employment is in sight.

The early response to recession was necessarily focused on holding up income and demand. The next step is properly focused on support for efficiency-raising reform.

Fiscal reform is rarely feasible without initial revenue costs. The last substantial structural reform of the Australian taxation system was John Howard's GST in 2001. Buying support for the introduction of the GST cost the revenue and the budget a full percentage point of GDP – almost $20 billion in today's terms. In the pandemic recession, any cost of reform can contribute necessary stimulus to demand. Now is the time to do it, especially if the reform leads to higher revenues after achievement of full employment.

7

THE BIG PICTURE: INVESTMENT, OPENNESS AND A TAX REVOLUTION

Getting rid of unemployment is our first priority. But unemployment is not our only big problem. Stagnation in productivity and average incomes will loom as important and challenging issues as we approach full employment.

Concern for productivity and future incomes growth requires much of the increase in aggregate demand to achieve full employment to come from business investment in the trade-exposed industries. This, in turn, requires a large increase in competitiveness.

The COVID-19 crisis has encouraged myriad official interventions in business decisions. Foreign investment review processes go far beyond the national interest tests upon which the legitimacy of the review depends. Ministerial discretion plays a major role in deciding which companies and projects in the energy sector receive government support.

It is important to maintain an environment open to foreign competition, in which corporate leaders rise to the global challenge, or fail. It is important that when government support for industry serves the public interest, it is provided through general mechanisms that do not require the exercise of official discretion.

There are opportunities for investment and expansion in trade – exposed industries if competitiveness is right.

The first big step in improving competitiveness is getting the macro-economic settings right. This chapter highlights the most important microeconomic reform that we could implement to supplement the macro-economic policies for increased competitiveness: a shift to cash flow as a base for corporate income taxation. This would provide incentives for new business investment as strong as having no corporate tax at all – without reducing long-term revenues.

Time for the big picture

Most policy change is incremental. It grafts small adjustments onto a complex body of policy, law and regulation. Complexity grows over time, and many lose a sense of why each part is there. Each incremental change trips over others and reveals a new problem, requiring another adjustment. In good periods for policy, the small changes make things better in a small way. In bad periods, the corrections introduce more stumbling blocks than they remove, leading to the stagnation to which economist Mancur Olson drew attention.

The depth of the pandemic recession and the extent of the economic stagnation that preceded it give us unusual reasons and opportunity to make fundamental changes in the structure of the economy. Some of the most important possible reforms would cost the budget a great deal of money before they brought large benefits. Now, when it is prudent to run large deficits to lift demand, economic activity and employment, is a good time to consider such reform. Now, when a great deal of normal economic life has been disturbed by the pandemic and the recession, is a good time to introduce disturbing productivity-enhancing change.

Once confidence has been established in the community that the economy is on a path to full employment with equitable distribution, a reform program can be expanded to embrace many productivity-raising changes that were never possible before. In discussing the reform task before us in the 1980s and early 1990s, I sometimes deploy a cricket metaphor, about how a century comprises plenty of singles as well as a few big sixes over the fence. Many opportunities for singles are described in reports from many institutions and by many analysts. My own favourite singles include conversion of state stamp duties to annual taxes on land value. They include road congestion taxes to replace other charges on motorists. They include reform of our federal fiscal arrangements to remove overlapping and diffuse responsibilities between the Commonwealth and the states. Actually, that last one – federal reform – is a four, if not a six, rather than a single. Another four is the application of realistic discount rates when assessing public investment in transport and other infrastructure. Maybe that is a six.

I do not downplay the importance of the singles, doubles and fours. They are essential contributions to a century. But there are some balls from which we can score sixes. Hit them early in the innings, and we break up the field and make the singles easier.

It is certainly a six to introduce sufficiently expansionary fiscal policies. So far so good. Let's see what happens if and when employment returns towards Dog Days levels. The Reserve Bank ceasing to run tighter monetary policy than the rest of the world is another. Let's see, but so far only partially good.

There are four big sixes in structural reform waiting for us to hit them over the fence. One is the shift from conventional corporate taxation to a tax on cash flows. That is the main focus of the remainder of this chapter. It would have large, positive effects on business investment, productivity, and output per person. The second is the integration of personal taxation and social security through the concept of a negative income tax, which these days is often called a universal basic income. Here it is called Australian Income Security (AIS). The third and fourth remove barriers to exploiting Australia's immense advantages in the emerging low-carbon world economy.

Replacing corporate income tax with a tax on cash flows

The Business Council of Australia has never given up seeking a cut in corporate income tax. If the 25 per cent corporate tax rate for small business were to be extended to big business, as favoured by the Business Council and the big end of town, that would have some positive effect on investment and output. Yet the careful independent analysis of Dixon and others,[1] in a presentation to the Melbourne Economic Forum, show that this effect on output would be small – so small it would be outweighed in its effect on national income by the transfer of tax revenue to foreign owners of businesses benefiting from the tax cut. Tax revenue and the average incomes of Australians would fall.

Business income can be divided into two parts. One is economic rent. The other is the normal return on investment in businesses operating in a competitive environment. A cut in corporate income tax does not encourage investment and economic activity to the extent that the tax falls on rent. Small businesses are more likely to face effective competition. This provides a crude rationale for the current practice of taxing small businesses at a lower rate than big businesses. If we find a more efficient way of reducing the tax burden on businesses operating in a competitive environment and increasing the tax on rent, we remove the rationale for the differential rate of tax favouring small business.

Rent, unlike the income from competitive investment, can in principle be taxed without reducing national output. To the extent that the assets generating rent are owned by foreigners, the tax increases national income. The reconciliation of principle and practice requires an efficient form of rent taxation. This is the cash-flow tax.

The importance of economic rent in total income varies over time. It has become more important in the developed economies in the twenty-first century,[2] helping to explain why inequality in the distribution of wealth and income has increased in those countries.

Robert Solow, long-time professor of economics at the Massachusetts Institute of Technology, received a Nobel Memorial Prize for work in the 1960s. This research developed what is now the standard way of measuring productivity growth, and the contributions respectively of labour and capital to economic value. In a letter to Max Corden on 17 November 2017, Solow said that he hadn't got it quite right:

> we conventionally allocate all of the value added to either compensation of labour or return to capital (debt and equity).
>
> That would be fine if there were perfect competition. In reality, there is a third component, monopoly rent … it gets allocated to labour and capital in unknown proportions.
>
> What one would like is a three-way breakdown in market return to labour, market return to capital and rent.

The increasing role of rents also featured prominently in Olivier Blanchard's 2019 Presidential Address to the American Economic Association.[3]

What is economic rent?

Rent is income in excess of that necessary to attract capital to and retain it in the activity in which it is engaged. It persists because supply of goods and services from the activity cannot expand because:
 › a specific resource or input contributes more to value than alternatives and cannot be reproduced by investment (superior urban or agricultural land, mineral deposits)

› regulation blocks entry of newcomers (banks, patents, controls on the location of pharmacies, taxi licences)
› established investors find a way of blocking newcomers, or
› overwhelming economies of scale relative to the size of a market stop newcomers becoming competitive (natural monopolies such as electricity transmission or railway lines, IT networks.

The insight that rent can be subject to taxation without deterring investment or production came initially from the classical economist David Ricardo two centuries ago.[4] It has attracted greatest attention and has had largest practical application in relation to natural resources and urban land.[5]

There are many challenges in using rent as a base for taxation. One is to distinguish between rent and what the great late-nineteenth-century economist Alfred Marshall called quasi-rent. Investment in a new technology that gives an investor an advantage for a period of time, but only for as long as it takes for knowledge of the technology to spread through the community, is an example of quasi-rent. Quasi-rent also represents a return in excess of what is necessary to hold a factor in the use in which it is engaged. However, the rent is temporary because its continuation depends on continuing investment. Tax a quasi-rent and you reduce investment in innovation and future income and output.

Some rents inhibit growth in output and incomes. These include rents from artificial barriers to competitive supply of goods and services. National economic performance can be improved if these are removed by government action.

However, some rents are a byproduct of efficient operation of the economy. There would be national economic loss if the economic conditions that gave rise to them were removed. These rents can still be taxed without reducing investment and future incomes.

Three sources of rent are associated with the efficient operation of the economy. The first is where government enforcement of exclusive property rights in land and natural resources avoids a free-for-all in use of the resource. For example, the state of Western Australia owns the rich iron ore resources of the Pilbara. By giving exclusive rights to a single company to mine each part of the resource, it allows development at minimum cost. If there were no state-created monopoly, and all citizens were allowed free entry, the resulting 'iron rush' would increase the cost of utilising the resource. Unlimited access would dissipate economic value.

The second is where copyright and patents generate economic rent but provide incentives for innovation. Here, there is a trade-off between the public interest in dissemination of knowledge, and incentives for investment in development of new knowledge. Good policy strikes the right balance with protection of exclusive rights to new knowledge for an optimal period.

The third is where overwhelming economies of scale mean that far fewer economic resources are necessary for incremental expansion of an established source of production than to establish a new source. Examples include transmission and transport systems for electricity, gas, water and telecommunications systems embodying physical infrastructure. These are sometimes called natural monopolies.

Networks are a variation on the theme of overwhelming economies of scale. The information technology platforms that have become so important in the modern economy are recent examples of network rents.

The search for neutral, non-distorting taxation is a search for tax on rent. For rents to be taxed without reducing investment, we must have a tax system that is well designed for capturing rents, which does not fall on either normal competitive returns or quasi-rents.

Australia has had successful experience in a limited sphere with a rent tax on offshore petroleum production.

I have been working with several colleagues over recent years to develop an alternative to the Australian corporate income tax that falls on economic rent.[6] It draws on some features of the petroleum resource rent tax, but is more closely suited as a general tax on rent. Unlike the petroleum rent tax, it is two-sided. It compensates negative cash flows at the same rate that it taxes positive flows. It is highly suited to achieving full employment and, subsequently, incomes growth after the pandemic recession.

A rent tax based on cash flow

The new tax would allow immediate deductibility of all capital expenditures; deny deductibility for all interest payments and financing costs; allow deductibility for imported services (including royalties, marketing and management fees) only if the taxpayer demonstrates that the costs have been incurred directly in producing the service for the taxpayer; and provide a cash credit for any negative cash flows, payable at the time of processing the tax return. Undepreciated capital expenditures under the old tax system would continue to receive depreciation credits at the old rates.

Firms could elect to enter the new arrangements at any time within the first decade after its introduction. All would be taxed within the new regime after the tenth year.

Banks and financial firms would be treated separately. They would continue under the old system, except that they would be allowed immediate expensing of capital expenditure.

Companies with large investment plans could be expected to elect to go immediately onto the new system. Companies suffering losses because of the pandemic recession would elect to move early into the new system and immediately receive back part of their negative cash flows. Companies with low investment and large interest deductions would delay transferring to the cash-flow tax.

The cash payments for negative cash flows would provide support for firms experiencing financial difficulties in recessionary circumstances, as well as for those undertaking high levels of capital expenditure.

The paper I wrote with my colleagues that was published in the *Australian Economic Review* in 2020 presented estimates of the change in revenue through the ten years of transition. We received some help from the Parliamentary Budget Office, but recognise that authoritative estimates can only come from the Australian Tax Office and Treasury using complete datasets.[7] We assumed for the purposes of the calculation that the rate of tax on cash flows is the current corporate tax rate of 30 per cent.

We had to make some assumptions about two major behavioural responses. We assumed that taxpayers generating half of all corporate income being assessed for taxation would switch in year one, and half in year ten. And we assumed conservatively for the revenue estimate that there would be no increase in investment beyond what otherwise would have occurred. We confidently expect the cash-flow tax to lead to substantially higher investment. This would lead to lower revenue in the early years, and much higher revenue in later years.

Prior to the investment incentives introduced in the October 2020 budget, we estimated that the tax change would cost about $50 billion in revenue in the first year. Some of the costs are now water under the bridge, funding the immediate expensing of some capital expenditure introduced at that time. The early loss of revenue would be fully recovered in later years without any discretionary change in policy. Introduction now of the new way of taxing corporate income is ideally suited to the time profile required by the economic circumstances: big early reductions in taxation liabilities before the establishment of full employment, and higher liabilities contributing to reductions in the budget deficit after that. Large initial stimulus would be automatically withdrawn through the 2020s. Large cash payments would be made now to firms that had been greatly damaged by pandemic recession.

The fact that negative cash flows are compensated at the same rate at which positive flows are taxed means that the expected rate of tax on businesses operating in a competitive environment is zero. The effect of the corporate tax on investment in competitive areas of the economy is the same as if there were no taxation at all. This insulates Australia against loss of investment to countries with lower rates of corporate taxation.

Companies earning rents are much more likely to pay tax on profits than be compensated for losses. The denial of deductions for interest and on some imported services means they would expect to pay much more tax than under established arrangements. They would threaten to reduce their activities in Australia. However, they would forego high earnings by doing so, and reduce their global profits. They would expect to pay more tax if they continued to operate in Australia, but would still have attractive Australian income and returns on investment after tax. So they would continue to operate as before in Australia, once it was clear that the threats to depart had not been effective in deterring reform. The taxation reform would insulate Australia from the 'race to the bottom' in corporate tax rates that has corroded the public revenues in many countries in recent decades.

Efficiency advantages of the two-sided tax

The cash-flow tax would provide incentives for business investment as big as a cut to zero in the corporate tax rate. It would do this without incurring the large permanent loss of revenue that would follow even a relatively small cut in the standard corporate tax rate.

The cash-flow or rent tax favours rational risk-taking, by ensuring that losses are compensated at the same rate at which profits are taxed. This removes a powerful advantage that low-risk investments have over those where the prospect for great success is balanced by a chance of loss. This is advantageous for innovation, including in research and development.

The proposed tax system removes a systematic bias in the old system in favour of established firms and against new ones. It ensures that all investments that fail receive credits for 'tax losses'. Under the established system, old firms with established cash flows can expect to receive a valuable deduction for capital expenditure on a new investment that fails. New firms without established cash flows cannot.

The proposed system removes the main opportunities for corporate tax avoidance and evasion, by removing deductions for interest, and for payments abroad in the nature of rents for services. In the process, it removes a systematic bias in favour of multinational over small domestic companies. Foreign or international firms, including Australian-owned companies with international operations, currently have a competitive advantage over smaller Australian firms which pay their fair share of tax. The international operations may include incorporation of affiliates in tax havens. It is currently hard for an Australian tax-paying entity to compete in the same industry with a company that has geared its affairs to pay zero tax.

The standard corporate income tax systematically favours short-lived over long-lived investments. This is because the capital deductions associated with long-lived investments have lower value the further we go forward in time. The immediate deductibility of capital expenditure removes this discrimination against investments that take longer to bear fruit. It happens that the trade-exposed industries, including energy-intensive manufacturing, from which Australia needs to draw high levels of investment to achieve income growth after full employment, are long-lived.

The proposed tax system removes a systematic bias in the established tax system in favour of less-capital-intensive firms and against more-capital-intensive ones. This is because a smaller proportion of expenditures of capital-intensive operations are fully deducted in corporate income tax assessment without losing value from the passing of time. The immediate deductibility of capital expenditure removes this discrimination against capital-intensive investments.

The standard corporate income tax systematically favours the use of debt (interest on which is deductible) over equity (which attracts no deductions for returns on investment). Among other problems, this encouragement of debt increases corporate vulnerability in times of financial crisis. The cash-flow tax removes this distortion, and so reduces enterprise and systemic risk.

The movement from standard corporate income tax is more equitable among businesses. It is also more equitable across the community. Rents are earned disproportionately by those with relatively high wealth and incomes. Shifting the taxation burden towards rents and away from returns to competitive business leads to fairer distribution of income.

How does the change in the tax system affect the Australian debates about negative gearing and franking credits? Negative gearing disappears, because interest is not deductible. Investors relying heavily on negative gearing tax deductions would presumably delay transfer to the new tax system. Franking credits are not affected. Franking credits make corporate tax a withholding tax, recouped on payment of personal taxation on dividends to domestic taxpayers. They lower the effective rate of taxation on domestic relative to foreign investors. For this reason, they tend to bias Australian investors' decisions in favour of domestic investments. There is no obvious disadvantage in that to the Australian national interest.

The 2020 budget is a first step

The October 2020 budget introduced versions of two elements of the proposed reform: immediate expensing of capital expenditure, and the carrying back of losses. It introduced these elements in ways that were less effective in promoting investment and less equitable than corresponding elements in the proposed cash-flow tax. The budget did not introduce two elements of the cash-flow tax proposal: exclusion of interest from assessment of income; and limiting deductions for imported services. Both these elements would have offset the losses of tax revenue from the introduction of immediate expensing of capital expenditure and carrying back of losses.

The budget measure fell short of the rent-tax proposal on immediate expensing of capital expenditure in several ways. It excluded large firms – those with global turnover exceeding $5 billion. It applied only to investments installed ready for use by 30 June 2022. It excluded banks.

The budget measures are helpful to early investment, but the help is limited. The time limits exclude any investment that is not ready now. The carrying back of losses allows compensation for negative cash flows in a crude way, but incompletely. The carrying back of losses is only for established companies with a history of profits, and because it relates to current and not future losses it does not affect incentives for investment.

The limitations of the budget measures mean they will not have a large impact on investment and future production – as recognised by the estimates for investment in the budget papers themselves. The budget measures can be seen as a first step in comprehensive corporate tax reform. They are in the right direction. The completion of the proposed corporate tax reform in either of the next two budgets would be the second and more important step. With the introduction of the full cash-flow tax, a range of businesses with losses from the COVID-19 disruption would be able to recoup some of them even if they had not been making profits in the past. That would remove a discriminatory element of the budget arrangements. I would expect that the switch from the standard corporate income tax to the cash-flow-based rent tax would give a large impetus to capital expenditure.

Much established business would oppose the change. Australian business income is now dominated by rents from mining, urban real estate, government regulation (banks), private natural monopolies (gas, electricity, telecommunications, tollways and IT networks) and private monopoly (retail trade). Our business schools teach the advantages of avoiding competition. Our superannuation funds seek zero risk and high returns – only available with oligopoly now that interest rates are low. Among larger businesses, entrepreneurial activity is less vigorous than in many other developed countries. We have become a nation of rentiers, with big business accustomed to securing protection against competitive entrepreneurial challenge – from Schumpeter's creative destruction. Olson taught us to expect that three decades of unbroken economic growth would harden the arteries and slow economic growth. Other aspects of the ideological and technological environments have magnified those effects.

The cash-flow tax would remove the corporate income tax's bias towards large and established over small, new and entrepreneurial businesses operating in a competitive environment. It would reset business culture, as part of the restoration of Australian prosperity.

8

THE CASE FOR A BASIC INCOME

The pandemic recession has hit most heavily those Australians with no reserves of wealth, on low incomes and in insecure jobs. The biggest victims of the Dog Days have experienced greater hardship in the pandemic recession. The victims are disproportionately younger people.

From early April, JobKeeper and JobSeeker provided substantial protection against immediate want for most people. Incomes and consumption increased for many poor people. Most of the payments were quickly spent, so they injected massive demand into the economy, helping to keep the fall in economic activity in the first half of 2020 to lower levels than in most other developed countries. They were designed as temporary measures. The levels of payment were reduced in September and December 2020. At the end of 2020, they were due to end in March 2021. If their large contributions to domestic expenditure are not replaced, employment will fall. The biggest question has always been: what will replace them?

There are strong pressures and good reasons for increasing unemployment benefits. The Business Council of Australia, the Australian Council of Trade Unions and the Australian Council of Social Service are among the advocates. Increasing unemployment benefits was temporarily achieved with the JobSeeker payments. At a time of extraordinarily high unemployment this is a straightforward response to an obvious need. But a permanent increase in the unemployment benefit is not the best answer for the longer term. We have to find a way of raising the disposable incomes of low-income Australians while increasing rather than reducing incentives for participation in the economy in the future.

In the best of circumstances, by 2025, Australians will have lived through the longest period of real income stagnation in our national history. There is some support for a higher minimum wage. It is an unhappy reality that the number of available jobs is lower when wages are higher. A higher minimum wage would mean fewer jobs in Australia, where minimum wages are high relative to median earnings. The sensitivity of employment to an increase in minimum wages is much lower in the United States, where the starting point is much lower. Ways have to be found to raise the incomes of workers on low wages without increasing costs of labour to employers. This leads us to a minimum basic income, which can be augmented by earnings from employment which are taxed at a moderate rate.

Australians with established wealth have done extraordinarily well out of the low interest rates, rising asset values and high profit shares of the twenty-first century. They continued to do well through the Dog Days and have been affected only at the margins in the pandemic recession. Losses in the early months of the pandemic were restored for most assets by late 2020, and asset prices and profit shares were rising strongly late in the year.

We are kidding ourselves if we think that such extreme divergence of fortune among Australians is consistent with social cohesion and effective democratic government as we deal with intractable domestic and international problems.

Full employment and rising living standards require cooperation across disparate elements of our polity. They require acceptance of a long period of income restraint and unsettling structural change among the majority of people with little wealth. We know from our history that it is possible for this successful, old, conservative democracy to accept and even embrace the restraint and support for change that is required. Our history also tells us that it is only possible if there is widely held understanding that the restraint and change are necessary in the national interest, and that their benefits are being shared equitably. Building the widely held understanding requires public education from political leaders about the realities that we face and the advantages of proposed reforms.

On each earlier successful occasion, confidence in fair distribution of benefits was an essential ingredient. In the depths of the Great Depression, the flawed and eventually partially successful Premiers' Plan was built around the concept of shared sacrifice. Contracted interest rates on domestic debt were cut by 22.5 per cent as part of a wider program of restraint. Historic commitment to full employment and expansion of the social safety net underpinned the far-reaching changes associated with postwar reconstruction, extending into the long postwar prosperity. The third and most comprehensive success was the reform program of the Hawke government, continued until the beginning of the 2000s by its successors. This introduced Medicare, greatly increased access to secondary and tertiary education, and extended social security – most importantly, family payments for children. Public education on the need for restraint and structural change was centrally important to the reform program. This supported many years of wage restraint and acquiescence in massive disruptive change. It established the foundations for Australia's most successful period of productivity growth relative to the rest of the world, and the developed world's longest period of unbroken economic expansion.

For a while early in the pandemic, there was talk of Australians coming together to solve longstanding problems. The National

Cabinet, of the prime minister and all first ministers, for a while was effective in coordinating approaches to the health crisis. This recalled the Premiers' Plan of 1931 and the Council of Australian Governments' First Ministers meetings during the Hawke and Keating prime ministerships. The cooperation across the federation frayed over time. The call to broad cooperation in a national effort was revived and given an explicit economic recovery focus by the prime minister in an address to the National Press Club in late September 2020, just before the October budget. A successful bipartisan National Cabinet could play an important role in building understanding of and support for our necessary reset.

Restoration has to be built around a plan for public expenditure and competitiveness that delivers full employment on the earliest possible timetable. Competitiveness requires wage restraint. Keeping public debt at manageable levels requires restraint on transfer payments, as well as hard-nosed commitment to taxing economic rents. The whole system of policy has to be widely understood as being fair, and it has to provide security of income and access to basic services to the large number of Australians whose material living conditions have been damaged through the long Dog Days and now the pandemic recession.

A year of public deficits growing without apparent limit has helped to sustain the economy. It has also obscured an awful reality: that we are a poorer country in late 2020 than we were eight years ago. Maintaining reasonable living standards for all Australians and democratic political support for the restraint and structural change necessary for restoration requires extraordinary discipline in policies. We will have to be clever and efficient in distribution as well as production. At the same time, policies for efficient production and distribution will have to align with the imperatives of full employment and optimal debt.

There are many proposals for partial interventions to deal with particular problems of poverty and inequity. Most have merit. Few could make major contributions to comprehensive programs that can hold Australians together while we establish foundations for full employment and rising incomes.

We give Australia its best chance of meeting the challenge by moving now to integrate the social security and personal income taxation systems around the idea of a negative income tax, or universal basic income. This is an old idea, which has faced reasonable practical objections in the past. The most important was always that it could not be introduced in a 'revenue-neutral' manner except at a rate of tax which is unattractively high. But the arithmetic has changed. Changes that have been introduced in the tax and social security systems over the past quarter-century have reduced the cost of introducing a minimum basic income. Increases in the tax-free threshold have reduced the incremental budgetary cost of making a basic payment to all Australians. Widening the range of beneficiaries of social security has had a similar effect. And now the pandemic recession makes it an advantage that it would be a substantial budget cost in the early years, providing stimulus in the approach to full employment, which then falls with employment and income growth through the 2020s.

The origin of the universal basic income

The idea of a universal payment was publicised by Milton and Rose Friedman as the negative income tax.[1] It was favoured by those on the free-market end of debates about the appropriate roles of the state and of market exchange in a modern economy. The Friedmans thought of it as a way of reconciling the inevitable political requirement in a democratic polity to provide for the basic material needs of all citizens, while still preserving scope for personal choice and markets. More recently, it has been favoured by people whose primary interest is adequate provision for the poor. In this context, it is often described as the universal basic income (UBI), or the minimum income guarantee.

In truth, the negative income tax and the universal basic income are for our current practical purposes the same. They deliver basic incomes to all citizens, in a way that minimises transaction costs while supporting economically optimal levels of participation in paid work. And whether it is called a negative income tax or a universal basic income, the concept has no political colour. The substantive political debates are about the appropriate level of the basic income and the rate of tax. Those placing larger emphasis on equity will want higher basic payments and tax rates. Those favouring minimum departure in the distribution of income from patterns that would emerge from raw market exchange will want lower basic payments and rates of tax. Introduction of the system achieves more efficiently the objectives of both those who prefer more equity and those who prefer less overt government influence on income distribution.

Let's get away from terms which have assumed political colour and call it the Australian Income Security (AIS).

I am going to suggest parameters that on the crudest of calculations are economically realistic. If the idea of introducing the AIS gains support, a next step would be for the Treasury to test the impact of various parameters on income distribution, labour force participation and public finances in the big models run by the Melbourne Institute of Applied Economic and Social Research, the Centre for Policy Studies and the Treasury itself.

The AIS would be highly stimulatory on its introduction in, say, 2022, and would automatically withdraw that stimulus as we approach full employment to 2025 and return to income growth after that.

The proposed reform would do this while increasing efficiency and participation and raising economic output after the achievement of full employment. It is equitable; provides underlying income security; encourages small business entrepreneurship; and avoids stigmatising the social security support that is necessary on a large scale to secure equitable income distribution as we find our way to full employment and sustained incomes growth after the pandemic recession. It is especially helpful for the greatest victims of the pandemic recession: young people, those not yet in secure work, women, and more generally second earners in households.

Earlier Australian discussion of a universal basic income

The integration of taxation and social security to provide all Australians with a secure basic income has been discussed from time to time over half a century. In 1975, the Commission of Inquiry into Poverty, chaired by the inaugural director of the Melbourne Institute, Ronald Henderson, favoured a universal basic income.[2] Bill Hayden, minister for social security and later treasurer in the Whitlam government, expressed interest in reorganising social security around the concept in 1973. The Priorities Review of the Whitlam government commended it.[3] Academic economists discussed it as an element in a set of policies to remove entrenched high unemployment in the 1990s.[4] The Business Council of Australia at that time saw it as a way of passing strong economic growth through to rising living standards for most Australians without damaging economic expansion.[5]

Early in the life of the Howard government, a group known as the Five Economists wrote to the prime minister advocating a combination of wage restraint and supplementary payments from the Commonwealth budget as a means of overcoming unacceptably high unemployment. This led to extensive discussion that came to embrace versions of the AIS.

I prepared a paper for the Business Council of Australia in 1997 proposing such an arrangement. I explained to the BCA that the guarantee of a basic income and low effective marginal tax rates would create an environment in which workers would be more inclined to cooperate with management in increasing flexibility and productivity.[6]

The problem then was that this integration of the tax and social security systems would have been costly to the budget bottom line, unless the initial marginal tax rates were set at a high level. Peter Dawkins, then at the Institute of Applied Economic and Social Research at the University of Melbourne, estimated that the initial tax rate required for revenue neutrality would be 57 or 47 per cent, depending on its scope. My own work for the BCA suggested that the marginal effective tax rate could have been brought down over a decade or so to low levels, so long as about a tenth of Australians were excluded on the basis of wealth. The tax rate could come down to 30 per cent, as incomes growth freed budgetary resources. But the high initial tax rate was still a barrier.

The AIS has re-entered public discussion in response to anxieties about continuing unemployment, and fears that technological change will entrench high unemployment. I do not think that technological change will necessarily lead to unemployment, but I do agree that the AIS will make for a fairer society and a more efficient economy, one that will more readily accept policies that are necessary to promote long-term increases in productivity.

How the Australian Income Security would work

Nearly all resident adult Australians would receive unconditionally into their bank accounts a fortnightly payment at the Newstart rate (about $15,000 per annum, indexed to the Australian Consumer Price Index). No tax would be paid on this payment. My preliminary estimate of fiscal costs is based on this rate of payment. The rate would be subject to review and subsequent policy debate.

Premiums would be added to the basic payment for citizens who currently qualify for payments in excess of the Newstart Allowance rate. These would include people:

> above a certain age, corresponding to the age eligibility for the aged pension

> with a disability, to the extent recognised for current disability pensions

> those with child dependents.

Existing payments for these categories of people would be absorbed into the AIS.

In the initial phase, until unemployment is brought below some specified thresholds – say, 5 per cent – there would be an additional payment to the unemployed. This could be implemented through the JobSeeker program.

To accompany the AIS, I suggested in the Barcaldine 'Reset' Lectures a tax or withdrawal rate of 37 per cent from the first dollar of income earned. Every dollar of Australians' personal income would be taxed at 37 per cent, up to $180,000. The tax rate would be 45 per cent on incomes above $180,000. I suggested that consideration be given to a lower basic rate of 32.5 per cent, corresponding to the dominant rate in the Commonwealth government's legislated revision of personal income taxation.

The budgetary cost of starting with a 32.5 per cent tax rate has been lowered by the Commonwealth government's announcement in the October 2020 budget that the second tranche of long-term tax rates legislated in 2018 would commence immediately. The lower tax rate would provide more stimulus in the early years, but would be more costly to the public accounts. But the revenues have already carried that cost following the Commonwealth's legislation attached to the 2020 budget to bring forward this tranche of tax cuts.

The AIS would maintain current basic payments for the aged, people with disabilities and those with child dependents. Provisions of services in kind, and payments for specific services, including those provided within the National Disability Insurance Scheme, would not be affected.

Equity inclusions and exclusions

The costs of the AIS would be reduced by excluding from basic payments resident non-Australians and people whose wealth and incomes remove any close connection between withdrawal of the basic payment and incentives to work. Eligibility would extend to all Australians who had been resident for at least half the financial year, with pro rata exclusion for people who had spent more than a quarter of the year abroad. Dual citizens would be included to the extent that they met the residency requirement and were not entitled to social security payments from another country in which they were a citizen.

The following would be excluded:

› people with taxable income above, say, $250,000
› people with net assets above, say, $2 million (superannuation, house, other assets minus debt). Assets could be shared among family members who have legal right to ownership of the assets.

Income security for all

The proposed arrangements would provide income security beyond that available in the current social security system. Receipt of the basic payment would not depend on passing a bureaucratic test of whether the recipient had put sufficient effort into the search for a job. Recipients could choose to look for a job in the knowledge they would keep 63 per cent or 67.5 per cent of every dollar of income from employment. The incentive to look for employment would be much stronger than under current arrangements with their high effective marginal tax rates arising out of the combination of taxation on income and withdrawal of social security payments as income increases. A recipient of the AIS could accept a job for a modest income, and the AIS payment would top up that income to a level that made life manageable, if parsimonious. This latter feature of the scheme would increase the attraction of agricultural and other rural employment to young Australians at a time of reduced availability of temporary migrants.

Someone losing a job would not face a gap between loss of employment income and receipt of the basic payment. Movement to reduced hours would not lead to a proportionate reduction of total income after tax and social security.

Greater incentive to work

The greater incentive to work comes from the low effective marginal tax rates, which would leave most income from employment or additional hours with the worker. That is not currently the case for the large number of people on social security benefits. The change from current arrangements would be greatest for part-time workers and secondary earners in households.

The AIS would be especially influential in encouraging self-employment and the establishment of new small businesses. Recipients of the AIS could, if they chose, live frugally off the payment while devoting all available resources to building their own business: for example, seeking to develop a farm, a restaurant, a gallery, a mechanical workshop or a band.

For small businesses, the combination of the AIS and the corporate tax reform proposed in Chapter 7 would be especially powerful. A musician seeking to build a livelihood around the success of a new band would receive the regular payments and be compensated for negative business cash flows at the corporate tax rate. The amounts of money are small to the financially secure, but large enough to make all the difference for the young entrepreneur.

There would be moderate effective marginal tax rates, at the same rate for all workers. This would remove 'poverty traps' from high effective marginal tax rates due to overlapping taxation liabilities and income tests on different social security payments. This is likely to substantially increase participation in work. As we approach full employment, it would increase participation rates by 2 per cent and total labour supply by perhaps 3 per cent. The increase would go disproportionately to low-income households. They would receive substantial incomes from increased employment while receiving the AIS as well. The change would substantially increase the incomes of such workers up to and immediately above the median. It would be especially favourable for part-time workers and those aspiring to work increased hours.

Ease and integrity of administration

The AIS would greatly simplify administration of taxation and social security for most Australians. Compliance costs would be reduced – both for taxpayers and the bureaucracy. There would be no work-search tests. This would save the time of officials, the unemployed and those businesses having to deal with artificial applications for non-existent jobs. The role of Centrelink officials would be to assist people in finding jobs, rather than policing failure to search hard enough.

The whole taxation and social security payments system would be administered as one, through the tax office. Arbitrary distinctions would no longer be drawn on student eligibility for income support. It would be much simpler for employers to calculate how much to deduct for the tax office in making up payrolls: it would no longer be necessary for an employer to know how much income was being earned from other employers. The lower effective marginal tax rates would reduce incentives for illegal non-disclosure of income.

A large and then diminishing boost to demand

The introduction of the AIS on the proposed terms (including 32.5 per cent tax rate) would add several tens of billions, perhaps $40 billion, to the budget deficit if introduced in mid-2022. At full employment, an estimated 3 per cent increase in hours worked and the growth in economic activity within restoration policies would recoup more than half of the shortfall. That would leave the net budget cost less than half that of introduction of the GST, as a share of the economy. Much of the budget costs would accrue to Australians on social security who are increasing their participation in work. With post-pandemic restoration policies, the net cost would fall over time.

As with the cash-flow tax, now – as we are recovering from the pandemic recession – is a good time to introduce the reform. A big initial cost to the budget is gradually clawed back. Unlike the cash-flow tax, it does not necessarily become a budget positive in the second half of the 2020s. But the general shape of this reform is a powerful move in the right direction for the achievement of full employment, and then for increasing budget revenues, reducing deficits and avoiding deterioration of competitiveness.

The budgetary cost would fall rapidly with progress towards full employment. The cost of the basic credits would rise roughly with population, and the revenue with incomes. The revenues would grow much faster than the costs through the 2020s within restoration policies. The measures would not be ready for implementation until perhaps mid-2022. In the meantime, the temporary JobSeeker measures to supplement payments to the unemployed would be continued at the reduced rate introduced in late 2020.

A boost to income growth

The reform would have several important effects on economic growth. One is the increase in labour force participation encouraged by lower effective marginal tax rates. The change would be highly favourable for new small business and innovation, especially when combined with a cash-flow tax on business income.

The AIS would provide a congenial environment for retraining and adult education. Workers taking time out for further education would continue to receive the AIS payment.

Most important of all, the AIS would help to build support for income restraint and structural change. This is crucially important to the achievement of full employment and subsequent productivity and income growth. It could form an element of a grand reset bargain agreed across party lines in the National Cabinet.

The AIS would fundamentally change – for the better – the whole context of income security in Australia.

Other ways to raise incomes and create jobs

In highlighting the AIS as part of Australia's reset, I do not mean to imply that no complementary measures have merit and that none should be introduced.

Peter Dawkins and colleagues at Victoria University have written about the high return on public investment in education and training to raise skill levels and preparedness for work in the emerging economy. This warrants substantial public investment in the post-pandemic recovery. [7] Dawkins and John Freebairn at the University of Melbourne have drawn attention to the anomaly in our taxation system whereby investment in physical assets, such as cars and computers and other machines, are deductible against taxable income, but business or personal investment in education and training is not. [8] The main cost of educational investment for the individual is income forgone, and that would be compensated by the proposed AIS. Fees and other external costs of education incurred by a student or employer obviously should be deductible against taxable income. [9]

That has merit independently of the reforms that I propose.

Alongside the AIS, there is a place for some government-sponsored employment-creating work while unemployment is high. The 2020 budget introduced large subsidies for employment of younger and unemployed workers. These would be phased out in the approach to full employment.

Many proponents of Modern Monetary Theory advocate a guarantee of employment for all residents, at a wage comparable to those available to low-skilled workers.[10] It would be funded by government borrowing from the central bank. This employment guarantee would require institutional arrangements to provide skills-enhancing and socially valuable work.

The link that proponents of Modern Monetary Theory have drawn between guarantees for employment and deficit-financing is an artificial one. If there is a case for public deficits to be funded for a while by expansion of the money supply by the central bank – and there is such a case while unemployment is high – the case is as strong for funding the introduction of the AIS as it is for public employment programs.

A key element of the restoration

The AIS, together with the replacement of corporate income tax by the cash-flow tax suggested in Chapter 7, would be a good use of a substantial proportion – around half – of the Commonwealth budget deficits required from 2022–23 to put the economy on a path to full employment. Together, they would do this in a way that is highly effective in increasing jobs per billion dollars of deficit spending. With continued growth for a few years after the achievement of full employment in 2025, the negative effect on budget revenue would be gradually and automatically reduced with growth in employment and incomes.

The very large costs to the budget in the early years are not money that disappears into thin air. The large deficits from the integration of the tax and social security systems would go disproportionately to workers on short hours or otherwise on low incomes, including those seeking more work. They would go disproportionately to people in insecure and part-time jobs, and to women earning low incomes, who have carried much more than their share of the burden of the policy response to the pandemic.

Both the corporate and personal income tax reforms have significant beneficial long-term economic effects, with an immediate cost to the budget. Neither could be introduced except at a time when a large negative short-term budget deficit was acceptable, and warranted by economic circumstances. The pandemic recession provides an unusual opportunity for reforms with short-term budgetary costs and long-term economic benefits. We have had no such opportunity for nearly thirty years. We hope to have no such opportunity for a long time into the future.

Let us take the chance while we can.

9

THE SUPERPOWER OPPORTUNITY

Full employment by the mid-2020s and rising incomes after that it requires large expansion of investment, production and employment in trade-exposed industries. There are barriers to expansion in much traditional trade-exposed industry. Nevertheless, there is a clear path forward: through utilisation of Australia's unequalled advantages in the emerging low-carbon world economy. There is no comparable opportunity for profitable expansion of business investment in other trade-exposed industries.

Getting carbon right becomes an integral part of getting economic policy right. There is no restoration without getting fiscal and monetary policy right for competitiveness, as discussed in Chapter 4. There is no restoration without getting incentives right for high levels of business investment, as discussed in Chapter 7. There are no high levels of investment in trade-exposed industries without getting the climate and energy transition right. Getting the settings right for the energy and industrial transition is the subject of this chapter. Supporting the transition of the Australian landscape is the subject of Chapter 10.

Until net emissions fall to zero, global average temperatures will keep increasing. If greenhouse emissions fall but remain positive, temperatures will rise more slowly, but the rise will not stop. The international community agreed at the United Nations Climate Change Conference in Paris in December 2015 to hold temperature increases below 2°C, and as close as possible to 1.5°C. The 2°C target requires zero global net emissions by 2050. Zero has to come significantly earlier to achieve 1.5°C. There was doubt about the international political will to achieve the Paris goals when Trump took the United States out of the Paris Agreement. That doubt has gone with Biden taking the US back in. It is now imprudent to presume that the Paris Agreement will fail. Countries of modest strategic weight that stand in the way of its achievement will be run over, by allies and foes alike.

Australia's low-carbon opportunity, even its role as a superpower of the low-carbon world economy, has come to be widely recognised through 2020 and early 2021. The Commonwealth government's Low Emissions Technology Roadmap shines a spotlight on five technological developments that are important building blocks for the superpower: energy storage; green hydrogen; green steel and aluminium; carbon capture and storage; and carbon in soils. The superpower potential was prominent in the NSW government's nationally important legislation on energy in November 2020 and the South Australian government's statement on climate change policy in December.

The roadmap is sound as a description of some of the technologies that will be important as we move forward. It is not yet a blueprint for success. It lacks a destination. It lacks a timetable. It lacks policy engines for moving across the map to a destination. Above all, it misjudges the time frames in which the transformation must and can occur.

The Low Emissions Technology Roadmap suggests that green aluminium, green steel and clean hydrogen-based manufacturing are for the long-term future. In fact, the transformation can and should begin on a large scale now – in time to play a major role in the restoration of Australia after the pandemic recession. It is feasible now to replace most of Australia's large imports of ammonia-based products. Building supply from new plants in rural and provincial Australia that rely on renewable energy and hydrogen – at prices that are competitive with high-emissions alternatives – can happen in time to contribute to full employment in 2025. Zero-emissions electricity at prices within the range required to keep established mainland aluminium smelters alive is possible now. By contrast, aluminium smelting at Gladstone, Newcastle and Portland would not survive through the 2020s with continued coal-based power supply. With funding of the kind envisaged in the 2020 budget but greatly expanded in scale, the first commercial-scale hydrogen-based iron-making plant can be built as part of the movement to full employment. Make a start on commercial-scale plants and more business investment will follow, in an international environment transformed by decisive political change in the United States and confirmation of new policy directions in China.

The Paris Agreement after the pandemic recession

It was not obvious in the early days that the pandemic would strengthen action on climate change. The pandemic distracted us from the climate and energy transition. The prices of fossil energy fell. These developments might have slowed progress.

However, other effects of the pandemic recession turned out to be more important. The pandemic drew attention to how natural processes can disrupt economic business as usual. It drew attention to the fragility of economic life in large, complex, modern societies. It drew attention to the value of anticipating and preparing for shocks from the natural world. It underlined the value of scientific knowledge in managing the impact of natural shocks. It destabilised the fossil energy industries. Most importantly, the pandemic undermined the political position of leaders that did not take science seriously. It greatly increased the force for change in US politics that destroyed the Trump presidency and Republican control of the senate.

Governments with leaders who have not taken science seriously have been rendered politically vulnerable. Alongside Trump, President Jair Bolsonaro in Brazil stands out. The United States and Brazil are important countries in global climate change mitigation. Trump and Bolsonaro rejected scientific knowledge of climate change – as they rejected expert advice on the virus and the economy.

Under President Biden, investment in accelerated decarbonisation of the US economy will be a central component of economic recovery. Biden has committed US$1.7 trillion – an amount much larger than the total Australian economy – to investment in the transition to lower emissions as part of the recovery from the pandemic recession. Commitments from the European Union, the UK, Japan and South Korea are proportionately similar in scale. Chinese policies for the zero-emissions economy are currently being developed within the fourteenth five-year plan, to be unveiled at the National People's Congress meeting in March 2021.

With Biden's policies for the United States, all developed countries except Australia are committed to zero net emissions by mid-2050. All are committed as well to trying to get to zero emissions earlier than 2050, and therefore to getting as close as possible to the 1.5°C objective. Australia is an exception only at the federal level: all state and territory governments are committed to zero emissions by 2050. If each state and territory meets its target, Australia achieves net zero emissions by 2050.

President Xi Jinping in an electronic address to the UN General Assembly in September 2020 announced that China would have zero net emissions by 2060. China has accounted for more than half of growth in global emissions-intensive industry in the twenty-first century so far, and now for around half of global production of most emissions-intensive industrial products: iron, steel and the whole range of metals; cement; and chemicals using hydrocarbons as feedstocks. Such a commitment by the General Secretary of the Chinese Communist Party to such a forum was not made lightly. China has renewable energy resources that are absolutely large, but small for its population and economic size. This is similar to its fossil-energy profile: the world's largest producer of coal by a large margin, and a significant producer of oil and gas, but also the world's largest importer of fossil energy.

Chinese demand drove the shortage and increase in prices of world energy and minerals in the first dozen years of the twenty-first century. This fuelled Australia's resources boom. While the decarbonisation of Europe, the UK, Japan, South Korea and North America will play a crucial role in developing new technologies and commercial models for the zero-emissions economy, changes in the structure of Chinese demand and production will be most influential in driving the emergence of massive new zero-emissions exports from countries with the natural and human resources to produce them competitively.

Australia faces fateful choices. It is the developed country that is most vulnerable to and has already been most damaged by climate change. It has the developed world's richest endowment of fossil energy relative to economic size – the world's largest exporter of coal and at least for a while, LNG. At the same time, it has by far the richest endowment of renewable energy and potential for capturing carbon in the landscape relative to economic size. As I explained in *Superpower*, unlike our riches in fossil energy, our renewable resources can convey permanent and large advantages in local minerals processing and other manufacturing industries.

In recent years, interests built around the economic structures of the past have dominated Australian policies. Australia's interests in successful climate change mitigation and the industries of the zero-emissions future have lost out. That will have to change for geopolitical as well as economic and climate reasons. We are seeking a comprehensive trade agreement with the UK, when Prime Minister Boris Johnson has made it clear that his central international policy objective in 2021 is a successful outcome from the Glasgow meeting of the United Nations Framework Convention on Climate Change. We are seeking a trade agreement with the European Union when the EU has made it clear that transition to zero emissions will be a central focus of post-pandemic recovery policies, and that border taxes on imports of carbon-intensive products will be part of future trading rules. Biden has made investment in the zero-emissions economy the central feature of domestic economic recovery policies in the US, and leadership of global progress on climate change the central new objective of US foreign policy. The United States is likely to join Europe in imposing border taxes on high-emissions imports. All of this at a time when Australia is seeking close links to the US at a time of problems in the bilateral relationship with China.

It is not realistic to think of Australia holding out against these powerful international trends. We will not do it. The question is whether we will embrace the immense opportunity offered by this change, or, crablike, shuffle sideways into acceptance of reality. Embracing the opportunity will greatly improve the prospects of restoration.

How has the pandemic recession affected fossil and renewable energy use?

There was a far larger fall in global emissions in 2020 than in any earlier year. The International Energy Agency in October estimated the fall at over 6 per cent. Travel by plane just about ceased for most of the year and by car fell sharply. This led to substantially lower oil use. Lower industrial production has reduced demand for all energy. Renewable energy production held its ground and increased a bit, and the whole decline in energy use fell on fossil fuels.

Prices fell for coal, oil and gas – at one point, dramatically. This, in isolation, encourages use of fossil carbon in established activities. But it reduces investment in exploration and development, which detracts from the future supply and competitive position of fossil carbon.

Chart 9.1 Estimated global energy demand, CO$_2$ emissions and investment indicators, 2020 relative to 2019

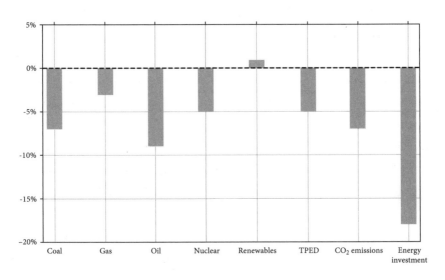

Chart 9.2 Electricity generation by source (%) in Australia

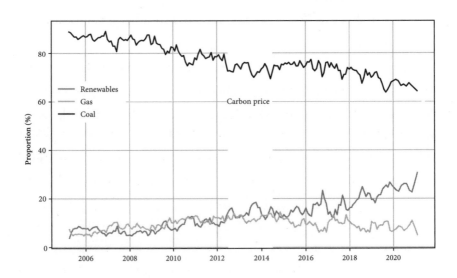

Data source: openNeM, data from the Australian Energy Market Operator

The story for Australia is broadly similar. There was a large fall in coal use in power generation. There was a substantial fall in gas use, but a moderate increase in renewables. Low electricity prices helped reduce the rate of new investment in renewables, but no established plants with access to the grid substantially reduced production. Grid-scale renewables investment fell considerably, but decentralised household and business investment continued at a rapid pace – with policy support.

In the first decade of this century, most renewable generation was from hydro-electric plants (Chart 9.2). Solar and wind supply gradually rose from about 2010. Data for 2020 are month by month, whereas earlier years are annual averages.

The rising renewables share makes wholesale power prices more variable. Coal generators cannot quickly or cheaply vary the level of output in response to price. Gas generators are more flexible. The expansion of renewables production with extremely low operating costs is reducing average wholesale costs of power, and taking them close to zero for extensive periods when the sun is shining and the wind blowing. The combination of lower price, lower market share and increased variability of price increases pressure for early coal generation closure. Market pressures are encouraging early large investment in electricity storage (batteries and pumped hydro-electric storage) to soak up surplus power when prices are low and to make it available to the grid when prices are high.

The total capital and operating costs of power from a combination of new solar, wind and firming (from pumped hydro, batteries or demand management) is much lower than from new fossil generators in all Australian states, even with the low fossil energy prices during the pandemic recession.

The market pressures are all in the direction of new production capacity being entirely renewable.

Chart 9.3 Global energy prices

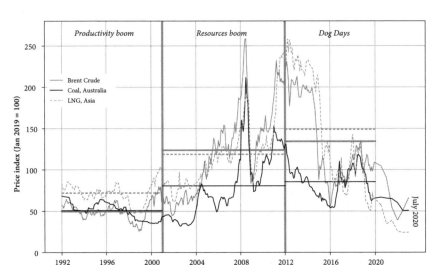

Data sources: Primary Commodity Price System, International Monetary Fund, Federal Reserve Bank of St Louis

Chart 9.3 looks at global coal, oil and gas prices in 2020 and the three periods of the long Australian economic expansion. All prices are in real terms, adjusted for inflation. The horizontal lines are the averages respectively for the productivity boom, resources boom and Dog Days.

Coal prices increased prodigiously during the resources boom, crude oil prices even more. Fossil energy prices stayed high during the Dog Days. By mid-2020, oil and gas had fallen more than half from early 2019, and coal by more than a third. Coal was well below prices in the resources boom and the Dog Days, and a bit above the productivity boom. The prices of all three fell month by month through the first half of 2020. There was some lift for all three later in the year, but less for coal, which was caught up in the problems in Australia's relationship with China.

These price developments and pressure from investors for faster climate action led to large falls on global and Australian stock exchanges for fossil energy companies. In mid-2020, the market capitalisation of the largest US coal company, Peabody, was not much more than 10 per cent of that in January 2019. The oil majors, Exxon, Chevron and Shell, were down between 10 and 30 per cent. For comparison, the Standard & Poor's average of all stocks was up by over 10 per cent.

In Australia, the share price of the coal company Whitehaven fell about two-thirds between January 2019 and mid-2020. Gas companies Santos and Woodside fell by a sixth and a third respectively. For comparison, the Australian All Ordinaries share price average was about the same in mid-2020 as at the beginning of the previous year. The prices of gas companies lifted later in the year.

Wholesale electricity prices fell sharply in all Australian states in the pandemic. When all mainland states depended on coal for their electricity, South Australia, with poorer and more costly coal, almost always had higher wholesale prices. It now has no coal electricity generation, and about 60 per cent of its electricity comes from renewable energy, and that figure is increasing. Since mid-2019, average prices in South Australia have been substantially below those in New South Wales and Victoria. Lower prices in South Australia will persist. In January, during the bushfires and before COVID-19 reached Australia, wholesale power prices rose sharply in all states due to heatwaves and the bushfires greatly increasing demand and disrupting coal generation and transmission. Average prices went much higher in New South Wales and Victoria than in South Australia,

Low energy prices and recognition of carbon risk reduce the incentive to explore and develop new oil, gas and coal sites. There have been announcements of the cancellation or postponement of several large gas developments. There were some shovels breaking soil at a proposed new mine in the Galilee Basin in the second half of 2020, but more action in contraction and closure of production elsewhere. Low spending now on exploration and development means that if there were strong future demand, prices would be higher than they otherwise would be. This becomes one more inhibition blocking investment in new plants using coal.

The richest renewable resources

For its economic size, Australia has by far the richest renewable energy resources of any developed country. The proximity of world-class wind and solar resources in several Australian locations is unusual. Managed well, the cost of energy will be lower in Australia than in any other country. Australia will have an advantage in a wide range of industries where energy is a major cost. The advantages are especially large in the processing of Australian mineral ores, including iron, aluminium, silicon, copper, cobalt, lead, zinc, magnesium, nickel, lithium, vanadium, graphite, titanium and other mineral sands, and rare earths. They are large in the many other industries in which hydrogen plays an important role because of its chemical properties, including making fertilisers and explosives from ammonia.

Australia also has the world's richest coal resources and some of the world's richest gas resources relative to economic size. These fossil resources were once the source of comparative advantage in Australian manufacturing industries. No longer. Exports have lifted Australian domestic coal and gas prices up to – and in some circumstances above – prices in the countries which import our energy.

Australia's industrial advantages from renewable energy are more durable. They will not be removed by the export of Australian energy. It is likely that Australian renewable electricity will become an important export to Asia. The Sun Cable project is planning to export large amounts of renewable electricity by high-voltage, direct-current (DC) submarine cable from the Northern Territory through Indonesia to Singapore. The Asian Renewable Energy Hub in the Pilbara aims to convert wind and solar power into hydrogen and ammonia as a hydrogen carrier for Asian markets. These direct-energy exports will be important in meeting niche requirements for a zero-emissions economy in countries with poor renewable energy resources relative to domestic demand. Japan, South Korea and Singapore are the most important examples in Asia, and Germany in Europe.

The costs of transmitting electricity by submarine cable or converting it to hydrogen or hydrogen carriers for shipping to overseas markets will make the price of Australian renewable energy much higher – usually more than twice – in other countries than it is in Australia. This means that Australian renewable electricity will not be taken to Singapore, or renewable hydrogen to Pohang, Kobe, Shanghai or Dortmund to make steel or aluminium. Australia is the economically efficient place to turn many Australian mineral ores into metals in the zero-emissions world economy. This makes the economic advantage from using Australia's natural endowments in industry much larger for renewable energy than for coal or gas. Coal is cheap and easy to transport between continents. The cost of shipping metallurgical coal from Queensland or New South Wales to Kobe, Pohang or Shanghai is less than 10 per cent of the value of the material and lower than shipping it to Whyalla in South Australia.

New and old advantages

Australia had comparative advantage in energy-intensive manufacturing for much of the twentieth century. The world's best per capita endowments of coal made Australia the economically logical home for processing many mineral ores. Gladstone, Townsville, Portland, Newcastle, Port Pirie and Kwinana hosted world-class metals processing facilities. Large discoveries of oil and gas in Bass Strait coincided with the emergence of natural gas as an important feedstock for plastics and other petrochemical production. With no export market, domestic gas was available in southeast Australia at globally competitive prices. Major manufacturing industries using gas as a feedstock emerged in Melbourne, Geelong, Adelaide, Newcastle and Brisbane.

The state electricity commissions made power available to the metals-processing industries at attractive prices. New transmission capacity was built connecting industrial centres to the coalfields when required by new industrial development. A high-voltage transmission line was built across Victoria from the Latrobe Valley in the east to Portland in the south-west at no cost to the smelter.

The support for industry was not always transparent to the community, and it was rarely applied consistently. It was not always governance at its best. It could have been executed with less official discretion and more transparency with no loss of development impact. Yet it was effective in supporting industrial development.

Australian energy changed in the twenty-first century. The biggest shift was the opening of the coal and then gas industries to an international market. The best thermal coal resources had once been allocated to the state electricity commissions, which generated power at low cost for sale through their own networks. With the opening of domestic markets to exports, thermal coal prices rose to export parity, and local power generation had to pay an international price for coal. The world's best metallurgical coal and iron ore had been allocated by the states which owned them to Australia's privately owned steelmaker, BHP – or iron ore to Rio Tinto on condition that part would be processed into iron and steel in Western Australia. BHP decided to focus on the more profitable mining of iron ore and metallurgical coal and sold off steel-making assets to separate companies that paid world prices for their raw materials.

An LNG export industry was established at Gladstone based on unconventional coal-seam gas. In 2015 and 2016, domestic gas prices rose from one-third of world prices to export parity – and above that for a while when a shortage of gas drove domestic prices higher. These Australian gas developments contrasted with the United States. US exports were tightly controlled, so new 'unconventional gas', which was smaller in proportion to established capacity than the Australian developments, led to prices falling by two-thirds. For industries serving international markets and using gas as feedstock, US gas prices went from being three times the eastern Australian price to one-third.

The second big change was the increase in electricity costs associated with the privatisation of Australian electricity assets. There was a sound case in principle for privatising electricity and gas generation and retail supply where there was opportunity for prices to be disciplined by market competition. As it turned out, oligopolistic supply of generation led to oligopolistic control of retail electricity, so practice was not as clear as principle.[1] But transmission and distribution of gas and electricity were natural monopolies. Prices and service quality could not be disciplined by competition. Securing the public interest required regulatory processes and instruments using knowledge, analysis and policy-making discipline in high degree. For this reason, the Productivity Commission cautioned against privatisation of the poles and wires and pipelines without effective price regulation.[2] The finance minister in the Hawke government, Peter Walsh, was rigorous in his economic rationalism. At his funeral, Australia's longest-serving finance minister, Mathias Cormann, generously described Walsh as Australia's best ever finance minister. Walsh opposed privatisation of transmission and distribution on economic rationalist grounds. In the event, Victoria, South Australia and later New South Wales privatised the poles and wires without economically efficient price regulation. Some jurisdictions produced even worse outcomes by corporatising state-owned assets and instructing the businesses to maximise profits as if they were privately owned. The outcome was massive overinvestment in transmission and distribution and huge increases in transmission and distribution costs. Australia went from having among the lowest-cost transmission and distribution systems in the developed world to among the highest.

Gas pipelines became a private monopoly without price regulation. Gas producers and users faced insecure and expensive access to pipeline services. Investors formed the view that it was cheaper to liquefy gas overseas, transport it by ship to Australia and pay for its regasification, than to transfer gas through established pipelines from one eastern Australian location to another.

Australia went from having about the lowest costs of energy for industrial activities in the developed countries, to higher than most. All metals processing was challenged by high energy costs. Competitiveness declined further with the appreciation of the real exchange rate during the resources boom, which was only partially reversed in the Dog Days.

The problems of established metals processing on the mainland were magnified by reliance on coal energy. The major owners of the largest aluminium smelters – Rio Tinto at Newcastle and Gladstone and Alcoa at Portland – are committed globally to early transition to zero emissions. The smelters will close without access to electricity that has a globally competitive price and low carbon-intensity. The post-pandemic acceleration of decarbonisation in developed countries, and the prospect of border taxes on emissions-intensive goods, focuses minds on early transition to low emissions. If the Australian aluminium smelters do well enough on price reduction and decarbonisation for survival over the next few years, the foundations will have been laid for expansion of this industry in Australia.

Australia takes other advantages into using renewable energy to rebuild old industrial strengths on a much larger scale. There are transport cost advantages in processing raw materials mined in Australia locally – so long as the energy and mineral resources are located near each other, which they were not for metallurgical coal and iron ore but are for renewable energy. It is an advantage that these processes are capital-intensive. Australia, like other developed countries, generally has access to capital at globally competitive prices. Australia also has rich reserves of human capital across the range of expertise required for processing resources on a large, globally competitive scale: engineering, financial, geological, metallurgical and project management.

Australian energy-intensive processing can be globally competitive when the transport cost savings on raw materials, lower energy costs and Australian skill advantages outweigh the drags on our competitiveness. They did outweigh them in aluminium and other energy-intensive manufacturing for a period late last century. They ceased to do so earlier in the twenty-first century, as energy costs and the real exchange rate rose. We now have an opportunity to achieve competitiveness far beyond any earlier experience, using our advantages in renewable energy. There are many large industries in which the price of electricity is or could be a major factor in global competitiveness.

Aluminium is currently the most electricity-intensive product entering world trade in large volumes. At 2020 market prices for aluminium metal, $50 per megawatt hour of electricity accounts for about one-fifth of the product's cost. China produces more than half of the global annual total of about 60 million tonnes, nearly all for its own use. China downgraded the priority of investing in new aluminium capacity in its post-2012 economic model. China's retreat from the new model of growth from 2017 stalled the adjustment out of energy-intensive industries. The adjustment will soon be resumed if China is to achieve zero net emissions by 2060. As growth in world demand for aluminium resumes with recovery from the pandemic recession, a substantial proportion of new capacity is likely to be placed in the most competitive locations outside China.

Aluminium is smelted from alumina – pure aluminium oxide from the natural mineral bauxite. Australia is the world's largest producer of bauxite and alumina (about a quarter of the world's total). Most of it is exported to smelters overseas. There are substantial cost advantages in smelting aluminium adjacent to alumina refining. This is only feasible if globally competitive power is available at those locations. This is achievable now, using renewable energy. Hence, Australia is now the economically rational home of new large-scale smelters.

The Australian advantage will strengthen as the world moves towards zero-emissions electricity, causing costs to rise in other countries but not in Australia. Smelting half of Australia's alumina exports at home would require us to construct four or five world-scale plants. This would increase aluminium production several times over, and total Australian electricity supply by around a quarter.

The largest superpower opportunity is in producing iron metal or steel from iron oxide ores. Australia is by far the world's largest producer (nearly two-fifths of the world total) and exporter (nearly three-fifths) of iron ore. China takes about 70 per cent of Australian exports. China has supplied most of the increase in global steel production in the twenty-first century, and now accounts for around half of the global total output of about 1.8 billion tonnes.

Much of the steel produced in the old developed countries in North America, Japan and Western Europe is now made from recycled scrap, through the electricity-intensive electric arc process. This can be zero-emissions steel if it is powered by renewable electricity and the small pure carbon additives are drawn from renewable biomass. But China and other developing countries do not yet have the steel consumption legacy that produces large proportions of scrap, and most of their output is from the highly emissions-intensive reduction of iron ore using coal.

In a zero-emissions economy the technology candidates for processing iron ore are direct reduction using renewable hydrogen, and a coal-based blast furnace with carbon capture and storage (CCS). Using a blast furnace and then capturing and safely storing carbon dioxide emissions would generally be more expensive than direct reduction using hydrogen. Exceptions may be found where good locations for blast furnaces are adjacent to excellent geological structures for carbon storage. There is pandemic oversupply of steel in world markets, and no economic pressure for new capacity, until a number of years of economic growth have substantially increased world demand. The acceleration of decarbonisation in the northern hemisphere brings forward the opportunity for profitable commercial investment in zero-emissions iron and steel.

Investors are now alert to carbon risk. None would invest now in new blast-furnace iron-making in a developed country without having access to globally competitive CCS opportunities. Several European governments have committed large grants to zero-emissions iron-making based on hydrogen, and China is at an advanced stage in commercialisation of the technology.

The strongest immediate commercial opportunity in Australia is for building new direct reduction iron-making facilities near iron ore resources in South Australia, Western Australia and Tasmania. In Western Australia, these could initially use a high proportion of natural gas, which is available at low prices as a result of domestic reservation policies. The renewable hydrogen proportion would be increased over time. Initially, the hydrogen component would require public financial support for innovation, pending the expansion of the scale of electrolysis and the associated reductions in cost. Natural gas contains methane, and methane's hydrogen and carbon atoms both reduce the oxide ore to iron metal. The presence of hydrogen reduction (where the exhaust is water, not carbon dioxide) reduces emissions from iron-making by about half. The emissions fall proportionately as the use of hydrogen rises in the mixture.

Other advantages of old industrial locations in the eastern states may justify large iron-processing industries there as well, using iron ore from elsewhere.[3]

Producing pure silicon from sand or quartz is one of the most energy-intensive industrial processes. Australia is a small silicon producer in the global context, but commands interest and high prices for exceptional quality. Demand for high-grade silicon has increased rapidly with the production of computers and solar photovoltaic (PV) panels – in both of which pure silicon is the critical material input. The economically efficient development of the global market would see expansion of production in places with access to globally competitive power and adjacent to supplies of high-quality quartz and sand. Several Australian locations meet these criteria.

Ammonia plays a large part in the global production of nitrogenous fertilisers, explosives and other chemical products. It is produced from hydrogen. Global annual production of around 150 million tonnes of urea, the fertiliser and stock food supplement, is overwhelmingly made from hydrogen from fossil fuels, and produces large quantities of carbon dioxide emissions. The production of hydrogen and then its conversion into ammonia is highly energy-intensive. Hydrogen can be produced with zero emissions through electrolysis using renewable electricity. Ammonia can be produced with zero emissions from renewable hydrogen. Renewable ammonia production would gravitate economically towards low-cost renewable energy in Australia. The first focus would be to supply around four million tonnes per year of ammonia-based fertilisers and stock-feed supplements and substantial amounts of ammonia-based explosives, most of which are currently imported. Commercially viable production in favourable northern locations is in reach now, using debt from the Commonwealth's Northern Australian Infrastructure Development Fund. High transport costs from ports to local users favour a substantial number of plants across the agricultural, pastoral and mining areas of Australia.

New industrial capacity will be built more easily in provincial cities with strong industrial traditions, and established energy, port, other transport and training infrastructure. This points to Collie–Bunbury in the southwest and Geraldton in the midwest of Western Australia; the mining ports of the Pilbara; the Upper Spencer Gulf in South Australia; Portland and the Latrobe Valley in Victoria; Port Kembla and Newcastle in New South Wales; Gladstone and Townsville in Queensland; and the established materials-processing centres on the Tamar and Derwent rivers in Tasmania. Some new industrial strenghts will emerge at the centres of electricity transmission built for coal generation – where transmission lines will be used to bring in renewable energy rather than to take out coal energy.

Breaking the transmission constraint: Transforming old and building new

Low prices for zero-emissions electricity are the foundation for global competitiveness in new manufacturing. It is the cost of power delivered to the factory that matter, including the costs of moving power from the point of generation. Our established transmission system was built to move power from generators on the coalfields to users in the cities and industrial towns. It is poorly located for linking high-quality renewable energy resources to load centres. It has become expensive by world standards and there are risks of costs rising over time. The location and high costs of transmission are a barrier to the global competitiveness of Australian energy-using industry, despite the exceptionally high quality of the renewable energy resource and the low costs of wholesale power.

From the early days of discussion of the energy transition, established energy interests recognised the crucial role that the transmission system could play in resistance to change. The established, coal-centred system was paid for by taxpayers and consumers. The Prime Ministerial Taskforce Group on Emissions Trading established to advise the Howard government, chaired by Peter Shergold and with its private membership dominated by representatives of large producers and users of fossil-fuel energy, wrote into their recommendations that all new transmission joining renewable generators should be paid for by the generators. The regulatory principles guiding assessment of new transmission gave no value to reductions in the cost of wholesale power to consumers, because there was a corresponding loss to established power generators. Accepting the deep roots of and working within the constraints, my Climate Change Review suggested 'scale-efficient network expansion'. I absorbed my suggestion from discussions with Governor Arnold Schwarzenegger's California. The approach was considered positively by many parties to the policy discussion, and then rejected without much explanation by the rule-maker (the Australian Energy Market Commission).

The rest is history. We don't use at all our best renewable energy resources. Transmission constraints now severely downgrade energy flows from the good renewable energy resources that are closest to established transmission. Many new solar and wind projects remain unconnected for long periods after construction; others are subject to unexpected exclusion of much of their production. Meanwhile, the costs to users rise.

Under the executive leadership of Audrey Zibelman, the Australian Energy Market Operator has done a great deal to sort through the issues. Work is proceeding on a number of important extensions of the established, regulated transmission system: in North Queensland, the copper string from Mount Isa to Townsville, which would be strengthened by a loop from Hughenden through Barcaldine to Gladstone; Dubbo and New England in New South Wales to Newcastle and Sydney; the solar and wind resources of the north and west of Victoria to Melbourne; a new cable joining Tasmania to Victoria (the Battery of the Nation); an interconnector from southern New South Wales to South Australia; NSW–Victoria; and NSW–Queensland. There is some discussion of the need to improve efficiency and timeliness in the connection of large new solar and wind generators. The technology is available to enable continued strong growth in decentralised solar generation and battery storage, including incorporation of the manifold demands and contributions of electric transport. There could be substantial reduction of system costs by use of new technologies to replace high-cost and unreliable low-volume connections in rural areas by more reliable local renewables and storage systems.

But the barriers in the path of change are so high and heavy that progress will be slow. And immovable parts of the institutional legacy mean that in the best of circumstances, transmission costs will be higher than in other countries with which we compete in producing low-emissions goods.

If we put large efforts into reforming the established regulated system, we can substantially reduce costs to users. This will help the competitive position of established businesses in metropolitan Australia and modestly improve the standards of living of citizens.

Let's do all the efficiency-raising reform that we can in the established regulated system.

But let's face the reality that this will be too little too late greatly to expand energy-intensive industry to capture our superpower opportunity.

Full utilisation of the Superpower opportunity requires transformational changes in electricity transmission. Making full use of Australia's opportunities will require a several-fold increase in electricity generation by 2030, built on our best renewable energy resources in all states. Several-fold in the next decade and much more after that.

Australia needs new high-voltage transmission with globally competitive technology and costs joining multiple sites of world-class solar, wind and storage to multiple nodes of energy-intensive industry. Each of the sites and nodes would have low-cost local sources of renewable energy and use the new grid to cover periodic imbalances in local supply and demand. The scale would be so large that there may be several different subsystems, joining and adding strength to each other.

For the moment, let us talk as if there were one new superpower grid system, the Supergrid. The principles would be similar if there were several, each connected to the other at one or more nodes.

The Supergrid would use high-voltage direct current (HVDC) technology, allowing movement of large volumes of power over long distances at low capital cost and with low transmission losses. The downside of the HVDC technology is that it is costly to break the line to take on new generators or users. For this reason, power would be taken up and downloaded at the nodes. There would be one or two nodes in each state. The nodes would be in major sources of zero-emissions generation and power use, in most cases both. Regulated (HVAC) transmission lines would join the Supergrid at the nodes.

The wide geographic spread of the Supergrid would allow substantial balancing of wind and solar resources – balancing different times of sunlight and wind movement across the continent. The services of storage, industrial curtailment and other firming capacity would be rendered more valuable by dispersion through a larger and more diverse system. The diversity of the system would make it more reliable and secure than any of its regional parts. It would come to operate as a large-scale firming support for power-generation and power-use systems at each of its nodes.

With forethought, the regulated grid and the Supergrid would be helpful to each other in reducing costs and increasing security and reliability. The Supergrid would participate in the regulated National Electricity Market as a generator at each of the nodes where it connected to the regulated grid. It would provide reliable low-cost zero-emissions electricity in large quantities, and supply grid security services. The Supergrid and the regulated system would be able to trade power to each other, and would pay for grid stability services supplied to each other.

So, for a while, we would have two transmission systems. One is the old, regulated system. It serves established users of powers in all of the major cities. If it were managed as well as now seems possible, this could supply users of power more reliably at lower costs as we move through the 2020s.

Manage the transition well, and the old power system supports consumption per person of a quarter or more additional power by the end of the 2020s with little or no investment in new capacity beyond connecting to a limited number of high-quality renewable energy zones, and to the new transmission interconnectors sketched above. The largest growth in demand would come from electrification of transport. There would be a modest increase in industrial demand inside the capital cities. Managed well, the old system would make efficient use of high proportions of decentralised power. The role of the regulated grid would evolve into providing platforms for balancing local requirements among large numbers of producers and users – the regulated system with many participants. The Supergrid would have much larger total capacity but a much smaller number of participants.

Transmission links through Moomba, the petroleum production centre of the Cooper Basin in the northeast corner of South Australia, would play a large role in the Supergrid. It has excellent solar and wind resources, and may provide the one large-scale example of economically justifiable zero-emissions gas power generation, with nearly all carbon emissions captured and stored in geological structures depleted of gas. If deep geothermal power ever fulfills its early promise, the connection at Moomba would provide access to markets for Australia's richest resource. Hydrogen would be made at Moomba by electrolysis from local solar and wind resources, augmented through the transmission links. Hydrogen would be fed into the gas pipelines to South Australia, New South Wales, Victoria and Queensland to reduce the emissions intensity of those energy flows. Oxygen waste from the electrolysis would be used to fire a gas generator, which would inject power into the grid when required for balancing. The combustion of gas from pure oxygen would generate a pure carbon dioxide exhaust, captured in a form already suitable for injection in the well-prepared geological structures established by Santos in the old gas fields.

Transmission is what we described in Chapter 7 a natural monopoly, naturally owned and managed by the public sector. There is no prospect of the Australian public sector building the new grid to serve the industrial superpower at a cost and on a timetable that is compatible with capturing the opportunity for Australia's restoration. Nor is there any prospect of the new system being provided cost-effectively through the current regulated system. The recent privatisation of state assets and the interests built around them mean that transformative investments will have to come from unregulated private initiative. Major industrial users at or feeding off the nodes would play a role in backing the new system. Such developments fit within the Commonwealth's Technology Roadmap and the policies announced by the state governments of South Australia, New South Wales, Queensland and Victorian.

There will be time after the restoration of Australia in the early 2030s to think about the advantages of deeper integration of the old and new systems.

In the meantime, building the Supergid and the industrial expansion that it supports can make a large contribution to full employment by 2025 and rising incomes after that. Transmission, renewable energy and storage capacity to support the new energy-intensive industry would attract private investment of more than $50 billion by the mid-2020s. This would be accompanied by more than $60 billion of investment in low-emissions alternatives to emissions-intensive industrial production in the northern hemisphere that are retiring. These are large numbers, but not much more than those those required to build the Gladstone LNG export capacity in the previous decade, over a similar time frame. They are not much bigger than the sums invested in expanding the capacity of the established transmission and distribution system in the decade after the commencement of the current regulatory system in 2006. Investment on this scale is easily managed by the private sector within a supportive policy environment.

These and related developments would contribute much of the private business investment required for full employment. They would lay the foundations for much larger developments in the second half of the 2020s and beyond, providing realistic prospects for a long-delayed return to rising Australian living standards.

The prospects are unhappy if we fail to correct the transmission problem. Continue to manage the regulated electricity system with the current degree of imperfection, and costs will rise, as new sources of power demand, including electric cars, force large investments in expanded grid capacity. Manage the transmission system badly, and Australia will destroy its superpower opportunity. Manage it badly, and Australian industry will shrink with the closure of aluminium smelters and other energy-intensive industries. Manage it as badly as we have over the past decade and a half, and rising power costs will contribute exceptionally to declining living standards through Australia's post-pandemic Dog Days.

Firming intermittent renewables

It has been clear from the beginning of the energy transition that storage, demand management and flexible thermal power generation would play major roles in balancing intermittent renewable energy as the emissions intensity of Australian electricity fell. This was a theme of my first Climate Change Review in 2008. It was difficult to develop the regulatory and planning systems to utilise fully the available technologies when there was deep resistance to decarbonisation within the institutions and sometimes the governments at the heart of Australian energy policy and regulation. There was resistance to more efficient electricity pricing (five-minute averaging), because the old, less flexible thermal generators would not be able to compete with instantaneous industrial curtailment or batteries able to respond to changes in grid requirements in a fraction of a second. In the month before the South Australian government announced the process that led to the installation of a 100-megawatt battery for grid stabilisation, AEMO acknowledged a role for battery storage for the first time, in units less than a single megawatt. The regulatory system's response to falling costs and of decentralised generation and storage was to slow its development rather than to plan for its introduction.

Progress was nevertheless made. The progress has accumulated into transformational change. The success of the Neoen–Tesla big battery in South Australia has led to announcements about its emulation on a larger scale in all mainland states. Prime Minister Malcolm Turnbull, blocked by his party room from direct support for low-cost renewable energy, announced and supplied momentum to large pumped hydro storage projects in the Snowy Mountains and Tasmania. State government initiatives in South Australia and then Victoria accelerated take-up of decentralised batteries. The NSW government introduced laws that would underwrite decarbonisation and a massive reduction in firm power costs. Federal energy minister Angus Taylor included several pumped hydro investments in his list of projects for Commonwealth underwriting in the Underwriting New Generation Investments program. AEMO led the introduction of market processes for expanding industrial demand management. We have come a long way in a few years.

We would go further and faster if we had transparent policies designed to encourage investment in balancing intermittent solar and wind. The big bull in the paddock is Snowy Hydro, now owned wholly by the Commonwealth. Snowy already controls large capacity for increasing power output when prices are high and absorbing power when prices are low: the established Tumut pumped hydro storage (about 470 megawatts); substantial gas generation; and the potential to use conventional hydro within Snowy 1.0 for peaking. Snowy 2.0 has been given advanced approval by the Commonwealth government and seems likely to proceed. The Commonwealth energy minister has said that Snowy Hydro will construct a 1000-megawatt gas peaking plant in New South Wales in time for the closure of the coalfired Liddell power station if the private sector has not committed to sufficient additional peaking capacity by April 2021.

Snowy Hydro already has a dominant position in the peaking markets of New South Wales and Victoria. Snowy 2.0, with or without a gigawatt gas generator, would increase that position. With access to the Commonwealth government's financial resources and the potential for policy direction of what would otherwise be commercial decisons, Snowy Hydro has become a major deterrent to private investment in peaking assets.

In *Superpower*, I recommended that Snowy Hydro's peaking assets be separated out from the conventional hydro into a separate statutory corporation. Its role would be to guarantee power reliability within parameters that are transparently defined. For example, it could be given the role of guaranteeing that power would always be available to meet demand within the National Electricity Market at a specified price, say $300 per megawatt. It would deliver this reliability service at the lowest possible cost.

This still seems to me to be the best way forward. This would have the unfortunate effect of removing private investment from storage and other peaking investments for which the business case depends on large variability in prices. But such investment is being discouraged anyway – and more besides – because of knowledge that Snowy 2.0 is coming and absence of knowledge about how it will operate. It would make the market safe and attractive for private investment in peaking capacity that can be made to work with moderate variations in price.

The transport transition

Electrification of transport over the decade ahead will reduce emissions while contributing to greater competitiveness in the economy and a higher standard of living. There are health benefits from less air pollution. There are security gains from reliance on local sources of solar and wind energy and storage, rather than oil supply chains traversing politically unstable regions.

Technological improvements and falls in the manufacturing costs of battery and hydrogen-fuel-cell electric vehicles (EVs) are driving an early transition to the EV in parts of Europe, North America and Northeast Asia. Australia is a laggard in this transition.

There is competition between two EV technologies: batteries and hydrogen fuel cells. Batteries are moving more quickly in countries where the transport transition is most advanced. Hydrogen fuel cells may emerge as an important technology for heavy vehicles and long-haul freight.

The two policy requirements for greatly increased use of EVs are the availability of charging infrastructure and the early adoption of time-of-use electricity pricing. A start has been made with support for charging infrastructure in several states. The Commonwealth government added to this, with an allocation of $74.5 million in the 2020 budget to a 'future fuels' program. Electricity pricing reform is more easily introduced early, before patterns of EV use have settled. One day there will be a need for fiscal policy reform, to replace the revenue now raised by governments from the sale of petroleum products. Given the external health, climate change and security costs that petroleum use places on the community, without compensatory taxation, and the advantages in accelerating innovation in the transport sector, the movements now in Victoria and South Australia to road-user taxes for electric vehicles seem premature.

The initial capital costs of EVs are still substantially higher than vehicles with internal combustion engines (ICEs). The electric motor is inherently simpler than the ICE and capital costs will fall below those of ICEs with a larger scale and a longer history of production. Capital costs of EVs will fall below ICEs in the mid-2020s and continue to fall. The EV lasts longer, has lower maintenance costs and uses less energy and a cheaper form of energy (electricity, which can become renewable energy produced at home). Once parity in capital costs is established, EVs will soon dominate new vehicle sales in other developed countries. Research and development within vehicle manufacturers is already focused overwhelmingly on EVs. Australia no longer produces its own ICE cars. The advanced producers of cars will not produce an old-fashioned ICE for a lagging Australian market, so we are bound to follow the rest of the world into the electrification of transport.

Early electrification of transport will, sooner rather than later, substantially lower transport costs for businesses and households. Electrification of transport could either reduce or increase the costs of delivering power through the grid to households and business. EV charging at peak times for grid usage would increase investment in grid capacity and increase costs for all users. EV charging at times of the day when there is surplus capacity in the grid would cause unit costs of grid services to fall by a large amount. Use of storage from EV batteries would increase the security and reliability of power supply. Good outcomes require the early introduction of time-of-use pricing to consumers. Experience in the UK shows 75 per cent of EVs are charging for less than 40 per cent of the time they are plugged in. This suggests that demand can easily be shifted away from peak periods.

The gas chimera

Early in the pandemic, the Commonwealth government established a National COVID-19 Commission (later Advisory Board) to advise on economic recovery policies. It has been best known for reports that it favoured greater use of natural gas. There were suggestions that the

Commonwealth government could use its statutory powers to restrict exports, so as to lower gas prices to around $4 per gigajoule. It was said that this would encourage the expansion of manufacturing activities using gas as a raw material, as well as increase the role of gas in balancing intermittent renewable power generation.

Western Australia has had domestic gas reservation policies from the beginning of its LNG industry, retaining them against strong pressure from the Commonwealth government for removal.

The Commonwealth has the legal power to secure globally competitive prices for a while. There is no sign that it is prepared to use that power. In any case, new investment in gas-using industries requires confidence in prices staying low, which is unlikely to be possible for large quantities given Australian costs of production. Eastern Australian gas can only be globally competitive for a limited period of time before it comes to depend on high-cost coal-seam gas, which cannot be made available at a low price even with strong reservation.

Eastern Australian gas prices used to be the lowest in the industrial world – around two dollars per gigajoule in the first decade of the century. Chart 9.4 shows prices in real terms (2019 prices). Back in the first decade of the century, we had competitive gas-using manufacturing industries, mainly in Melbourne, Geelong, Adelaide, Newcastle and Brisbane. With the establishment of the Gladstone LNG plants, gas became scarce and expensive. There was a big lift in price from 2016, which made gas-using industries uncompetitive in eastern Australia. With the slump in global demand in the pandemic recession, eastern Australian wholesale gas prices fell. That is unlikely to unlock high levels of manufacturing investment because it remains near the lower international price, and so does not provide an advantage for operating in Australia, and in any case it is unlikely to be maintained.

Gas is not a low-emissions source of energy unless accompanied by carbon-dioxide capture and sequestration. Capture is cheaper from gas

Chart 9.4 Gas prices in Western Australia and Victoria, 2010–20

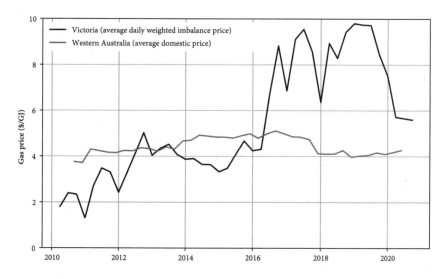

Data sources: Australian Energy Regulator and Department of Mines, Industry Regulation and Safety (WA)

than from coal combustion. Safe and reliable long-term carbon-dioxide storage is technically feasible. Australians tend to be sceptical about a technology until they have seen it working in their own country. CCS is working at the Chevron project in the Pilbara gas fields. The CO_2 Cooperative Research Centre at the University of Melbourne has demonstrated technical feasibility in the Otways. CCS is expensive. It may get cheaper with larger scale and experience in use. Government support for innovation is warranted in early sequestration projects to bring costs down and to inform assessments of potential for future cost reductions. It is likely that capture of emissions and geological storage will be competitive for only a few gas uses and in only the most favourable locations. Australia has more than its share of favourable locations, including near potential sources of carbon emissions in the Pilbara gas fields and the Harvey River Basin near Collie in Western Australia, the Otway Basin near Portland, and East Gippsland near the Latrobe Valley in Victoria.

The most advanced for early use at low cost is in the Cooper Basin in South Australia. Every bit of economically competitive zero-emissions production helps full employment and incomes growth, and the global mitigation effort. It will be a niche technology in Australia, but it is worth investing in the technology to find and make use of the niches. It may be more important in countries with less-rich endowments of renewable energy, including China. Australian development of the technology could underpin the export of services that would assist the international mitigation effort.

There is some transitional role for gas in peaking power, balancing intermittent renewables. But a small one. Gas-based power generation has declined over recent years and it is unlikely that the decline will be reversed. The lower the gas price, the larger and more valuable the role. The COVID Commission focused on a domestic price of $4 per gigajoule for internationally competitive industrial use, and there would be a larger transitional power generation role at that price, which is available on a sustained basis in Western Australia. Where gas production from a geological structure that is suitable for low-cost sequestration is located near high-voltage transmission lines, zero-emissions gas power generation is possible. Such confluence of conditions can be found in several Australian locations. The best available now would be in the Cooper Basin if it had access to transmission services.

At Western Australian gas prices, there is a transitional role for gas alongside hydrogen in the direct reduction of iron metal. Using gas for direct reduction of iron oxide in place of coke from coal in blast furnaces is an established technology. About 70 million tonnes of iron is produced globally each year from this technology. Direct reduction using gas reduces emissions to about half of those from a blast furnace. The rest can be reduced proportionately by mixing renewable hydrogen with gas in the reduction feedstock. Up to 70 per cent hydrogen can be used without modification of the equipment. That reduces emissions from blast furnace levels by about five-sixths. With small modifications, the plant can use 100 per cent hydrogen. The transitional role of gas would phase out as the costs of hydrogen came down.

Beyond niche roles including those in power generation with CCS attached to new transmission in the Cooper Basin, and for supply alongside hydrogen of direct reduction iron processing plants, it is unlikely that gas can contribute much to restoration.

Finally, it is my melancholy duty to inform my readers of a contradiction in the Commonwealth government's favouring of carbon capture and storage and opposing carbon pricing. I support public assistance for innovation and the commercial application of carbon capture and storage. This can bring down the cost of applying the technology. But it will not bring the cost of carbon capture and storage down to zero. And if the cost is above zero, it will never be as cheap as venting emissions freely into the atmosphere. Emitters with opportunities to capture and store carbon dioxide will have no incentive to do so, no matter how low the cost, without a carbon price or regulatory restrictions on emissions into the atmosphere. Public investment in carbon capture and storage is wasted unless it is followed by carbon pricing or regulation that provides incentives for its use.

Where Australian emissions policy stands now

My book *Superpower* noted that the Australian political discussion of climate change policy had poisoned the well for economically low-cost policies involving carbon pricing. The Commonwealth Coalition government has been reluctant to support any development explicitly to mitigate climate change, beyond the budgetary allocation to the Emissions Reduction Fund. Some commitments of the government cut across transition objectives – for example, to support a feasibility study of a new coal-based generator in central Queensland. The government remains committed to the emissions-reduction targets that it took to

Paris, which are the weakest of the developed countries.

Superpower suggested that we could make substantial progress in the climate and energy transition over the term of the parliament elected in 2019 within the policy commitments of the Coalition government. Progress without a carbon price would require increased funding for innovation, extended to low-emissions industry; public underwriting of new long-term electricity retail supply contracts along the lines recommended by the Australian Competition and Consumer Commission (2018, Recommendation 4); offsetting fugitive emissions from the mining and coal sectors by the purchase of credits from the Australian land sector; and facilitating private investment in new transmission, especially by allowing payment for services provided to the regulated system.

The Commonwealth has introduced variations on some of these suggestions. The Minister for Energy's Underwriting New Generation Investments (UNGI) program applies a variation on the theme of the ACCC's Recommendation 4, with the Commonwealth underwriting investment in pumped hydro storage and other technologies to balance intermittent renewable energy. The Low Emissions Technology Roadmap supports five technologies that it expects to play a role in the decarbonisation of the Australian economy. All five technologies in the Commonwealth's Low Emissions Technology Roadmap were identified in *Superpower* as having a role in the zero-carbon future. There is much right and nothing wrong with these technologies. The Australian government's fiscal commitments to the roadmap are minuscule alongside those envisaged by all our developed-country trading partners and China, after adjusting for population and relative economic size. This is anomalous, given the immensely greater scale of opportunity for Australia, and Australia's stake in avoiding dangerous climate change.

The Commonwealth would be wise to adjust its commitments now on its own initiative, before the emerging global pressures force it to do so. Meanwhile the states are leading the way. All states and territories are aligned with the developed countries of the northern hemisphere in committing to zero net emissions by 2050. All have substantial policies and fiscal mechanisms for advancing the transition.

Tasmania already has a near-zero-emissions electricity system based on hydro-electric power. The Tasmanian government is supporting the expansion of intermittent renewable power generation, which is turned into low-cost firm (twenty-four hour) power by judicious use of the hydro-electric capacity for peaking rather than base-load purposes. This will be important in attracting zero-emissions industry to Tasmania, as well as for the transmission of peaking power to the mainland.

South Australia has gone further in the use of solar and wind resources than any other state. It is the most advanced in building the security and reliability of a power system based on low-cost intermittent renewables through support for battery and pumped hydro storage and demand management. The state has made itself a favourable and well-known focus for investment in a wide range of zero-emissions industrial and other economic activities. This, in combination with the availability in the Upper Spencer Gulf of a rich combination of solar, wind and pumped hydro-electric storage resources, established industrial capacities and adjacent mineral resources, allows South Australia to move more quickly than others on new zero-emissions energy-intensive industrial development. The South Australian Climate Change Action Plan, released in December 2020, consolidates the state's leading position.

The ACT is a long way towards zero net emissions and has policies to get further. In many ways, it has the easiest task, and has used its advantages effectively.

The Northern Territory has immense opportunity for solar. It would be surprising if this was not matched by some high-quality wind resources. It has considerable although underdeveloped mineral resources for local processing. The proximity of its main industrial centres to Asian markets is an advantage. A rich endowment of natural gas has focused attention on low- rather than zero-emissions paths to economic development. The Territory hosts the immense Sun Cable Australia–ASEAN Power Link project, designed to export electricity from solar and battery capacity. Progress on this project would focus attention on the economically stronger case for local processing of mineral ores and concentrates.

Western Australia is home to a high proportion – possibly a majority – of Australian superpower opportunity. It has immense quantities of excellent wind, solar and biomass resources and mineral ores for processing. It has done well as a mining state, in which business and government focus strongly on access to and extraction of resources. New mindsets are required for success in using the state's incomparable advantages in minerals processing.

The three eastern states have to live with the legacy of large industries built on coal and gas. All have excellent potential for pumped hydro storage near industrial centres, using the elevation of the Great Dividing Range. All have strong government commitments to the transition.

Victoria and Queensland have made good progress in providing incentives to expand renewables generation along the way to meeting strong renewable energy targets. Both face formidable transmission constraints in bringing low-cost renewable energy to major industrial centres.

Queensland has used a new state corporation, CleanCo, to bring the state balance sheet to account in reducing the cost of renewables and storage capacity. Gladstone, in central Queensland, has the natural capacities, including a world-class port, the location in relation to inland renewable resources, the established infrastructure and the industrial history to emerge as a major global industrial centre based on renewable energy. Townsville has advantages after the strengthening of transmission links to renewable resources to the west and southwest.

Victoria's special advantages relate to its history as an industrial and commercial state, with well-developed capacities for business innovation and response to complex new opportunities. The transmission network built around established power generation centres gives the Latrobe Valley access to renewable energy and storage capacity across the state, and local biomass resources of exceptional quality, together with advanced industrial skills and traditions. Portland, in the southwest, has industrial capacity built around the long-distance transmission line from the Latrobe Valley. The Portland transmission infrastructure has greater economic logic and value in the zero-carbon world economy than in the fossil energy economy for which it was built. Portland is located among world-class wind and biomass resources and not far from excellent solar resources inland.

New South Wales's industrial cities of Newcastle and Port Kembla have the energy and port infrastructure and the industrial skills and traditions to become major centres for zero-emissions industry. New South Wales has recently gone further than other states in articulating and legislating a set of policies that can accelerate emergence of globally competitive manufacturing industry. These have emerged explicitly from a vision of Australia as an energy superpower of the low-carbon world economy.[4] New South Wales is developing the financial model that can underpin emergence of the superpower, and which other states can emulate to secure their share of emerging opportunity.

The states are doing much and can do more on their own. There are large gains for Australia if the Commonwealth puts its fiscal strength behind the states and their ambitions to build new export industries from their renewable energy endowments. This would fit easily into the Commonwealth post-pandemic economic strategy.

I said in *Superpower* that the Commonwealth could make a good start towards using the low-carbon opportunity without violating its electoral commitment not to introduce carbon pricing. With all the developed countries committed to zero emissions by 2050 and Europe and the United States proposing to introduce border taxes for high-emissions imports, there would be large economic gains for Australia entering the European carbon pricing scheme at an early date. Earlier election statements from the Coalition that they would not introduce carbon pricing need not be the last word. At the 1996 election, John Howard promised 'never ever' to introduce a GST. He then won the 1998 election promising to introduce a GST. He was able to explain to the electorate the advantages of taking this step. The Coalition could choose to use the next election to change its stance on carbon pricing. This would assist market access in the developed countries for the products on new energy-intensive industrial plants.

Commonwealth policy has moved forward in useful ways through the current parliamentary term. There are large advantages for the restoration of Australia if the Coalition uses the next election to remove constraints on going further. That would help. But the states will go a long way towards using Australia's opportunity. Better with the Commonwealth. But if necessary, alone; if necessary, for years.

10

CARBON IN THE LAND

Australia is exceptionally well endowed with land and sea for absorbing carbon and growing biomass. This follows from our large landmass and long coasts relative to population. The mountain ash forests of Victoria contain the densest carbon stocks in the world. But the opportunities are also large elsewhere, in less productive soils and climates – where much of the land is semi-arid, and of low value for agriculture. Large areas of slow-growing plants add up to large quantities of carbon. Some of the Australian natural heritage is unusually well suited to efficient growth of biomass in dry environments.

Private and public investment in absorption of carbon in the landscape can provide early employment for large numbers of people and also for long-term growth in output and incomes. The high labour-intensity of planting trees made it a major focus of public investment for employment creation in several Australian states and in the United States during the Great Depression. From that time, plantations provided materials for industrial employment for several generations.

Australian farmers and pastoralists are our most inventive, flexible and energetic entrepreneurs. They respond rapidly to new opportunities. They absorb new skills quickly. Investment in absorbing carbon in the landscape can provide a substantial number of the jobs required for full employment by 2025. Investment in the years leading up to this provides the resource base for later expansion of zero-emissions industrial activity.

Although the current policy framework is inimical, the policy innovation required to make a start is straightforward and relatively uncontroversial and could be put in place quickly. Most of it could be introduced without breaching explicit electoral commitments of the current Commonwealth government. However, full utilisation of the opportunity requires participation in a global market for carbon. This could be achieved more reliably with Australian land-sector participation in domestic carbon-pricing arrangements which impose mandatory requirements on major emitters to purchase carbon offsets.

Growing awareness of the landscape carbon opportunity

Awareness of Australia's potential for growing and sequestering carbon in land and sea has grown considerably over the last few years from small beginnings. Knowledge of the advantages of soil carbon and richer vegetation for land productivity has increased, alongside interest in restorative agricultural and pastoral practices and systems. The development of deeper voluntary and mandatory carbon markets in Europe and North America and the business search for carbon offsets to achieve zero-emissions commitments have driven Australian entrepreneurial interest in new sources of farm value. There is early recognition in rural and provincial Australia of the potential for new industrial activities based on low-cost renewable energy and biomass. Rural Australia is ready for the rapid expansion of investment in carbon in the landscape.

The new awareness has several origins. One is recognition that declining land productivity on many farms and stations is due to degradation of soils and plant stocks. Australians have contributed to expanding global interest in restorative farming and land management. Books by Charles Massy, David Pollock and others have become bestsellers and spread the word of new approaches.[1] Australian farm and rural communities have observed the undeniable reality of warming and changing patterns of rainfall and their effects on crops and pastures, and have become more concerned about containment of disruption from climate change. This concern has been reinforced by consumers in developed countries becoming much more interested in the carbon-intensity of the supply chains for food and other rural produce. And active interest from corporations in the northern hemisphere seeking carbon neutrality and traders in purchasing legitimate carbon credits has spurred commercial interest in adding carbon value to other agricultural revenue streams.

More and more farmers and rural residents are discussing climate change, its effects and its mitigation. Common early perceptions that city elites were exaggerating the importance of the issue or promoting a falsehood have given way to increasing recognition of rural Australia's interest in containing the problem and benefiting from participation in the solution. The National Farmers' Federation in August 2020 announced support for zero net emissions by 2050. In early 2020, Meat and Livestock Australia set the objective of zero net emissions for its producers by 2030, and said that it was an achievable goal. It will do this by applying recent advances in biological knowledge of digestion in ruminant animals to reduce methane emissions (food additives, including char and some kinds of seaweed); genetic improvement; shorter life cycles of animals for meat; and managing land to increase carbon in soils and plants. Methane is a short-life gas, so zero net emissions are achieved with sustained falls even if absolute annual emissions remain above zero.

Absorption of carbon in soils was one of the Low Emissions Technology Roadmap's five priority technologies. The roadmap saw sequestration potential of 35 to 90 million tonnes per annum of carbon dioxide. It said that low-cost measurement technologies would unlock commercial potential. It set a goal of bringing costs down to $3 per hectare. These were sound perspectives and objectives, but conservative in relation to sequestration quantities.

How land carbon and biomass work for zero and negative emissions
There are two main ways in which plants contribute to net zero emissions. One is by increasing the amount of carbon in soils and plants. The basic arithmetic tells us that the amount of carbon held in soils (about 1500 gigatonnes in the top two metres but falling with modern economic development) and living things (about 500 gigatonnes and falling) is two and a half times as large as that held in the atmosphere (about 820 gigatonnes and rising). It follows that an increase in the percentage of carbon in soils and plants can have a disproportionate effect in reducing the amount of carbon in the atmosphere.

A major 2017 study from the US National Academy of Sciences[2] highlighted what it calls 'Natural Climate Solutions'. These can provide one-third of the cost-effective climate mitigation needed between now and 2030 to stabilise temperature increases below 2°C, and one-fifth of the required reductions between now and 2050. Absorption of carbon in the landscape will be essential to correct any overshooting of emissions beyond the Paris goals.

Managing land to increase carbon in soils can also retain water and enhance productivity. Small increments of carbon in plants and soils over large areas add up to significant amounts, so there is great potential in the dry rangelands. Native Australian plants, including saltbush, Mitchell grass and mallee, provide exceptional opportunity for adding carbon to the land and soils while providing materials for industrial use or feed for farm animals.

Mangrove forests store carbon for longer than terrestrial forests, and revegetation of such ecosystems can provide up to four times as much carbon per hectare as rainforests. Increase of carbon stored in native vegetation provide landscape carbon sinks. Change in land and farm management can store additional carbon and reduce emissions while increasing the value of farm and station production.

A second contribution to net zero emissions is the harvesting of biomass in a way that does not diminish the landscape carbon stock, and using the material to replace fossil hydrocarbon or carbonate for construction, energy, industrial processes and transport. New biomass can do everything in the economy that fossil carbon and transformed carbonate do: produce heat; power electricity generators; fuel cars, boats, planes and trains; supply the hydrocarbon or other carbon base for making plastics and other petrochemical manufactures; provide the material for buildings. But not all at once. New biomass cannot be grown and harvested sustainably at the rate at which the modern industrial economy is drawing down stocks of fossil carbon. We are now drawing down those fossil carbon stocks at an incomparably faster rate than they were created by natural forces hundreds of millions of years ago.

Fortunately, we now have access to relatively low-cost alternatives for many uses of fossil carbon that do not require biomass: renewable energy, replacing fossil carbon in electricity generation, land transport and many industrial processes (including the reduction of iron ore into iron metal). This allows us to reserve biomass for those processes in which there are no low-cost alternative paths to zero emissions. We can expect biomass to be increasingly scarce and valuable as the world moves to zero net emissions, and for it to be reserved by its high price for those uses for which there are no low-cost alternatives.

Technologies for negative emissions

The most promising opportunities for large-scale negative emissions are in the land sector. We have discussed the increase in carbon stocks in soils and living plants. Three others warrant special attention.

Pyrolysis can be used to convert biomass into a combination of pure carbon, or char, and a liquid or gaseous hydrocarbon. Both the char and the hydrocarbon can be sources of energy and other industrial inputs. Char is a valuable addition to the productivity of land, supporting moisture retention and in other ways contributing to greater farm output. If part or all of the char is returned to the soil, it can hold the carbon out of the atmosphere over a long period – hundreds and thousands of years. While in the soil, it attracts biota that are instrumental in augmenting the soil carbon. As a supplement to feed for ruminant animals (cattle and sheep), it leads to more complete digestion of food, greater conversion of food into meat, milk or wool, and reduced methane emissions. Passed through into animal manure that is deposited on the ground, the carbon is retained in the soil.

Accumulation of carbon in soils through the spread of char is potentially a large and continuing source of negative emissions. The sequestration capacity of char is being accepted in global voluntary and some compliance carbon markets. It is legitimate sequestration, and can be expected to become more important in carbon trading systems.

The incomplete digestion of feed by sheep and cattle and its emission as methane is the major source of greenhouse gases from Australian agriculture. Research over the past decade has established that not only char from pyrolysis but also seaweeds and algae can reduce methane emissions from cattle and sheep while increasing commercial production. For example, research in South Australia demonstrates that the native seaweed *Asparagopsis* yields much more per hectare than any land-based crops. When added to feed for cattle and sheep, it can reduce methane emissions by around 90 per cent – converting methane into valuable animal protein.

A second possibility for negative emissions is harvesting biomass in a sustainable way, using it in place of fossil carbon for energy and industry, and then capturing and permanently sequestering the carbon dioxide emissions from its combustion. Geological sequestration is technically feasible, but expensive at the current state of knowledge. It will be important only in favourable locations, where good sites for industrial use of biomass are close to suitable geological sites. When use of bioenergy in industrial processes occurs in the same place as the production of hydrogen through electrolysis, the large amounts of oxygen waste (eight times the mass of the hydrogen produced) can be used for combustion of the bio-oil or biogas. This produces a pure carbon-dioxide exhaust stream that is already captured and ready for geological storage. This is potentially a low-cost source of negative emissions given the presence of suitable sites nearby.

A third option for negative emissions is the use of timber in long-lived construction. Technological improvement is widening the range and extending the life of timber-based alternatives to cement in construction. Cement emits about 8 per cent of global carbon emissions. Alternatives involve low-emissions cement, glue-laminated timber (GLT) and cross-laminated timber (CLT). Several areas in our country – including the southeast of South Australia, Gippsland and the southwest of Victoria, the southwest of Western Australia, areas adjacent to the eastern slopes of the Great Divide along the east coast, and parts of Tasmania – are well placed as hubs for plantation timber production.

Rewarding landowners for carbon sequestration

Utilisation of Australia's rich potential for sequestering carbon in the landscape requires access to carbon markets. That is much more straightforward if Australia itself has a carbon market, with landscape carbon being accepted as an item of trade. That has been ruled out politically for the time being. If it was reinstated, rural Australia would have a large new source of income.

How can we get moving pending the integration of Australia into official international carbon markets? The federal government's Clean

Energy Future package, which introduced carbon pricing from 1 July 2012, established the Carbon Farming Initiative. This allowed carbon credits certified by the Clean Energy Regulator to be offset against liabilities for emissions within sectors covered by carbon pricing. Within the rules, there was unlimited opportunity to sell credits at the Australian carbon price – initially fixed at $23 per tonne of carbon dioxide, but to be integrated into the European carbon trading system and therefore to attract a European price from mid-2015 (later mid-2014).

The Climate Solutions Fund, administered by the Commonwealth's Clean Energy Regulator, survives from the period of Australian carbon pricing. The regulator has defined acceptable approaches to carbon sequestration which could be awarded carbon credits – or Australian Carbon Credit Units (ACCUs). The Clean Energy Regulator is seen internationally as a credible agency for certifying carbon credits. That supports the trade of ACCUs in international voluntary markets, which are becoming deeper as more and more major corporations seek to establish that they are 'carbon-neutral'.

In Australia, the market for ACCUs has been the Emissions Reduction Fund, introduced after the abolition of carbon pricing in 2014. This is funded through the Commonwealth budget, with an initial allocation of $2.5 billion. The Clean Energy Regulator periodically runs auctions to purchase ACCUs from the lowest bidder. The regulator enters into contracts to purchase credits for up to ten years. A secondary market in ACCUs developed around the periodic auctions. Ten years is less than half the period over which carbon stocks are accumulated from the planting of trees.

The initial budgetary allocation was close to exhaustion in late 2020. The government announced in early 2019 that it would be augmented by an additional allocation of $2 billion over ten years. The Emissions Reduction Fund was renamed the Climate Solutions Fund. Its scope has been extended to cover many low-emissions industries and geological carbon capture and storage, so the additional funding has to be spread more thinly. It will not be possible to continue even the limited amount of land carbon purchases that have been possible over the past half-dozen years unless vast new revenue sources become available.

To unlock more of the carbon sequestration potential of the Australian landscape, farmers must be able to sell all that they produce, and not rely on success at periodic auctions. A first step could be to bring forward access to the new budget allocation. The $2 billion could be made available to all who meet the Clean Energy Regulator's eligibility criteria, rather than being released periodically over a decade as currently envisaged. That would keep things moving for a while.

What would keep the market going after that? Expanding the budgetary resources of the Climate Solutions Fund would be a reasonable use of post-pandemic economic stimulus. However, it is unrealistic to think that expansion of the budget allocation would meet anything like the potential demand. The Climate Solutions Fund contains provision for major emitters of greenhouse gases to hold emissions below a defined baseline. Emissions above this baseline are to be acquitted by surrender of ACCUs. This adds a small amount to demand for Australian carbon credits. It would have been larger – and may yet be much larger – were it not for undemanding baselines and a loose approach to enforcement of obligations. The review in 2020 by a committee chaired by Grant King for the Commonwealth government recommended changes that could increase demand for ACCUs, although it would also increase supply by allowing sale of credits by companies reducing emissions below their baselines. It is open to the Commonwealth government to interpret these recommendations in ways that unambiguously increase demand for ACCUs.

I suggested in *Superpower* that the Commonwealth – or the states, if the Commonwealth did not wish to lead – could require fugitive emissions from coalmining and natural gas production to be offset by the surrender of ACCUs purchased from the Australian land sector. Some producers have chosen to reduce emissions from their own operations to zero by specified dates, and all are under pressure to do so from investors and many from purchasers of their products. Some purchase offsets against at least some of their emissions. They would face no extra costs from mandatory requirements, and would not face competition on an uneven playing field from competitors that had chosen not to commit to zero emissions. I suggested phasing in the obligation over a decade to ease the adjustment burden on producers. By the end of that time, the producers would be carbon-neutral in their Australian operations. Some sources of fugitive emissions would choose carbon neutrality by an earlier date. That would be supported by many shareholders. It may become a requirement for entry into many markets before 2030. Fugitive emissions in Australia are growing more rapidly than any others, and now rank among the largest sources of emissions. Requirements to offset emissions would provide a large boost to carbon farming.

Ultimately, the solution is to join the large carbon markets that have emerged in other developed countries and which will expand rapidly under pressure from the Biden administration in the United States. The European market is now generating a carbon price around A$40 per tonne of carbon dioxide equivalent. This is similar to the US Department of Energy's central estimate of the social cost of carbon before the Trump ban on its calculation. It is similar to my estimate in 2008 of the cost of carbon in a world seeking to hold temperature increases below 2°C. At this price, the Commonwealth roadmap's 35 to 90 million tonnes would represent a new rural industry worth $1.5 billion to $4 billion per annum for soil carbon alone. I myself think that with a $40 price for carbon, soil carbon sequestration would comfortably exceed 90 million tonnes per annum by the mid-2020s. Other landscape carbon – the accretion of carbon in plants – could be as much again. As acknowledged in the Commonwealth's roadmap, large additional rural income could be achieved while increasing the value of traditional income streams.

Export of carbon credits

There will be no large-scale carbon trading in Australia for the foreseeable future. That well of sweet water has been poisoned by the political history and it will take time for the toxins to dissipate to non-fatal concentrations.

Australia will come under great pressure to do more on climate change mitigation as our trading partners accelerate their own efforts. The costs of staying outside the new global effort will be high. It may be acceptable to accelerate our own progress in ways that do not involve carbon pricing, and to establish our credibility on climate change in the post-Trump world by showing that we are making progress towards targets that are in line with those of the European Union, the UK, Japan, South Korea and Biden's United States. That may open a path to other countries' carbon markets without Australia having a carbon market itself. But once we are doing all of that, the political penny may drop: that we would be better off economically if carbon pricing were part of the mix.

To prepare for expansion of economically rewarding carbon farming, including through making the best use of voluntary markets and requirements for some emitters to purchase offsets, we should make two changes to the rules for accrediting ACCUs. They would make a great deal of difference. The second depends on the first.

The roadmap focuses usefully on the first: developing reliable low-cost means of measuring carbon in the landscape. The technological effort should go beyond the soil carbon discussed by the roadmap and encompass carbon in plants. Current measurement costs are prohibitive for producers seeking to sell small amounts of carbon sequestration. We need, first of all, a major Commonwealth commitment to research on low-cost, reliable measurement of carbon in soils and plants. The soil component is supported in the 2020 roadmap: the government has got this right as far as it goes. Low-cost measurement of carbon in plants is also required. We need innovation in the way we measure things: for example, remote sensing from drones or satellites. Research on this and other means of reducing measurement costs is being conducted at the University of Melbourne, the CSIRO and elsewhere. The technologies are available. What is required is their verification alongside traditional approaches to measurement, and commercialisation. Now that the Commonwealth government has made this a priority, success is not far away.

The second change is to introduce what I call comprehensive carbon accounting. Owners of land would register for a carbon pricing scheme and be rewarded for all accretion and penalised for all depletion of carbon above and below the surface. Participation would be voluntary. Comprehensive carbon accounting will allow land owners (and people with property rights over biomass in parts of the sea) to opt in to carbon-pricing arrangements. A decision to opt in would be irrevocable, with contingent revenues and liabilities being attached legally to the land title. Participants could deliver an unlimited number of ACCUs to the market at an announced price. Later, the price could be set in a market. This opens immense economic potential by placing autonomy of carbon management in the hands of private landowners, and encouraging innovation and diversification.

This contrasts with current approaches, in which accretion of carbon is rewarded only if it can be demonstrated to have occurred within one of a range of specified ways ('methodologies'). There is no current mechanism applied by the Clean Energy Regulator for continuing calculation of carbon stocks, nor reward for accretion or penalisation of depletion. Comprehensive carbon accounting should be introduced now, based on established approaches to measurement. Its use will grow with the expansion of access to remunerative carbon markets.

The tortured political history of the Climate Solutions Fund has served us ill. The low prices generated, the uncertainty about success at auction, the high transaction costs, and the limitations on the size of the market have been deeply discouraging for Australian farmers. Early removal of barriers to the expansion of carbon in the Australian landscape would make a major contribution to the restoration of Australia.

Planting a secure future

Investment in plants to sequester carbon, in reforestation or plantations, takes many decades to generate high value – and may take decades to generate any value at all – from traditional markets for trees. Such investments are favoured by zero and low real interest rates. It is a good time to make major long-lived investments. Of all capital expenditure, the most labour-intensive is planting trees. Such investment is ideally suited to job creation in recession.

We have already discussed how the real cost of riskless long-term capital is now the lowest it has ever been for sovereign investors in developed countries. However, the cost of capital has not fallen correspondingly for private investors. This partly reflects irrational responses to the increasing abundance and falling value of capital, as investors retain high expectations for return on investment that were formed in different conditions. To some extent it reflects increased premiums for risk since the Global Financial Crisis, especially for small and medium-sized firms that are most likely to be active in innovation. Risk premiums have increased again for long-term private investment in the uncertain post-pandemic economic conditions.

If investors are certain that government policy will support the emergence of a low-carbon national economy participating in a low-carbon world economy, they will have confidence that future prices of carbon and biomass will be high and tending to rise until zero net global emissions have been achieved. A government that is committed to playing its full part in a global climate change mitigation effort has that confidence. However, a private investor must take account of sovereign risk. Discounting of future sources of income for sovereign risk is especially high in matters related to forestry and carbon, where past changes in policy have been frequent and large.

For all of these reasons, a government committed to a goal of zero emissions values future income from long-term investment in carbon sequestration in the landscape and biomass for industry much more highly than private investors. Indeed, private firms are unlikely to invest in expanding these areas. This is the historical experience. Almost all past Australian investment in plantations has been made by governments or directly encouraged by large subsidies – or by anticipation of, and briefly the reality of, a carbon price. The differential between public and private assessment of the value of plantation investment is larger now than ever. This makes government the logical investor in or underwriter of long-term carbon sequestration and production of biomass.

Should the Commonwealth or states be the investor or underwriter? There is a case for either or both. The Commonwealth has entered this field for renewable energy and now some low-emissions industry through the UNGI program, the Clean Energy Finance Corporation and Snowy Hydro. It has entered the field for northern Australian development through the Northern Australian Infrastructure Development Fund. The states benefit from contributions to state carbon sequestration goals and from expansion of local industry and are justified in using their balance sheets for the purpose if the Commonwealth does not.

The overall aim is to increase incentives for investment, in partnership with owners of suitable land, and thereby expand the market.

Biomass for manufacturing

The building of low-emissions manufacturing industries based on biomass raises similar issues to land-based sequestration. However, it will be more challenging because of more complex interaction with trade policies. In the Australian market, grants for innovation can assist early investments in new biomass-based manufacturing industries. Similarly, a Clean Energy Finance Corporation with a wider mandate that allows lending for investment in low-emissions manufacturing can help. In the low-carbon world economy, biomass will replace fossil carbon in manufacture of plastics and petrochemicals and some other industrial uses.

But the most important question is whether low-emissions Australian manufactured products will have access to international markets that favour low-emissions over traditional products. The European Union is committed through the early 2020s to introduce a border tax on imported products that are more carbon-intensive than European products. Producers here would benefit if the European tax system acknowledged Australian products with zero emissions and did not apply duties to them. Goods made with Australian biomass would be exempt from border taxes. But there is a risk that the new arrangements will not be applied with great subtlety, and that Australian products will be excluded on the basis of general judgements about Australia's progress in reducing emissions. It is likely that UK climate policies will remain closely aligned with Europe's after formal withdrawal from the European Union. Following the election of President Joe Biden, the United States will follow a similar path to Europe on ambitious emissions reductions and border taxes.

We need to do everything we can to support participation in voluntary and official international carbon markets with rigorous certification. The development of credible methodologies is a precondition for large-scale entry into these markets. We have a strong base in the Australian Clean Energy Regulator.

Other environmental values

In all of this, we should never lose sight of nature's other roles – in life on earth and in our human lives and society. The benefits of biodiversity will not be secured by growth in forests and woodlands that only takes account of carbon value. Forests and woodlands have value for humans whether or not that value is captured in market exchange through sale of carbon and the products of tourism and other industries. Just as failing to consider carbon externalities allows practices to develop that destabilise our climate, so valuing carbon as a commodity runs the risk of depleting other sources of value. In making suggestions for climate mitigation, we should take care to protect the landscape's other values.

Some voluntary markets place a higher value on carbon credits if they are accompanied by certification of biodiversity, catchment protection and other environmental values. Such certification is a role for state agencies with responsibility for protecting environmental services beyond carbon. The Queensland Land Restoration Fund (LRF) provides a model, where co-benefits are rewarded with premiums. Certified contribution to multiple environmental objectives allows a 'Gold Standard' of carbon sequestration units, which trade at a premium in international markets.

A core industry in restoration of rural Australia

Carbon farming to produce carbon credits and biomass for industry could become a major Australian rural industry in the 2020s. The early stage is highly labour-intensive and could contribute a substantial proportion – a sixth or more– of the growth in primary jobs required for full employment by 2025. Success would require development of new systems for measuring and accrediting carbon in the landscape. Prior to Australian rural businesses securing access to deep carbon markets, a significant start could be made through official underwriting of long-term investments in biomass production. The progressive replacement of fossil hydrocarbon feedstocks for petrochemical industries by biomass and the increasing realisation of the need for negative emissions to reach global carbon needs would provide opportunities for growth in Australian living standards for decades after the achievement of full employment in 2025.

11

PROTECTION DEAD-END VERSUS FREE-TRADE HIGHWAY

Recall Albert Camus saying that plagues and wars – and we added recessions – are so common, and yet they always take us by surprise. So stupid that they can't last. And yet they last. This book covers plagues and recessions. This chapter is about the international market opportunity that is necessary for Australian economic success after the pandemic recession. Matters of national security, sovereignty and international political influence affect trade policy and lie behind the tensions in Australia's relations with China that are discussed in this chapter. I leave analysis of these important matters for other times, places and voices.

This chapter explores the links between international trade relations and how we emerge from the pandemic recession.

Pandemic tensions in the global trading system

Earlier chapters demonstrated the importance of expansion in the trade-exposed industries for Australia to achieve full employment and rising standards of living. Australia can only do well if other economies are growing strongly enough to absorb more of the goods and services that we produce. The international trading system has to work in ways that give Australia access to growing markets. That does not happen without effective leadership of an open international economy. If these international conditions are present, Australian goods and services then have to be competitive against supplies from other countries.

Here we focus first on the detail of market access for major Australian industries. Later in the chapter we look at leadership of the international system, and the opportunity for correction of current weaknesses following Biden replacing Trump as US president.

In the several years before the pandemic, there were powerful tendencies towards increased restriction on international movement of goods, services and capital. World trade volumes increased by an average of 4.2 per cent per annum from the formation of the World Trade Organization in 1995 to 2019, a period that covered the Asian and global financial crises.[1] Trade in goods actually fell slightly in 2019.[2]

In the United States, President Trump ran a sustained assault on the rules-based international trading system from 2016 until his departure in January 2021. This provided a congenial environment for an upwelling in protectionism everywhere, including in Australia. The most extreme measures were the US tariffs against China and the Chinese restrictions against imports from Australia.

In the midst of the US–China trade war, the United States and China entered a bilateral trade agreement that had the potential to divert large amounts of Australian rural and energy exports to US suppliers. This was in breach of Article 24 of the General Agreement on Tariffs and Trade, which was absorbed into the WTO on its formation. The trade deal was never implemented while Trump was in office.

The tendency to increase restrictions on trade and investment was intensified by the pandemic and the recession.

The restrictions on trade and investment with China have significant implications for the Australian economy. My summary numbers on the economic future under 'The fateful choice in numbers' in

Chapter 3 presume that the restrictions and associated uncertainty about trade and investment conditions stay roughly as they are at this time for a number of years. Things may get worse: Dog Days would then be more damaging, and restoration less fruitful. That strengthens the case for avoiding Dog Days and all their risk for Australian political cohesion and stability as well as material comfort

There does not seem to be any early prospect of the restrictions in the Sino–Australian trade lifting to leave clear air. There are real issues of Australian security to be managed. There are real Chinese responses to Australian initiatives. Australia and China will respond from time to time in ways that are influenced by the shifting dynamics of US politics and international engagement. What might be possible is a narrowing of restriction to the minimum necessary for meeting clearly defined and essential security interests, as analysis and the passing of time causes us to see them. This will make heavy demands on Australian knowledge and analysis. It will take subtle and intense diplomacy. It will require Australians to adjust to the realities of living in a perilous world, in which peace and prosperity, and our effective sovereignty, depend on understanding the world as it is and not as we wish it to be. This is a world that has been inhabited by other countries of modest size alongside great powers since the beginning of the nation state. It is a world that is understood from the history by our Western Pacific neighbours South Korea, Vietnam and Thailand – and by the neighbours of great powers in Europe and Central and North America.

It will be less costly for Australia to find alternative routes to trade expansion in a smoothly functioning multilateral trading system. Second best would be a smoothly functioning and outward-looking Western Pacific trading system. This could emerge from the Regional Comprehensive Economic Partnership (RCEP), in which a majority of Australia's trading interests are located. The most difficult is currently looking too likely for comfort: continued fragmentation of the multilateral trading system into bilateral arrangements in which might is right, and in which Australia's old trade interests in East Asia are carved up among weighty powers, just as the Ottoman Empire was carved up at Versailles. Here, our task is to work with the new Biden administration to rebuild an open multilateral trading system, and with our ASEAN and Northeast Asian neighbours to make the most of the 2020 agreement on RCEP. We come back to these systemic questions later in the chapter.

The special role of trade-exposed industries

We saw in Chapters 4 and 6 that full employment and sustained growth in living standards require high levels of investment and output in the trade-exposed industries.

Investment in domestic industry reaches a limit when the home market has been filled. The market for trade-exposed production is global. Establish a globally competitive plant, and investment and output in that industry can expand immensely. If investment in trade-exposed industries is made in Australia without protection, it is very likely to raise future Australian incomes. Where it succeeds, it can expand almost without limit – subject to Australian producers having access to markets on similar terms to their competitors. In contrast, investment with protection is almost certain to reduce future Australian incomes.

The trade-exposed industries are demanding. They require globally competitive costs of production. They require access to international markets. They are much more demanding of knowledge, world-class risk management and other business performance.

These demands on trade-exposed industries encourage the idea that we should reduce the demands on them. We can make them more like domestic industries, with protection. They will be confined to the small local market, but will then be secure, unbothered by demands on knowledge, world-class performance or risk. Where is the harm in that? After they are established, they can expand investment to supply global markets.

We have seen how that plays out – on Australian and many other stages. The protection of one trade-exposed industry raises the real exchange rate and reduces the competitiveness of others. Growing awareness that profitability depends on government decisions case by case diverts management attention from improving competitiveness in global markets to influencing governments. That shifts the political system away from the search for policies that advance the public interest. Corporate leaders cease to keep abreast of global trends in markets and technologies, as this is no longer centrally important for survival and growth. The endpoint is slower growth in incomes, economic instability and distorted democracy.

Australia's productivity boom was unleashed by the removal of protection in goods, services and capital markets. For two decades from 1983, the volumes of services and manufactured exports increased at compound rates of over 10 per cent per annum. The composition of the exports was highly diverse, as Australian business made its way in a competitive global economy. We were supported by the liberalisation of trade in our natural markets through the Western Pacific region during the 1990s, underpinned by the concept of open regionalism that Australians had developed mainly with colleagues in Indonesia and Japan.[3]

That led into the second decade of Australia's long expansion. Here the opportunity was provided by China's growth and voracious appetite for industrial raw materials and energy. We were well placed to make use of the opportunity, and did so. The resources boom kept Australian incomes rising until the shift in China's growth strategy in 2013.

By spending most of the increase in incomes as it arrived during the resources boom, we raised the Australian real exchange rate excessively and brought the diverse export growth of the productivity boom to an end. That led us into the Dog Days.

In earlier chapters, we have discussed what needs to be done to strengthen competitiveness in general and in the industries of the low-carbon economy in particular. In this chapter, we focus on the market access required for expansion of the trade-exposed industries as we seek post-pandemic restoration. Will economic growth be strong in countries which have economies that are complementary to Australia's and which are geographically located to give Australia advantages in market access? Will these economies be open to increasing international trade? Will Australia have access to these markets on similar terms to other suppliers?

Will global import growth be strong?

Future growth in global international imports depends, of course, on the trajectory of the pandemic. My guess is no better than the Australian Treasury's: that after a horrific northern winter across Europe and North America, by the end of 2021 the pandemic will no longer be hugely disruptive of economic life in the developed countries. Economic life will not return immediately or soon to what it was before the pandemic: cautions will remain about long-distance travel and large concentrations of people. But the health problems that remain are at the margins of the economy, except in some developing countries.

The pandemic and recession will have left a costly legacy in all countries. But for the immediate future, these costs will have disappeared into fiscal and monetary expansion of unprecedented dimension right through the developed world and China. China had already returned to strong growth in the second half of 2020. Massive fiscal expansion – avoiding what are seen as errors of timidity after the GFC – will see strong growth later in 2021 in the United States, Canada, Japan and South Korea. It may not be so strong in the European Union, internally conflicted over fiscal policy, or the UK, battling after Brexit and a bad pandemic. The loss of growth momentum is likely to end up being heavily concentrated in the developing world.[4] These are the immediate prospects. Whether the strong growth in developed countries driven through 2021 into 2022 by fiscal and monetary stimulus is sustained depends on what else is done in policy.

Developing economies expanded after the GFC at average rates not much below those in the eight years leading up to the crisis. This momentum was broken by the pandemic recession. We saw in Chapter 2 that from mid-2020 deaths from COVID-19 were overwhelmingly in the developing countries and Anglo North Atlantic, and Europe joined them in the northern autumn.

The underestimation of COVID-19 deaths is much greater in the developing world. Developing countries have weak public health systems with which to respond to the pandemic. They have fragile financial systems that are vulnerable to flight of capital and downgrading of international investors' appetite for risk. They have shallow fiscal and monetary policy capacity with which to counteract recessionary pressures. The managing director of the International Monetary Fund, Kristalina Georgieva, said in early 2021 that up to that time developed countries had deployed the equivalent of 20 per cent of GDP in fiscal support to offset the effects of the pandemic recession; developing countries had been able to deploy only 2 per cent.[5]

Not all external growth is the same for Australian trade opportunity. The value of a billion dollars of economic growth for Australian trade is greater if it occurs in countries with resource endowments that are closely complementary to Australia. That is first of all China and other densely populated economies of Northeast Asia. Behind them are the countries of South and Southeast Asia, and then Europe – much more complementary to Australia than North America, with its lower population density and richer per capita natural resource endowment. Australia is better able to take advantage of expanding markets if the expansion is located nearby, in Asia. Complementarity and geographic location are the largest influences, but the value is also less if it is in countries that are inside deeply internally integrated regional trading relationships of which we are not part – such as the European Union and the North American Free Trade Agreement.

Australia's current geographic pattern of trade reflects these underlying economic realities and not some policy or strategy deliberately to focus trade and development on China and other countries in Asia. It is economic gravity that causes China to absorb more value in Australian exports than the next nine countries combined – eleven if Hong Kong is included in China rather than the rest of the world. One can stop a massive object falling to earth, but at a cost. This particular object has extraordinary mass and is nearby, and the pull of gravity is correspondingly strong.

It is greatly to Australia's economic advantage that China has recovered early and strongly from the pandemic recession – even if the tensions in relations dull the value that we can build from bilateral trade. Strong Chinese imports hold up prices in regional and global markets for important Australian exports. At the same time, it is an advantage for us that China's neighbours in Northeast Asia have had a good pandemic. It is a problem for us that the more populous countries of Southeast and South Asia have not done so well. Asian developing countries beyond China are major Australian export markets: the Association of Southeast Asian Nations (ASEAN) is more than 50 per cent larger than the EU and the United States combined; India roughly as large as the US or the EU.

Will our trading partners remain open to trade with us?

All countries choose how open to keep their markets, and which markets are kept more open than others. Economic growth is generally stronger in countries that choose free trade; the costs of highly restrictive trade are extremely high. All countries are influenced in these choices by domestic pressures from vested interests. They are influenced as well by perceptions of the risks of heavy reliance on international supplies – including risks to the security of the country against foreigners seeking to take advantage of dependence on trade. All countries restrict some trade on security grounds. The wise take care to define essential security interests and restrict trade only to the extent necessary to protect these interests. If international supplies are judged to be unreliable, all countries retreat from them. All countries are poorer from any country's retreat – most of all smaller economies, economies outside established trading blocs and economies with endowments of resources that are different from those in the world as a whole. Australia loses exceptionally from any retreat from open trade on all counts – and gains exceptionally from all countries relying more heavily on global markets. Our gains and losses are affected most by restrictions that we ourselves impose, and compounded by the restrictions of others. Greater confidence in the reliability of foreign trade leads to increased trade shares in production and expenditure and greater gains from trade for all countries and especially for us.

Major Asian economies' decisions on how heavily to rely on foreign trade are of immense importance to Australian trade opportunity. Acceptance of deep reliance on imports for food and major inputs into industrial production takes time and a congenial international environment. It is richly rewarding when the conditions for confidence in the reliability of trade are met.

As Australia's ambassador to China in the early years of China's reform of Maoist autarky, an important part of my job was to explain to leaders of government and business that international trade was a cost-effective and reliable way for China to secure goods and services that were necessary for development.

Maoist doctrine favoured self-reliance for security reasons. The doctrine had been reinforced by experience. The United States blocked trade with China from the early 1950s into the 1970s and sought to restrict its allies' trade with China. The Menzies government with John McEwen as trade minister resisted restriction in areas where they judged trade with China to be in our national interest. When I presented my credentials to the president in 1985, Li Xiannian said that he greatly appreciated Australia's supply of wheat through the Great Famine of the early 1960s. I responded by noting the consistent support of Australian farmers and their political representatives for trade with China.

From then, the Australian embassy engaged comprehensively with Chinese leaders on how reliance on international markets would improve the chances of China realising its high ambitions for economic development. We focused at first on the advantages to China in moving away from self-reliance in food, steel-making raw materials, and textile fibres.

When interviewed by the Shanghai *World Economic Herald* to mark the fifteenth anniversary of diplomatic relations in December 1987, I was asked whether Chinese leaders could succeed in their ambitions for self-sufficiency in food.

'Yes,' I replied. 'All that is necessary is for the reforms to fail and for the Chinese people to remain poor. But if the reforms succeed, and the Chinese people on the mainland grow rich like their compatriots in Hong Kong and Taiwan, it will not be possible to provide all of the high-quality food that 20 per cent of the world's people want from 7 per cent of the world's good agricultural land.'

My comments were accurately reported in the paper. I was invited to discuss the article over lunch in the Great Hall of the People by Du Runsheng, venerable adviser on agricultural reform to Deng Xiaoping and Zhao Ziyang at the apex of party and state. Du brought along as interpreter a recent graduate in agricultural economics from the University of Chicago, Justin Lin. Lin was later founder of the China Center for Economic Research at Peking University and then World Bank senior vice president and chief economist.

By the mid-1990s, official statements were saying that import of 5 per cent of grain consumption was acceptable. That was more than the Australian wheat crop in a good year. China's imports of food are now so large that, by the account of a former US national security adviser, Trump believed that China buying more or less would influence the outcome of elections in US Midwest states.

Australia's efforts in persuasion were more emphatically successful with iron, steel and wool than they were with grain. In my last year as ambassador, I said in a lecture at the Wuhan Iron and Steel University in January 1988 that China would get much more value from its steel mills if they used high-quality imported iron ore. China would benefit from importing 100 million tonnes per annum of high-quality iron ore by the end of the century. A couple of weeks later, Premier Li Peng in Beijing was quoted by Xinhua: 'Some foreigners say that China will import a hundred million tonnes of iron ore by the end of the century, but they don't understand the Chinese situation.' In 2019, China accounted for most of the world's imports of iron ore: 1009 million tonnes, with almost two-thirds coming from Australia.

On wool, we explained that imports of fine fibre would enable China to produce high-quality fabrics for export markets, and for an increasingly prosperous and demanding domestic population. From small levels, then, China came to buy three-quarters of the Australian wool clip, much of it for local consumption.

Leaders of the Chinese metallurgy industry eventually became comfortable about our iron-ore story, but cautioned against pushing steel-making coal. That was a bridge too far. Autarkical attitudes were too deeply established, the security argument too deeply entrenched. China had plenty of metallurgical and thermal coal, even if not all was as high-quality as the best Australian. We persisted anyway. In 2018, before the recent deterioration in Sino–Australian relations, China was Australia's largest market for coal.

China became more and more confident in reliance on international markets in the quarter century after 1992. Its confidence was enhanced by entry into the WTO in 2001, itself an outcome of long-term Sino–Australian cooperation. Australian exports of high-value food have been greatly enhanced by Chinese implementation of the bilateral free trade agreement. China's own objectives in the FTA were heavily weighted towards access for Chinese investment in Australia. The twenty-first-century shift in the Western Pacific away from multilateral trade liberalisation to bilateral so-called free trade agreements was generally a setback for opening markets to international trade.[6] The China free trade agreement is one in which gains were initially large. This all went into reverse at high speed through 2019 and 2020.

Where does Chinese trade policy go now? Over recent years the trade wars with Trump's United States and increasingly common protectionist reaction to rising Chinese exports elsewhere raised questions in China about the feasibility of maintaining the earlier rate of trade expansion. China's thirteenth five-year plan looked forward to increasing the services share in production and expenditure, which would have a smaller foreign trade component. All of these forces and President Xi Jinping's nationalist proclivities were in the direction of less reliance on export markets for future growth. Slower export growth would mean slower import growth as well.

Nevertheless, China's total imports of goods increased through the early years of the Trump presidency, by over a third from 2016 to 2018. They fell by a few per cent in 2019 in the midst of the trade wars. Chinese trade with the United States and Australia was subject to increasing policy restriction through 2019 and 2020, but not China's imports from the rest of the world. Total imports fell sharply during the pandemic shutdown in the first half of 2020 but have lifted strongly to above pre-pandemic levels since then.

If China is closing its markets against us, it is much better for

Australia that China maintains imports from the world as a whole. Strong Chinese import demand holds up global prices and therefore prices for Australian products in third markets. There would be larger gains from direct sales to China, but we still benefit from Chinese imports from the rest of the world.

China's response to the US trade war has included increased focus on other partners in Eurasia and elsewhere. European trade relationships have been strengthened by the investment agreement signed late in 2020. China and Japan have intensified high-level communications. Annual trilateral meetings of Chinese, Japanese and Korean heads of government continue, most recently on Christmas Eve 2020. Chinese diplomacy with a large element of trade has been active in Indonesia and elsewhere in Southeast Asia.

It is likely that we will see continued growth in China's total exports and imports during the 2020s, but at a lower rate than in the 2010s, and with a continuing fall in the trade share of Chinese GDP. Slower import growth in a larger economy will leave China contributing a high proportion of world import growth during this period.

Seen as a single entity, ASEAN is Australia's largest export market after China. There is no strong tendency towards changing trade policy in ASEAN after the pandemic recession, ASEAN is at the heart of the new Regional Comprehensive Economic Partnership (RCEP) grouping, which includes Australia, New Zealand, China, Japan and South Korea in addition to the ten Southeast Asian countries. RCEP is built around an ASEAN conception of open regionalism. RCEP may be helpful to keeping East Asian markets open on a non-discriminatory basis. ASEAN and its members will remain deeply and increasingly engaged economically with China. It is crucial that Australia is also deeply and increasingly engaged with Indonesia and ASEAN. Australia will have to invest more in understanding and treating with respect Indonesian values and strategic perspectives. Deep integration with

ASEAN, with close and productive relations with Indonesia in particular, allows Australia to avoid isolation from Asia during a period of tensions with China. Engagement in the ASEAN-centred RCEP is the most promising opportunity for Australia to hold on to large gains from direct trade with China through the current disruption of the bilateral relationship.

Japan (our second-largest export market if ASEAN members are viewed separately) and South Korea (third-largest) remain reliable open economies in sectors important to Australia. There is no reason to expect significant change, except in the area of access to low-carbon industrial imports. Both are committed to zero emissions by 2050. Neither has large domestic renewable energy resources. Both will need to import large amounts of zero-emissions energy and energy-intensive metals and other products as well as land-based carbon sequestration credits if they are to meet their climate commitments. Both have indicated an intention to do so. Imports of zero-emissions hydrogen in liquid form or embodied in ammonia or other hydrogen carriers are the focus of early attention. Japan has commissioned a ship for transporting hydrogen from Australia. The economics argue more strongly for imports of energy-intensive industrial products than for hydrogen itself, as discussed in Chapter 9. Established trading arrangements can support the new trade in zero-carbon energy and industrial inputs.

India has been the focus of periodic strong Australian trade policy attention for three and a half decades. Indian protectionism has deep roots in the political economy and has been resistant to efforts to loosen it. Prime Minister Hawke had a close personal relationship with Prime Minister Rajiv Ghandi and invested effort in enriching the content of Australia's economic relationship with India. In my October 1989 report to the Australian prime minister and foreign minister, 'Australia and the Northeast Asia Ascendancy', I wrote: 'The strong conclusions drawn in the Report about the implications of sustained Chinese economic growth for trade in foodstuffs and raw materials would hold in similar form at lesser degree should sustained rapid economic growth become entrenched in India.'[7]

My friend and sometime colleague Jagdish Bhagwati, professor of economics at Columbia University in New York, America's leading analyst of international trade policy, advised against expecting much from Indian policy reform. His first job after graduating with a PhD in economics from the Massachusetts Institute of Technology had been in the Indian Planning Commission. He thought the Indian commitment to inward-looking approaches to economic development too strong to allow the sustained rapid economic growth we had seen in one country after another in East Asia. Jagdish came up to an empty seat beside me on a flight from London to New York in late 1991. He was returning after several months in New Delhi with the new finance minister (later prime minister) Manmohan Singh. 'Forget everything I have said to you about the impossibility of Indian reform and development,' Jagdish said. 'I think it might be happening.' He then laid out in fascinating detail the Indian government's program in response to the macroeconomic crisis of 1991. On my return to Canberra, I made the case to education minister Kim Beazley for the Commonwealth contributing to a new South Asian Research Centre in the Economics Division of the precursor to the Crawford School at The Australian National University. With substantial contributions from the university, the Australian and Indian business sectors and the Commonwealth of Australia, we set out to build an institutional and intellectual foundation for engagement with the reforms in India, as we had done at other times in Indonesia, Thailand, the Philippines, Papua New Guinea and China, and in different ways with Japan. The research and related work from that time lifted Australian scholarly and public policy interaction in economics with India. There was early progress on the Singh reforms. Trade increased more rapidly than output, and economic growth lifted above the famed 'Hindu rate of growth'. But India's own protectionist gravity pulled the Singh liberalisation back to earth.

In the twenty-first century, India has put effort into and then stood out against liberalisation within the Doha round of trade negotiations, a bilateral free trade agreement with Australia and participation in RCEP. It is worth continued effort. And in any case India is already a significant market for Australian exports – as big as the United States and almost a tenth the size of the huge Chinese market. It is a substantial market for coal at a time when the largest established markets in Northeast Asia are closing – although our coal sales are now being challenged by the rapid growth of renewable energy in India and the availability of abundant coal supplies from adjacent Indonesia. Development of close economic relations warrants all the effort that we can give it. But only undisciplined hope would lead us to expect that expanded trade with India would play a major part in the restoration of Australia in the 2020s.

The main prospects for expanded exports to the EU derive from the continent's commitment to zero carbon emissions by 2050. Europe's mediocre renewable energy resources relative to economic size are complementary with Australia's abundance of zero-emissions energy resources, minerals requiring energy for processing, and opportunities for growing and storing carbon in the landscape. The Community and Germany and France within it are promoting rapid decarbonisation of industry and allocating large public grants and loans to its acceleration. Of special importance to Australia is their interest in hydrogen. European governments and business leaders see Australia as a potential source. Importing zero-emissions iron metal from Australia is not yet on the radar of governments, but it is in the minds of steel businesses. This would allow international movement of hydrogen embedded in metal at much lower cost than movement of hydrogen itself.

Australia is seeking a free trade agreement with the EU. That would be more fruitful if we had an emissions-reduction target in line with Europe's own: net zero by 2050, and interim targets that represent credible progress towards the destination. (The EU's 2030 target is minus 55 per cent on 1990 levels.) The European Union and its most influential member governments will be demanding on compliance. They see the Australian Clean Energy Regulator as a credible institution for accreditation of carbon units, which makes the CER a valuable Australian asset. Australian participation in the European Emissions Trading Scheme alongside a new Europe–Australia free trade agreement would have large economic benefits for Australia. Australia would emerge as a large exporter of carbon credits. This would underpin the development of a major new industry in rural Australia. If such new arrangements on trade and carbon emissions were established early between Australia and Europe, Australia would emerge naturally through competitive processes as the source of zero emissions iron and of some other metals for European industry. If Australia chose not to have its own ETS linked to Europe, it would be harder, but there would be other bases for trade on which we could seek agreement with the EU. Australia could trade carbon credits through a government window. Private firms could export zero emissions products to Europe on the basis of certification from the Clean Energy Regulator.

The UK may expand imports from non-European sources despite a weak post-pandemic economy as trade arrangements are restructured after Brexit. Like the EU, it provides opportunities for trade in zero emissions industrial inputs and carbon credits alongside a new free trade agreement with Australia. As with Europe, success will require credible commitment to zero emissions by 2050.

The US under President Biden is likely to be a steadier participant in international trade and a supporter of the WTO. The Democrat Congress is unlikely to support substantial early trade liberalisation. Since early in the twenty-first century, Australian governments have invested a great deal of political and diplomatic capital in trying to expand the economic relationship with the US. The US–Australia free trade agreement came into effect at the beginning of 2005 amid expectations from government (but not from independent analysts) that it would greatly expand Australian gains from trade. The US is proportionately a smaller export market for Australia now than then. There is no large opportunity for expansion of traditional trade. The Biden administration, like the EU, is likely to introduce strong measures for decarbonisation of the US economy. The US is more richly endowed than the EU with opportunities for zero emissions energy, and also for land sequestration, absolutely and relative to economic size. The US will provide some export opportunities for expansion of post-carbon trade with Australia, but fewer than the EU and probably than the UK. US economic growth in response to massive fiscal and monetary expansion over the year ahead will expand traditional imports in line with the economy.

How much international market access does Australia need?

To support restoration, Australian total exports will have to be much higher in 2030 than they were in 2019, before the pandemic dragged down the value. Exports would need to grow at least as rapidly as the economy to support full employment with rising living standards and a manageable burden of debt – accumulating to an increase more than a third in the volume of exports over the decade. This is daunting; but in the language we have learned from viewing the American election, there is a path to victory. We will have to do a lot of things right, and a lot of things will have to go right. But there is a path.

Let us look at the market opportunities for the main current and prospective goods and services, which will help us to define the path to victory. Let us take as our base 2019–20 exports of about $480 billion, for a minimum target of about $650 billion in 2030 in 2019 prices.

Headwinds in fossil energy and services

We start with some strong headwinds.

Coal, gas and crude petroleum exports contributed over 22 per cent of total exports in 2019–20. There will be a decline in global use of coal and probably no increase in gas over the next decade, as global decarbonisation gains momentum. Within the Indo-Pacific, the decline will be greatest in Japan and South Korea, where Australia has the least troubled access. Unless there is a marked change in the state of the relationship, Australia's share of declining Chinese imports will fall. Slower growth in Indian coal use is likely to be met from domestic supplies. It has been said by senior executives of Bravus (formerly Adani), the company developing the Carmichael mine in central Queensland, that its output will go to India. If the mine is built, and it secures a place in Indian imports, this will be at the expense of established international suppliers in Australia and elsewhere. There may be some growth in Southeast Asian imports. There, Australia's main competitor is Indonesia, which has advantages of proximity and ASEAN relationships. LNG exports may hold at current levels, although continuation of current tensions with China would see contracts going to other suppliers as old ones mature and require the building of new markets elsewhere. A moderate fall in coal exports and holding current levels for gas would be at the higher end of the range of possibilities for Australian exporters.

Services that involve international travel – education and tourism – contributed about 15 per cent of Australian exports in 2019. These were on a strong upward trajectory before the pandemic. They fell sharply with the travel restrictions in 2020. Behavioural responses to the pandemic will keep numbers down for several years, even if success with vaccines leads to the removal of formal travel restrictions. Tourism can be expected to resume growth after several years' hiatus.

Education faces other headwinds: the weakening of the standing of Australian universities from the financial crisis; and tensions in the China relationship. Australia is the third largest supplier of international education services in the world, behind the US and UK – a position out of all proportion to our economic and demographic size. Our major competitors have made the universities a central focus of their recovery programs. President Biden's initial stimulus package to go to the Congress soon after his inauguration provides $US35 billion for strengthening universities after the COVID damage. On a population basis, that is equivalent to about $A3.6 billion to the Australian universities. Australian and American universities are competing for the same pool of international students. Australian universities have been denied access to pandemic emergency support programs.

Australia's attraction for international students is supported by the high global rankings of the major universities. The rankings are way above Australia's population or economic size. The high rankings create an aura of quality around the system as a whole. It is unlikely that the rankings would survive without rethinking public support as part of a restoration fiscal strategy. Australia entered the pandemic with six universities in the Times global top 100, and China with two (four including Hong Kong). This is a major source of Australian prestige and influence among business, official and intellectual elites through Asia. After the pandemic recession passes into history, China may emerge with more top-ranked universities than Australia. The decline in rankings will weaken the attraction of Australian universities to overseas students. It will have the incidental effect of damaging Australia's regional standing and influence, especially in Southeast Asia, at a critical time in systemic competition with China.

The financial crisis of the universities will impose collateral and unintended downsides for other export industries. As an example, I draw attention to just one of many: the weakening of the intellectual support base of the mining and other natural resource-based industries. Mining is not only the source of a majority of our exports of goods. It is the one major industry in which Australian companies are probably the world leaders. We have large exports of high-value mining services and some equipment. International benchmarking shows the geosciences as an area of Australian scientific pre-eminence. Teaching of geosciences has been closed at Newcastle (the world's largest coal exporting region), discussed for closure at Macquarie, being merged into another faculty at Melbourne, and with large cuts in staff numbers elsewhere. Concerns have been expressed that there will be no major offering to undergraduate or graduate students in New South Wales. The high quality of Australian geology graduates contributes to Australia's leading role in global mineral exploration, and has contributed over longer time spans to corporate leadership. Presumably under the government's radar, the financial crisis of Australian universities may see Australia surrender this leading position in the years ahead.[8] The geosciences are not essential only for excellence in the old mining industries, but also for the zero-emissions industries of the future, and for adaptation to the climate change that we will not avoid. I could have taken examples of consequences of the universities' financial crisis from other areas of knowledge that are important to Australian exports of the past and future, including agriculture and forestry.

Demand for international tourist and education services will continue to grow strongly with rising incomes through most of Asia. Tourism is likely to contribute its share of the required export growth after pandemic caution recedes. Education exports are unlikely to do so in the absence of reconstruction of financial support for the universities.

Expanding traditional exports

The international market prospects for other established Australian exports are mixed with greater opportunities if economic development momentum is re-established in the developing countries in South and Southeast Asia.

Chinese import demand for metals is temporarily strong through the Chinese economic recovery. Growth is likely to moderate as recovery programs give way to normal growth. On iron ore, China is now likely gradually to reduce dependence on imports of steel-making materials from Australia, through supporting new mines in other countries, extending or expanding output from higher cost domestic ores and accelerating the development of electric arc steel-making using local scrap. Growth opportunities for Australian metallic mineral ores and concentrates will come from two sources. One is the return to growth in Asian developing countries other than China – not certain, but a worthy focus of Australian support. The other is the growth of global demand for a wide range of metals and other materials resulting from the energy transition – inputs into electric vehicles, batteries, solar panels, wind turbines, electricity transmission cables. Progress towards zero net emissions in the developed countries will underwrite prospects for large investment in these industries to supply markets everywhere. Demand will be strongest if Australia can warrant zero-emissions supply chains – as it is in a good position to do without increasing energy costs for vehicles and plant, explosives (use of renewable ammonia supply chains) and other major inputs. Processing of most of these minerals with zero emissions will be cost-effectively located in Australia, substantially expanding the value of exports. Gold is an important special case; high prices in response to international economic and. political uncertainty are likely to continue to provide opportunities for large expansion in this old Australian industry. In the minerals and metals industries, strong growth in Chinese demand will expand Australian opportunity, even if Australia is excluded from direct access to the Chinese market. Chinese efforts to reduce total import demand are unlikely beyond iron ore.

Metals processing is much less important in Australian exports now than before the resources boom. High energy costs and commitment of owners and users to zero emissions make sharp decline likely in the absence of transition to use of low-cost renewable energy. But there are excellent prospects for maintaining and greatly expanding production if we use the new energy. Movement to efficient use of Australia's renewable energy resources removes both the carbon and the energy cost constraints on expansion of aluminium and a wide range of metals processing. This does not require technological change except in the supply and use of electricity. The potential is large—large enough to fill the fossil energy hole. Do enough to provide a future for established plants, and we build the foundations for major expansion of the industry. No innovations in market access are necessary, but two developments would add momentum to export growth. One would be the securing of access to European, UK, North American, Japanese and South Korean markets for zero-emissions metals as they come to command a price premium over production from carbon-intensive processes. This would come with new free trade agreements with the UK and European Union in which we made satisfactory commitments to reducing domestic emissions. Similar arrangements may be possible in South Korea, Japan and the US. The big prize for the long term would be access to Chinese markets on these terms; that is for the longer-term future when bilateral trade relations have been placed on a different footing. For the time being, obtaining access for green metals to developed country markets on terms that recognise the value of the low carbon would provide large opportunity.

High quality foodstuffs are in strong demand with growing incomes in Asia. China is the market with largest opportunity, but there are large markets in South Korea and Japan, and in Southeast Asia if and when the old development momentum is resumed. While traditional broadacre farming is dependent on weather, some of the new opportunities come from protected agriculture, providing greater security against variable and deteriorating climatic conditions.

For high-value food, direct contact between supplier and retailer is important for valuable outcomes. There would therefore be a rich prize from limiting constraints on Sino–Australian trade to areas that are essential to core security interests. Opportunities in Japan and South Korea would be enhanced by use of zero-emissions supply chains. North American and European markets are supplied from adjacent regions.

Wool is a special case. China has become overwhelmingly the main market for Australian wool, and also the main global centre of wool processing and use. The textile industry in the rest of the world has largely moved to other materials – led by the US shift to synthetics through high tariffs on wool in the early decades after the second world war. There is a risk that wool will be seen in China as an Australian commodity, and measures taken to reduce its use. The mutual interests of Australia and China that have underpinned the growth of the trade since the 1980s are as strong now as ever, and it is in the interests of both countries that the trade continues at its current scale.

Australia has a wide range of valuable services exports beyond education and tourism. They include financial, medical, engineering and general business services. These are highly responsive to Australian competitiveness: during the China resources boom, several of our leading legal firms supplying services to regional markets merged with British firms, and work is done now in London or Australia depending on the real exchange rate.

Like services, we have many manufactured exports from a wide range of mostly small firms. Among much else, a worthwhile number of jobs in the car industry has survived the closure of the plants of the three assembly companies by shifting to export of components.

There is much scope for large expansion of diverse manufactures if Australian competitiveness is strong. For these firms, the corporate tax reform proposed in Chapter 7 stands alongside depreciation of the real exchange rate as a way of improving competitiveness.

The blossoming of services and manufactures exports during the reform era into the early twenty first century 1983–2003 ended as we spent most of the new income from the resources boom as it arrived, driving the real exchange rate higher. Its restoration requires a disciplined focus on competitiveness.

International cooperation

We live in a global economy and society. The solutions to our most consequential problems require international cooperation. Most solutions depend heavily on the United States and China, but not only on them.

Economic growth after the pandemic recession everywhere would be strengthened by concerted fiscal and monetary expansion. Such support was present during and after the Global Financial Crisis. The formation in late 2008 of the G20 as a heads of government forum, with Australia as a member, was an important step. The G20 meeting in Canberra in 2014 was one of its most fruitful.[9] Concerted economic expansion without explicit understandings among states is possible, but less likely for the required duration. This time, the short-term stimulus applied in all developed countries is immense, and probably adequate for the support of immediate recovery in 2021. Concerted policies are important in continuing the stimulus for long enough to achieve full employment in many countries, and to build support for the restoration of conditions for economic growth in developing countries.

The appropriate forum is again the G20. The ad hoc group selected by President Trump in 2020, which excluded authoritarian China and sought to bring authoritarian Russia in from the cold, would not have been appropriate.

Post-pandemic economic development requires an open multilateral trading system. The system around the WTO is imperfect, but it has supported trade expansion and broadly-based economic growth on a global scale. Australia has been one of the largest beneficiaries of its work. Over the past few years, the WTO has been marginalised by US protectionism and crippled by the United States blocking appointments to the dispute-resolution mechanism, the Appellate Body. The tariffs against China, were a breach of the anti-discrimination provision (Article 24) of the GATT and its successor in the WTO. Under President Trump, it seemed that we could only seek to replicate WTO mechanisms in smaller groups, as happened with the establishment of a dispute-settlement mechanism outside the WTO. We now have a chance to support President Biden in rebuilding the multilateral trading system.

The international community found an effective instrument for climate change mitigation with the Paris Agreement in December 2015. Cooperation between the presidents of the United States and China played an essential role in the formulation and early implementation of the agreement. President Xi's address to the UN General Assembly in September 2020, committing China to zero net emissions by 2060, and President Biden's commitment to zero net emissions by 2050 provide the foundations for renewal of Sino–American leadership of the implementation of the Paris commitments.

Restoration of post-Paris momentum would contribute to post-pandemic global economic recovery and development. It would be especially helpful for Australia, assisting the emergence of low-emissions export industries in energy-intensive goods and land carbon credits.

The most immediate post-pandemic international challenge is the stabilisation of developing economies that have been disrupted by disease and its recessionary aftermath.[10] This is a task for which established global institutions, the World Bank and the International Monetary Fund, have capacities and experience. They will need greater funding. They will be more successful if supported by the whole range of regional organisations, and by bilateral donors in their spheres of interest. The new Chinese international development institutions can play large and positive roles. Japan makes large commitments to Asian development and is increasing its contributions. Demands on Australia in its immediate neighbourhood will be heavy. But the sum of the international efforts currently falls well short of the great challenge. A historic rupture of global development is likely, with significant damage to political stability and economic growth everywhere.

Trump's name recurs in discussing contemporary problems of international cooperation. Leadership personalities matter, and the change of president expands what is possible in dealing with global challenges. But personalities are not all that matter. Trump's election four years ago reflects underlying problems that will not go away with a change of leadership in Washington. There is less easy acceptance now than a generation ago, in all developed countries, of deep integration into an international economy. Many people in democratic developed countries are uneasy about increasing international trade, investment and movement of people.

We in Australia are not immune from distrust of globalisation. That distrust will be fuelled by persistent unemployment and the fall in ordinary Australians' incomes if we choose to live in post-pandemic Dog Days.

We can improve the prospects for the most important international cooperation by heeding lessons about what has worked and what has generated the most hostile domestic political reaction in recent decades. Voluntary international cooperation has often produced better results than binding legal agreements. This is true of trade policy. The voluntary cooperation based on the intimate exchange of information within the Asia-Pacific Economic Cooperation in the decade after 1989 saw important progress on trade liberalisation. The formal so-called 'free trade agreements' – bilateral agreements introducing preferential trade – that followed from the beginning of the twenty-first century generally did not.[11] The Regional Comprehensive Economic Partnership agreed in late 2020 embodies elements of APEC's voluntary cooperation, which is an asset in moving forward. The Paris Agreement on climate change, built on concerted independent action, is much more promising than the earlier Kyoto approach purporting to embody legally binding agreements.

The cooperative efforts on APEC, climate change and recovery from the GFC were concerted because many countries were agreeing to move in the same direction at once. The knowledge that others were moving in the same direction made it politically possible for each country to go further. The fact that cooperation did not involve a government binding itself to an international agreement allowed each domestic polity to judge proposals for cooperation on their substantive merits, without being overwhelmed by reaction against foreign forces. In all these cases, concerted unilateral cooperation was built on expansion of trust and knowledge through the exchange of information and analysis: the role of the Pacific Economic Cooperation Council in APEC; of the Intergovernmental Panel on Climate Change in climate change mitigation; and of the Organisation for Economic Co-operation and Development and the International Monetary Fund in cooperation on macroeconomic stabilisation.

Countries that do not wish to be part of the global effort can sit it out for a while, and be encouraged back by the progress others are making.

Concerted unilateral cooperation may allow the international community to make the huge transfers required to stabilise developing economies after the pandemic recession. Each country will be more active in areas of its greatest economic, political and strategic interest: China in the core countries of the Belt and Road Initiative; the European Union in Africa; Australia in the arc across our north. It would be helpful if the United States under a Biden presidency was deeply engaged.

The most challenging international environment

Australia has to build its post-pandemic restoration in the most challenging international environment for three quarters of a century. That greatly increases the difficulty of the task. It increases the importance of getting right everything that is in Australia's own control.

Australia's task was complicated by the Trump administration's retreat from established global arrangements on macroeconomic policy, trade, development, health and climate. The challenge is complicated by Xi Jinping being much more assertive than his predecessors in the projection of hard and soft power on and beyond China's own borders. It is hugely complicated by the tensions between our largest security and trading partners.

Doing everything right within our own control includes being a full and active participant in the new US president's efforts to rebuild the international organisations that have come under stress – the WTO, the WHO and the United Nations Framework Convention on Climate Change.

If we do everything right, there is a path to the large increase in exports that will be necessary to support full employment by 2050 and rising incomes for the rest of the decade. There are large headwinds from the decline of global markets for fossil energy, the financial crisis of the universities, and the restrictions in Australian trade and investment relations with China. These can be outweighed by making good use of the new opportunities opening to Australia: the use of our exceptional renewable energy natural resources and opportunities to grow and store carbon in the landscape to support the developed countries' commitment to reduce carbon net emissions to zero by the middle of this century.

12

POST-PANDEMIC DOG DAYS, OR RESTORING AUSTRALIA

There is a tide in the affairs of men which, taken at the flood, leads on to fortune. Omitted, all the voyage of their life is bound in shallows and in miseries. On such a full sea are we now afloat, and we must take the current when it serves, or lose our ventures.

Omitted, Australia's voyage from pandemic recession drifts into long post-pandemic Dog Days. But the passage is full now and old Australian knowledge has shown us where it lies. Better, take the tide at its height to the restoration of Australia.

The tide for restoration

Our full sea has been raised by the aligned pull of several moons.

Democratic governance remains strong enough to stop the spread of plague, when it was not so strong in the United States and UK.

Our economic performance for ordinary Australians was poor during the Dog Days, but not bad enough for long enough to create the conditions for Trump-like insurrection. We have come to a point of crisis at a time when it is still possible to make decisions that lead to good outcomes.

Enlightenment values and institutions have been battered here, as in the US and the UK, but knowledge and analysis still have a place in public policy. During the pandemic, Australians have turned to knowledge for guidance, increasing its legitimacy, and the populist appeal of simple distortions of reality has lessened. The sharp economic downturn and need for eyewatering amounts of debt have created conditions in which we could replace with knowledge the habits that held back our economy's performance in the seven years before the pandemic.

We need reforms of tax and social security that cost the public revenue a great deal in early years but return it over time. In normal times, these reforms are widely seen as being ruled out by immediate macroeconomic imperatives to contain the deficit and debt. It happens that the funding required to support reform meets the need to stimulate demand on the way to full employment. The reforms increase government revenues in later years, helping the reduction of stimulus that is needed to contain inflation once full employment is achieved.

And the biggest pull of all is Biden's victory as president and the Democrat majority in the US senate. There is a chance to rebuild the multilateral trading system through which we can find markets for our trade-exposed industries. Biden's commitment to zero net emissions and to forceful diplomacy in support of the Paris climate goals means that the worst damage from climate change may yet be avoided in Australia. The Biden climate change commitment on top of those from other developed countries and China means that Australian exports of zero-emissions products using our rich natural endowments can fill the holes left by the decline in fossil energy and the tensions in relations with China, and keep open to us a passage towards full employment and rising incomes.

These favourable forces are with us now. Some of them may not be with us long. They are the tide that we must catch now, at the flood, or lose our ventures.

The sixth fateful choice

Five times since Federation, Australia has run into economic problems of historic dimension and has had to make fateful choices about whether and how we would respond to them. On three occasions we dealt with the problem and greatly improved the material living standards of our people, and strengthened our democracy – although one of the three was half as successful as it might have been. On two occasions we let the problems run, and later governments had to deal with larger challenges in more difficult circumstances.

We now face a sixth such occasion. We have an opportunity for a fourth success.

The first success (or half success) was the response to the Great Depression in the 1930s; the second to the challenge of postwar reconstruction through the 1940s and into the 1950s; and the third to the entrenched unemployment, inflation and income stagnation from the mid-1970s through the first few years of the 1980s.

The first response, to the Great Depression, gave us a faster return to lower unemployment than in the large English-speaking economies of the northern hemisphere – albeit with prolonged high unemployment. We can look back and see how some elements of economists' policy proposals could have been changed for the better. We can also see how things would have been better if governments had accepted more of the best of the economists' advice. But a broadly-based program of reform substantially improved material living standards for most Australians. With unnecessarily high unemployment continuing until the outbreak of war in 1939, I rate this half a success.

The response to the second, after World War II, gave us full employment with moderately and steadily rising wages alongside a sustained high level of immigration for more than a quarter of a century. It transformed Australia in economic size and demographic diversity.

The response to the third gave us the exceptional productivity growth of the 1990s, at the top of the developed countries for the first time ever; the longest period of economic growth unbroken by recession ever in a developed country, coming to an end with the pandemic recession of 2020; and substantial increases in living standards of almost all Australians until we entered the Dog Days in 2013.

It is worth recalling the two occasions when we faced large problems and did not deal with them. The first was the stagnation of living standards and rising external debt through the 1920s, culminating in large deterioration in economic conditions in the year or two before the Great Depression. These were the circumstances described by Shann at the University of Western Australia in his bracing small book *The Boom of 1890 – and Now*. The second was the decade of simultaneous high unemployment and inflation from 1974 until the beginning of the reform era in 1983. The challenges facing us after the pandemic recession are as large as these, and have to be met in as challenging an international economic and political environment as we have ever faced.

If the response to the pandemic recession can become the fourth success – if we choose restoration of Australia – we will achieve full employment in about four years; rising wages and living standards in the second half of the 2020s; and lay foundations for a long period of prosperity that consolidates our democracy and national coherence through a time of international stress and systemic competition. If it becomes the third case of failing to face up to large and complex problems, we will have continuing high unemployment through the 2020s and ordinary Australians will have lower living standards at the end than on the eve of the pandemic. We will be a divided and cranky democracy in a world that will punish weakness and division.

The three Australian successes applying Australian knowledge

The three successful Australian responses to the challenges had several essential elements in common. They remain important today.

They define conditions for major structural reform in our democratic polity.

They applied what came to be known as the Australian model of macroeconomic policy. The Australian model saw full employment and a manageable level of debt as the crucial objectives, and levels of expenditure and competitiveness as the general levers available to policy-makers. This was implicit in economists' proposals during the 1930s, explicit in plans for postwar reconstruction, formalised in the Swan diagram (Chart A4.1), and a guide to policy thinking through the first decade of the reform era. The means of achieving the right levels of competitiveness and expenditure varied over time, and identifying the best ways of getting the right level of each was always a policy art. The exchange rate was always important in the mix – although the means of varying it (or not) were different in each case. Expenditure was always a crucial variable. Again, the means of varying expenditure changed over time.

The Australian focus on international competitiveness came from the larger role that foreign trade played in our relatively small economy – compared at the time with the UK and the United States, which were the homes of the most influential economic thought. Until the last few decades, American economists often thought of their country as having a closed economy when developing economic policy proposals. As Brookings Institution economist Larry Krause said at a meeting for a Brookings project in which we were both involved in the mid-1970s, 'No one ever got their forecasts wrong by miscalculating net exports.' In contrast, the British economy in the 1930s was one in which exports were of considerable importance, but John Maynard Keynes' famous *General Theory* did not discuss problems of foreign trade, because he was writing for the world as a whole.[1]

Keynes' deliberate undervaluation of the problems suffered by countries with difficulties in their foreign trade was important for Australia.

It had an unfortunate effect on the Premiers' Plan policies that helped to move us to lower unemployment in the 1930s. When I was at the ANU in the early 1980s, our economics department tearoom would often see three figures together: Professor Sir Leslie Melville, one of the leading economists to advise on the Premiers' Plan and its evolution in 1931 and 1932; Professor Sir John Crawford, a young economist in the 1930s and later research director of the Department of Postwar Reconstruction in the Curtin and Chifley governments and then Secretary for Trade in the Menzies government; and Professor Heinz Arndt, author of the authoritative economic history of the 1930s sponsored by Chatham House and published in 1945.[2] One morning we were discussing who had been the best Australian treasurer. Sir Leslie made a case for Ted Theodore, treasurer for the Scullin government during the early stages of the Premiers' Plan. I suggested that Joseph Lyons, treasurer of his own government in its early years, would have to have a claim, for putting the Premiers' Plan into law and making it work. 'No,' said Sir Leslie. 'The prime minister had accepted the economists' advice that there had to be another large devaluation in 1932. But Keynes published an article in the Melbourne *Herald* arguing against devaluation. That was the end of the matter for Joseph Lyons. The authority had spoken.' Sir Leslie thought that Lyons' deference to Keynes on the exchange rate kept unemployment unnecessarily high until the war. (In defence of the great Anglophile's intellect, Keynes' objective was not to define what was best for Australia, but for the global financial system with London as its centre.)

In all three successful responses to large economic challenges, concern for competitiveness was accompanied by recognition that markets had to be available for expansion of export industries. The first attempt was a disaster; the others abundantly achieved their goals. The 1932 initiative was the Imperial preferences agreed at the British Empire Economic Conference in Ottawa. This aimed to shift trade from external to intra-Imperial sources, and necessarily away from Australia's rapidly growing trade relationship with Japan. This was taken further with higher tariffs against countries outside the Empire in the 'trade diversion episode' of 1936. The economists were unenthusiastic about the use of preferential tariffs to enhance trade with a partner on the far side of the world, but the government warmed to this practical expression of common blood and history. The outcome was a shock to the government. What had been rapidly growing exports to Japan went into decline, and never recovered when the Australian government recognised its error and abandoned the later trade diversion. More surprisingly, exports to the UK fell and fell. Working on full employment in the Department of Postwar Reconstruction, Crawford had the lessons of the 1930s front of mind, leading to his partnership with trade minister John McEwen on the Agreement on Commerce between Japan and Australia only a dozen years after the cessation of war. The Hawke government's trade liberalisation in the reform era was accompanied by a strong focus on Asian markets that was soon reflected in rapid and geographically and industrially diverse export expansion. China eventually delivered the biggest numbers, but export expansion to Japan, South Korea, Taiwan and Southeast Asia went well beyond historical experience.

Reset on fiscal and monetary policy for full employment with the right amount of debt

The Australian model tells us that failure to make progress towards full employment during the Dog Days was the result of expenditure and competitiveness being too low. The economic effects of the pandemic mean that even more expenditure and competitiveness are necessary for full employment, which is a stage on the journey to rising incomes for most Australians.

The unprecedented speed of the fall in economic output and trade in the first half of 2020 undermined Dog Days approaches to employment. That now allows us to achieve full employment, which we could not do before. The Reserve Bank of Australia has started to acknowledge the costs of running tighter monetary policy than other developed countries. Sharp economic decline on its watch has allowed the Coalition federal government to accept eyewatering increases in public deficits and debt to counter high unemployment. An immense increase in spending by federal and state governments has held up economic activity for a while, giving us time to apply knowledge to decisions on what comes next.

The first and biggest change is in monetary policy. To meet its statutory and contractual obligations on full employment and inflation, our Bank must avoid running tighter monetary policy than other developed countries before we reach full employment. That will lower the exchange rate, support investment in trade-exposed industries and reduce the amount of expenditure that has to come from government and be funded by debt.

But a lot of public expenditure funded by debt is still needed on the path to full employment. Australians' preferences and needs for public expenditure include many services supplied by the states, so federal fiscal arrangements have to support state as well as Commonwealth expenditure. The levels of debt-funded expenditure in the first half of 2020 and budgeted through 2020–21 have held employment and economic activity well above where they would have been. The Commonwealth's immediate response to the pandemic recession is an economic policy success story. That success will be compromised if the level of stimulus is reduced by much before we are on a clear path to full employment. If JobSeeker and JobKeeper end on the current schedules (both gone by the end of March 2021) and nothing is put in their place, there is a strong risk that the fall in the rate of unemployment will stall. The two big programs have done their jobs in holding up living standards and economic activity during a tough time. What is needed now is a shift to forms of stimulus to measures that will boost productivity and labour force participation over time. The suggested introduction of the cash-flow tax and Australian Income Security are of the right scale, with the desired impact on the future efficiency of the economy. The cash-flow tax will claw back later as much revenue as it gives up now, automatically, when it is needed to constrain demand with the approach of full employment. The AIS will not quite do that, but will make steadily smaller demands on the budget as employment and incomes grow through the 2020s.

It would be helpful to the growth in living standards after the achievement of full employment to avoid relying excessively on tighter money to constrain demand. The cash-flow tax and the AIS will have their own inbuilt tendencies to raise more revenue over time. In addition, there are large advantages to putting in place now instruments for varying some tax rates up and down within defined limits, when required, to stop inflation or reduce unemployment.

Reset on equity

Equitable distribution of the fruits of reform is a necessary condition for successful reform to raise productivity and achieve full employment. Full employment itself is a large contributor to equitable distribution.

Beyond the achievement of full employment, the AIS would be the main instrument for securing equity in income distribution. It would become a supplement to wages for part-time, insecure and low-income workers. It would provide income security for all Australians. It would increase total economic output after full employment by attracting much more participation in the labour force, especially second earners in households, especially women. Prior to the introduction of the AIS, there is a strong case to phase down, rather than abruptly stop, supplementary payments to unemployed people.

The shift to the cash-flow base for taxation of corporate income tax would make its own contribution to equity in income distribution.

Improvements in access to early education and other educational reforms would be important steps to promote equity while contributing to stronger future economic growth.

Shifting away from the twenty-first-century expansion of temporary immigration, with its low average value of skills, would reduce downward pressure on wages of Australians on low incomes and support movement to full employment. Immigration has temporarily stopped with the pandemic. An attempt to restore it to pre-pandemic levels would be contentious, unpopular and distracting to reforms to achieve full employment and rising living standards. I suggest removing this as an issue by deciding now to move to moderate rather than high total levels of immigration when something like normal international movement of people returns – to about half a per cent per annum of the established population, the levels of the productivity boom in the 1990s.

Reset on trade

Full employment with rising living standards requires expansion of our exports at a faster rate than the whole economy. Many of our established exports face strong headwinds: fossil energy exports (now over a fifth of the total) will decline; education (third-largest in value before the pandemic) will decline without restructuring of the universities' financial base; and trade tensions with China will reduce the value of some important exports.

Exports of other products will have to increase prodigiously to meet our restoration goals.

There is nevertheless a path to the necessary export expansion. At its centre is general improvement in competitiveness, with monetary policy playing an essential role. The movement to a cash-flow tax on corporate income will be strongly supportive of competitiveness for expanding export industries.

Biden's reorientation of the United States back to full participation in the multilateral trading system is important to Australian interests and warrants our strong support. Full participation in the new RCEP could strengthen relations with our Southeast Asian partners and Japan and South Korea, while providing the most important means for the time being of maintaining as many gains from trade with China as we can and working to restore productive trade and investment relations with the world's largest trading economy.

None of this would be enough export growth for restoration were it not for the opening of vast opportunities in the emerging low-carbon world economy. Chapter 9 showed that Australia's natural strengths in renewable energy and its role as the world's main source of minerals requiring large amounts of energy for processing into metals establishes opportunity for large-scale investment in new export industries. Chapter 10 described how our riches in land and sea relative to our population and economic size create potential for large exports of zero-emissions chemical manufactures based on biomass, and for exports of carbon credits. The election of President Biden sees the United States join all other developed countries and China in committing to zero net carbon emissions around the middle of the century. Australia can make a major contribution to the global decarbonisation effort by providing zero-emissions goods and carbon credits to countries with poorer resources of the kind that we have in abundance.

Embracing our low-carbon opportunity fills the hole in our export growth, into which our ambitions for restoration of Australia might otherwise fall.

Reset on democratic culture

We are still living off the diminishing legacy of high incomes growth unbroken by recession through the productivity and China resources booms. It took three and a half decades of income stagnation to brew the conditions for a destructive Trump presidency. Fox News, the National Rifle Association and the Koch brothers are blamed for Trump. They were the immediate instruments, not the underlying cause. Top predators evolve to fill the evolutionary gap in any ecosystem that provides them with an opportunity. Our own Dog Days are less than a decade old, and too young yet to nurture to supremacy the predators on our democratic body politic.

In 2021, American democratic knowledge has grabbed the tiller back from the predators. It was a close-run thing. Now, there is a chance once more that in the country of Lincoln, government of the people can be by the people and for the people. The defeat in the United States of the forces that created and sustained the Trump presidency make then less influential in our own country.

The success of the world's largest democracy and economy does not determine Australia's prospects, but it does help to forge conceptions of what is possible.

President Biden has to find a way out of the pandemic and towards stabilisation and growth of the economy, with an electorate still poisoned by the division and misinformation that sustained the Trump presidency. Australians have a large interest in the success of his administration. Threats to US democracy and more generally to the United States' success as a nation are also threats to Australian democracy. The most important contribution we can make to the defence of democracy and to prosperity in the rest of the world is to make our own democracy work for all Australians – to choose post-pandemic restoration over post-pandemic Dog Days.

If the Biden presidency were to be dragged down by the legacy of division and predatory obfuscation, smaller democratic capitalist countries could still demonstrate the strengths of their political systems. After all, Australian democracy operated with a much wider franchise than the American or British did for much of the six or seven decades that concluded with the enfranchisement of women in the UK and the US in the early 1920s. The Australian experience was helpful to the democratic evolution of Britain and the United States.[3] If others fail, it is harder for us, but we can still succeed and demonstrate the advantages of the best democratic governance: if necessary, alone; if necessary, for years. But we would not be alone. There is a place for us in the Indo-Pacific with its many civilisations and political systems. We can make our way, if necessary for years, in a region where we are one of many different communities.

What matters most for ourselves, and for the attractions of our democracy to others, is that we make our political and economic systems work for most Australians. That means restoring Australia through the application of knowledge and analysis to public policy. It means building mechanisms to insulate policy-making in the national interest from the vested and foreign interests that have become much more influential and effective in the early twenty-first century. It means taking the tide at the flood, and avoiding the shallows and the miseries.

Reset of energy and climate change policy

The 2019–20 bushfires reminded us of what Australia has to lose from the world's failure to deal with climate change – we are more vulnerable than any other developed country. We also have more to gain than any other country from the world moving early to the zero net emissions necessary for cessation of warming, and from full participation in the global transition to zero emissions.

The United States under President Biden has joined China, the European Union, the UK, Japan and South Korea in committing to zero net emissions around mid-century. That makes now the time for Australia to move decisively to use its zero-emissions opportunity. This can provide most of the expansion of investment and production in the trade-exposed parts of the economy that is necessary through the 2020s to deliver full employment and then rising incomes with a reasonable level of external debt.

Australia is held back by the past decade of incoherence in energy and climate policy. But it is not unalloyed weakness. Renewable energy output has risen strongly despite policy headwinds. The Commonwealth's technology roadmap favours five developments that have places in Australia's low-carbon future.

Economists have no doubt that putting a price on carbon emissions equal to the damage that carbon does would be helpful to any cost-effective emissions-reduction strategy. A general carbon price is ruled out in Australia for the time being by our political history. There is a large economic prize for Australia if and when we remove that constraint. We will find it much easier to be a major trading partner of Europe and the UK, in particular. In the meantime, there is no alternative to carbon pricing in two areas included in the Commonwealth government's technology roadmap: sequestration of carbon in the landscape and capture of carbon in geological structures. A limited carbon price could be introduced in the absence of a comprehensive one, to provide incentives for sequestration in the land and geological structures. Funds for purchasing credits could come from requiring coal and gas producers to offset fugitive emissions, together with an increase in budgetary support for the Climate Solutions Fund and access to international voluntary and perhaps compliance markets.

Deep Australian participation in global carbon markets requires our acceptance of targets in line with other developed countries – now zero net emissions by 2050. Prime Minister Morrison says that we will reach zero net emissions as soon as possible without a carbon price or high costs to Australians. If that is going to happen anyway, there are large benefits in announcing that we share the target adopted by other developed countries. Commitment to it in the UN Framework Convention on Climate Change would facilitate access for our farmers and others to international markets for carbon credits.

The transition to zero-emissions electricity now has momentum without carbon pricing. The missing ingredients are efficient transmission links between rich natural resources and established and potential centres of demand. For decarbonisation of transport, the missing ingredients are battery-charging facilities and electricity pricing regimes that encourage charging of batteries outside times of peak demand.

The industry transition requires large investment in innovation. The Commonwealth government's expansion of the roles of the Australian Renewable Energy Agency and the Clean Energy Finance Corporation provides institutional foundations for support for new low-emissions iron, aluminium, hydrogen and other energy-intensive manufacturing. But funding for these institutions is not commensurate with the scale of the opportunity and the need. And the Abbott government's requirement that the CEFC achieve returns on investment that are high compared with those expected for similar activities in other countries reduces their impact. Biden's commitment of US$1.7 trillion, represents many times Australia's commitment under the roadmap when amounts are scaled for population. China, the UK, the European Union, Japan and South Korea are all doing much more than Australia. There is a danger that our superior human and natural resources in the low-carbon economy will be outweighed by the much larger fiscal commitments of the rest of the world.

We have a big advantage in our states' support for the energy and industrial transition. The NSW government has gone furthest, by committing to underwrite zero-emissions energy sales to users of power. Repeated across all states and supported by the Commonwealth, that would go a long way towards claiming our future as a low-carbon superpower. The NSW energy minister, Matt Kean, summed up the biggest dimension of Australia's choice when his historic clean energy legislation was before parliament on 25 November 2020:

we can set ourselves up to be not only a renewable energy super-power, but an economic superpower at the same time. We know the world is moving to decarbonize. With Joe Biden now in the White House 70 per cent of Australia's two-way trade will be with countries that have signed up to achieve net zero-emissions by mid this century. So that means markets that underwrite our prosperity are changing. And we need to be positioned, especially by the 2030s, to be able to take advantage of those opportunities. So, the choice is very clear, we can put our head in the sand and do nothing. Or we can grab these opportunities and make sure that we continue to be a prosperous, strong and successful nation.[4]

Seizing the chance

Early in the pandemic recession, our prime minister spoke of returning to the conditions that we left the year before. Chapter 3 explains why that is neither possible, nor good enough. Yet Morrison is right to assert that there is no need to turn our backs on the best of our past. Reset for restoration builds on the best of our past: use of old Australian economic knowledge and experience of how to face up to difficult economic challenges; open international markets for trade and investment; policy in the public interest, built on knowledge and analysis, guided by an independent centre of our polity.

Let us make this the fourth time that our democratic polity faces a great economic challenge, and wins.

ACKNOWLEDGEMENTS

This book was conceived and written during the time when Jayne and I were residing in the central-west Queensland town of Barcaldine, between March and December 2020. Warm, safe from the pandemic, under big skies through which you can see forever. We thrived in the company of good people who became friends, and from whom we learnt much about the natural and human riches of our country. Thank you to our hosts in the pandemic year.

Reset began as six public lectures from Barcaldine, conveyed to a large audience through the University of Melbourne's Institute of Applied Economic and Social Research. Thanks to Abigail Payne, director of the Melbourne Institute, and Paul Kofman, dean of the faculty of business and economics, for hosting the series. Professor Payne chaired the lectures and the discussion after each one. She demonstrated that a skilled chair, deeply knowledgeable in the subject, can bring discussion alive through the internet without the buzz of a full lecture theatre. Questions and comments at the lectures and subsequently by email rubbed some rough edges off my argument and sharpened the story.

Thanks to the Remote Area Planning and Development Board and to Morgan Gronold for access to facilities for presenting the lectures in

Barcaldine. Morgan and Louise Gronold managed many technical challenges with high competence and steadiness. Jenny Williams and her colleagues in the faculty of business and economics made things work at the Melbourne end. Many thanks to Morgan, Louise and Jenny. The first lecture generated most anxiety. Everything seemed to be going smoothly with a capacity audience on the line all over Australia and beyond as the clock ticked over to the start time of 5 p.m. Queensland time. Then, at 5.00.01 the grid through the central west failed. When the power was restored after ten agonisingly long minutes, I was able to describe my location as having beneath its feet the world's richest coal resource and above its head eastern Australia's richest solar energy resource; and to say that I looked forward to power being more reliable when the latter was its source.

Thank you to my colleagues in my academic home over the past decade, the Melbourne Institute and the faculty of business and economics at the University of Melbourne. Thanks especially to Max Corden, Paul Kofman, Abigail Payne, John Freebairn, Ian McDonald and Jeff Borland. Thank you to my colleagues in the Melbourne Economic Forum, who have heard me on these themes over several years, helped to straighten out my arguments and improved what I have to say. Thanks, also, to our Victoria University colleagues in the Melbourne Economic forum, Peter Dawkins, Craig Emerson, Janine Dixon and James Giesecke.

On the energy and carbon questions in Chapters 9 and 10, I am learning all the time from my colleagues in ZEN Energy and Sunshot Energy; from Mike Sandiford and Michael Brearley at the University of Melbourne; and from past chief scientists Robin Batterham and Alan Finkel.

Special thanks to the colleagues who have worked with me on the cash-flow tax presented in Chapter 7: Craig Emerson, Reuben Finighan and Stephen Anthony. And to Reuben for our work together on savings, investment and interest rates, and the problems of contemporary democracy.

Many thanks also to David Vines, Nancy Viviani and Jayne Garnaut for reading through the whole manuscript and helping me to improve it. To David Vines, emeritus professor of economics at the University of Oxford, thank you for interaction over many decades on the questions that frame this book, and especially for sharing what he has been learning along the way to his important, forthcoming book, *Transforming Australia's Global Role since Federation: Steering the macroeconomy, removing protectionism and responding to climate change.* David has helped me place the themes in the history of Australian economic policy. And to Andrew Elek for thoughts on international cooperation.

Thanks to John and Anthony Garnaut, who have each taught me much and caused me to think more about matters dealt with in the book, knowing that we have each had different life experiences and learnt different things. And thanks to Harvey Garnaut, who had a quick read of the final manuscript when his curiosity got the better of him and found a couple of errors for correction.

Thanks to Dylan McConnell for the charts in the lectures, adapted for the book – and for many insights along the way. Thanks to Isabelle Grant for keeping me up to date on Carbon in the Land and for much help with Chapter 10.

Susannah Powell and Louisa Gebbie have been with me on the whole journey, through the Barcaldine lectures, several drafts, and now the book. Theirs has been a big contribution, and a pleasure.

This is the third book I have published with Black Inc. Each has been an enriching experience, thanks especially to the strategic pen and wise judgements of Chris Feik. Big thanks also to Kirstie Innes-Will, for the skilful editing under great pressure including over Christmas and New Year.

I have dedicated the book to the memory of my close friend for fifty-four years, Mekere Morauta. In the years straddling independence in 1975, Mekere was the first secretary for treasury and finance in

Papua New Guinea and we learnt together how humanity is governed. Mekere was later Papua New Guinea's great reform prime minister, putting things together again at the turn of the millennium. I said in his eulogy just before Christmas, 'What he built was worth building though it might fall down, because it proved forever that it can be built.'

Ross Garnaut
University of Melbourne
1 February 2021

ENDNOTES

1 The Tree of Knowledge

1   John Kay and Mervyn King, *Radical Uncertainty: Decision-making for an unknowable future*, The Bridge St Press, London, 2020.

2   Malcolm Turnbull at McGrathNicol client forum, Sydney, 1 December 2020.

3   Nancy MacLean, *Democracy in Chains: The deep history of the radical right's stealth plan for America*, Penguin, New York, 2017.

4   Glyn Davis, 'Universities and the liberal imagination', *Meanjin*, 4 September 2020.

5   David Vines, personal communication, December 2020.

2 The Pandemic Recession of 2020

1   Ross Garnaut with David Llewellyn-Smith, *The Great Crash of 2008*, Melbourne University Press, Carlton, 2009.

2   Max Corden and Ross Garnaut, 'The economic consequences of Trump', *Australian Economic Review*, vol. 51, no. 3, 2018, pp. 1–7.

3   Ross Garnaut, Ligang Song and Cai Fang, *China's 40 Years of Reform and Development, 1978–2018*, Australian National University Press, Australia, 2018.

4   Quoted in David Penberthy, 'Australia leads on COVID, says Anthony Fauci', *The Australian*, 30 November 2020, pp. 1 and 7.

5   Charles Kindleberger, *The World in Depression, 1929–1939*, University of California Press, United Kingdom, 1973.

3 Wrong Way; Don't Go Back

1   Ross Garnaut, 'Full employment in a new century', lecture presented to the Australia Unlimited Conference, Melbourne, 4 May 1999, reproduced in Chapter 14 of Ross Garnaut, *Social Democracy in Australia's Asian Future*, Asia Pacific Press, Canberra, 2001.

2   John Howard, Reply to Question Without Notice: Howard Government Foreign Policy (Questioner K. Beazley), House of Representatives, Parliament House, Canberra, 28 September 1999; John Howard, address at the 1999 Minerals Industry Dinner, Great Hall, Parliament House, Canberra, 2 June 1999; John Howard, address at the official opening of the Sir Roland Wilson Building, Australian National University, Canberra, 1999; John Howard, address to business luncheon, Sydney, 17 June 1999.

3   Ross Garnaut with Rana Ganguly and Jongsoon Kang, *Migration to Australia and Comparisons with the United States: Who Benefits?*, Australian Department of Immigration and Multicultural and Indigenous Affairs, Canberra, 2003.

4 Full Employment with the Right Amount of Debt

1   T. Swan, 'Economic control in a dependent economy', *Economic Record*, March 1960, pp. 51–66. This paper was originally discussed in a seminar at the ANU in 1954. The famous diagram did not actually see the light of day for a couple of years. It was first published in T. Swan, 'Longer run problems of the balance of payments', which was chapter 24 in H.W. Arndt and W.M. Corden (eds), *The Australian Economy*, Cheshire, Sydney, 1964. That paper was originally mimeographed and circulated in May 1955, when Swan presented it to the ANZAAS conference in Melbourne.

5 Full Employment

1   Peter Dixon & Maureen Rimmer, *Doubling US exports under the President's National Export Initiative: Implications of successful implementation*, Contemporary Economic Policy, 2012.

6 An Eye-Watering Amount of Debt

1   Paul Samuelson, 'A note on measurement of utility', *The Review of Economic Studies*, vol. 4, no. 2, 1937.

2   John Maynard Keynes, *Essays in Persuasion*, Macmillan & Co., 1931.

3   Jason Furman and Lawrence Summers, 'A reconsideration of fiscal policy in the era of low interest rates', discussion draft, 30 November 2020.

7 *The Big Picture*

1   J. Dixon and J. Nassios, *A Dynamic Economy-wide Analysis of Company Tax Cuts in Australia*, Centre of Policy Studies Working Paper G-287, 2018, available at www.copsmodels.com/elecpapr/g-287.htm.

2   Ross Garnaut, 'Capitalism, socialism and democracy in the twenty-first century', London School of Economic and University of Melbourne public lecture, London 2014.

3   Oliver Blanchard, 'Public debt and low interest rates', *American Economic Review*, vol. 109, no. 4, 2019, pp. 1197–1229.

4   David Ricardo, *On the Principles of Political Economy and Taxation*, John Murray, England, 1817.

5   Henry George, 'Progress and Poverty: An inquiry into the cause of industrial depressions and of increase of want with increase of wealth: the remedy', D. Appleton & Company, New York, 1881, in Ross Garnaut and Anthony Clunies-Ross, *Taxation of Mineral Rents*, OUP Catalogue, Oxford University Press, no. 9780198284543.

6   Ross Garnaut, Craig Emerson, Reuben Finighan and Stephen Anthony, 'Replacing corporate income tax with a cash-flow tax', *Australian Economic Review*, vol. 53, no. 4, 2020, pp. 463–81.

7   Ibid.

8 *The Case for a Basic Income*

1   Milton Friedman and Rose Friedman, *Free to Choose*, Penguin, 1980.

2   Brian Howe, 'Australians support universal health care, so why not a universal basic income', *The Conversation*, 13 February 2018.

3   Priorities Review Staff, *Possibilities for Social Welfare in Australia*, AGPS, Canberra, 1975.

4   Peter Dawkins, *The Five Economists' Plan: The original idea and subsequent developments*, Centre for Economic Policy Research, Discussion Paper No. 450, November 2002.

5   Business Council of Australia, *Rebuilding the Safety Net, New Directions of*

Business Paper No. 1, 1999; The history of discussion of the idea has recently been the subject of a survey by the Commonwealth Parliamentary Library: Australian Parliament House, 'Basic income: A radical idea enters the mainstream', 18 November 2016.

6   Ross Garnaut, *Investing in Full Employment*, commissioned paper for the Business Council of Australia, 1997. Reproduced as Chapter 13 in Ross Garnaut, *Social Democracy in Australia's Asian Future*, Asia Pacific Press, Canberra, 2002.

7   Peter Dawkins, 'A five-point plan for lifelong learning', *Australian Financial Review*, 21 October 2020.

8   Peter Dawkins, Peter Hurley and David Lloyd, *Averting an Escalating Labour Market Crisis for Young People*, Mitchell Institute Victoria University, Melbourne, 2020.

9   Discussion at Melbourne Economic Forum, Victoria University and University of Melbourne, Melbourne, 22 October 2020.

10   Stephanie Kelton, *The Deficit Myth: Modern Monetary Theory and the birth of the people's economy*, PublicAffairs, New York, 2020.

9 The Superpower Opportunity

1   Australian Competition and Consumer Commission, *Restoring Electricity Affordability and Australia's Competitive Advantage: Retail electricity pricing inquiry – final report*, Commonwealth of Australia, Canberra, 2018.

2   Productivity Commission, *Energy Generation and Distribution*, vol 3, no. 11, Commonwealth of Australia, 1991.

3   Tony Wood, Guy Dundas & James Ha, *Start with Steel: A practical plan to support carbon workers and cut emissions*, Grattan Institute, 2020.

4   Matt Kean, 'Electricity road map will power prosperity', *Australian Financial Review*, 22 November 2020.

10 Carbon in the Land

1   Charles Massy, *Call of the Reed Warbler: A new agriculture – a new earth*, University of Queensland Press, St Lucia, 2017; and David Pollock, *The Wooleen Way: Renewing an Australian resource*, Scribe Publications, London, 2019.

2   Bronson W. Griscom et al., 'Natural climate solutions', *Proceedings of the National Academy of Sciences*, vol. 114, no. 44, October 2017, pp. 11645–50.

11 Protection Dead-End Versus Free-Trade Highway

1   World Trade Organization, 'Evolution of Trade Under the WTO', Geneva, 2021.

2   World Trade Organization, Press release, 8 April 2020.

3   Peter Drysdale, International Economic Pluralism: *Economic Policy in East Asia and the Pacific*, Allen & Unwin, Sydney and Columbia University Press, New York, 1988. Ross Garnaut, *Open Regionalism and Trade Liberalization: An Asia-Pacific contribution to the world trade system*, Institute of Southeast Asian Studies, Singapore, 1996; Andrew Elek, 'Trade policy options for the Asia–Pacific region in the 1990s: The potential of open regionalism', *American Economic Review*, vol. 82, no. 2; Ross Garnaut and David Vines, 'Regional free-trade areas: Sorting out the tangled spaghetti', *Oxford Review of Economic Policy*, vol. 23, no. 3, 2007, pp. 1–20.

4   McKibbin and Vines, 2020.

5   IMF, Weekend Read, Washington, DC, 16 January 2021.

6   Garnaut and Vines, 2007.

7   Ross Garnaut, Australia and the Northeast Asia Ascendence: Report to the Prime Minister and Minister for Foreign Affairs and Trade, AGPS, Canberra, 1989.

8   Personal communication, Mike Sandiford, emeritus professor of earth sciences, University of Melbourne.

9   David Vines, 'Cooperation between countries to ensure global economic growth', 13th Heinz Arndt Lecture, The Australian National University, 2014.

10   McKibbin and Vines, 2020.

11   Garnaut and Vines, 2007.

12 Post-Pandemic Dog Days, or Restoring Australia

1   Peter Temin and David Vines, *Keynes: Useful economics for the world as a whole*, MIT Press, Boston, 2014.

2   H.W. Arndt, *The Economic Lessons of the 1930s*, Oxford University Press, Oxford, 1945.

3   David Kemp, *Land of Dreams: How Australians won their freedom, 1788–1860*, Melbourne University Press, Carlton, 2018.

4   Energy Insiders, 'Matt Kean and the NSW Energy Transition', RenewEconomy podcast, 24 November 2020.

INDEX

Ross Garnaut is Professorial Research Fellow in Economics at the University of Melbourne. In 2008, he produced the Garnaut Climate Change Review for the Australian government. He is the author of many books, including the bestselling *Dog Days* (2013) and *Superpower* (2019).